MARKETING RADICALISM

PRINCETON STUDIES IN CULTURAL SOCIOLOGY

Clayton Childress, Angèle Christin, Paul DiMaggio, Michèle Lamont, Iddo Tavory, and Viviana A. Zelizer, *Series Editors*

For a full list of titles in the series, go to https://press.princeton.edu/series/princeton-studies-in-cultural-sociology.

Marketing Radicalism: The Cultural Production of Far-Right Populism in Contemporary Hungary by Virág Molnár

Data-Driven Hollywood: Algorithm Specialists in the Age of Streaming by Violaine Roussel

The Death and Life of Gentrification: A New Map of a Persistent Idea by Japonica Brown-Saracino

Revolution of Things: The Islamism and Post-Islamism of Objects in Tehran by Kusha Sefat

Resurrecting the Jew: Nationalism, Philosemitism, and Poland's Jewish Revival by Geneviève Zubrzycki

How Civic Action Works: Fighting for Housing in Los Angeles by Paul Lichterman

The University and the Global Knowledge Society by David John Frank and John W. Meyer

Billionaire Wilderness: The Ultra-Wealthy and the Changing Nature of the American West by Justin Farrell

Inside the Critics' Circle: Book Reviewing in Uncertain Times by Phillipa K. Chong

The Extreme Gone Mainstream: Commercialization and Far Right Youth Culture in Germany by Cynthia Miller-Idriss

Seeing the World: How US Universities Make Knowledge in a Global Era by Mitchell L. Stevens, Cynthia Miller-Idriss, and Seteney Shami

Under the Cover: The Creation, Production, and Reception of a Novel by Clayton Childress

A Fraught Embrace: The Romance and Reality of AIDS Altruism in Africa by Ann Swidler and Susan Cotts Watkins

Contested Tastes: Foie Gras and the Politics of Food by Michaela DeSoucey

Magazines and the Making of America: Modernization, Community, and Print Culture, 1741–1860 by Heather A. Haveman

Marketing Radicalism

The Cultural Production of Far-Right Populism in Contemporary Hungary

Virág Molnár

PRINCETON UNIVERSITY PRESS
PRINCETON AND OXFORD

Published by Princeton University Press
41 William Street, Princeton, New Jersey 08540
99 Banbury Road, Oxford OX2 6JX

press.princeton.edu

GPSR Authorized Representative: Easy Access System Europe - Mustamäe tee 50, 10621 Tallinn, Estonia, gpsr.requests@easproject.com

ISBN 9780691290379
ISBN (pbk.) 9780691290386
ISBN (epub) 9780691294209
ISBN (PDF) 9780691290393

Library of Congress Control Number: 2026936025

British Library Cataloging-in-Publication Data is available

Editorial: Rachael Levay and Tara Dugan
Production Editorial: Theresa Liu
Jacket/Cover Design: Heather Hansen
Production: Lauren Reese
Publicity: William Pagdatoon
Copyeditor: Anita O'Brien

Jacket images: Detail of Kalocsa embroidery from a traditional costume. Photograph © Virág Molnár. Background texture by Tewin Kijthamrongworakul / Alamy.

This book has been composed in Adobe Text and Gotham

Printed in the United States of America

10 9 8 7 6 5 4 3 2 1

CONTENTS

LIST OF FIGURES AND TABLE

Figures

Table

ACKNOWLEDGMENTS

It was in Montreal in 2010 at the Council for European Studies meeting that I first presented at a conference on the rise of right-wing populism in Hungary. At the time, I was still focusing on the proliferation and growing influence of right-wing civil society organizations. My talk was met by stark skepticism from a distinguished audience that included, for instance, a prominent German political sociologist who basically laughed at me and said that what I talked about simply did not exist. The spontaneous emotional backlash from the audience made me think that I might have put my finger on something that was worth exploring further. In the following years my attention shifted toward the right-wing culture industry that I discovered through my initial immersion in "uncivil" society. The foolishly ambitious idea to cover four (very) different sites of cultural production (fashion, heritage tourism, book publishing, horseback archery) destined me for a long and arduous journey. I was, however, lucky to benefit from ample financial, institutional, and intellectual support all along.

A generous fellowship from the American Council of Learned Societies helped to kick-start the fieldwork in Hungary. This was followed by a lavish stay at the American Academy in Berlin, where I could test my first ideas on an inquisitive and demanding audience. I was lucky to share a residence with esteemed scholars and writers that turned daily meals into enlightening conversations. My thinking about the project and scholarship were shaped by many stimulating chats, especially with Kate Brown, Marjoleine Kars, Wendy Chun, and Jane Newman, while the kindness and wit of Adam Johnson, Mark Pottinger, Chanan Tigay, and Molly Antopol always lit up gray days in Berlin. The AAB staff was also exceptional in making sure that fellows could focus their full attention on their work. And ironically, I could have literally never written this book without Peter Vajkoczy and his dedicated team at Berlin Charité, who saved my life effortlessly as part of their everyday routine during this otherwise idyllic spring on the shores of Wannsee.

Princeton's Institute for Advanced Study provided another crucial incubator for this book. Didier Fassin and Marion Fourcade brought together a diverse group of accomplished international scholars to think about economy and society in innovative new ways. They also deftly and affably developed this group into an intellectual community. Our exchanges did not only help me sharpen my analysis and arguments but sustained my enthusiasm about my research. I was heartbroken when our year was abruptly cut short by the outbreak of Covid and fellows were quickly dispersed into lockdowns. I am also thankful to Balázs Trencsényi, who hosted me at CEU's Institute for Advanced Study in Budapest, where I ended up completing the manuscript while beginning work on a new project.

My home institution, the New School, kindly supported my research leaves and awarded me small grants and priceless feedback through its in-house research institutes, including GIDEST, the Zolberg Institute on Migration and Mobility, and the Robert L. Heilbroner Center for Capitalism Studies. I particularly appreciate Hugh Raffles's unaffected leadership that has turned GIDEST into a uniquely creative and nurturing intellectual space at the New School. My excellent PhD students Ágnes Szanyi and Karolina Koziura provided vital research assistance at various points in the lengthy research process. And they still, luckily, both finished their dissertations before I finished this book.

Some materials in the book have previously appeared in print: Chapter 3 is in part derived from an article published in the *Journal of Cultural Economy* 18, no. 1 (2025): 68–91, copyright Taylor and Francis, and is available online: https://doi.org/10.1080/17530350.2024.2373158. Chapter 4 is in part derived from an article that appeared in *Comparative Studies in Society and History* 65, no. 3 (July 2023): 557–86, copyright Cambridge University Press, available online: https://doi.org/10.1017/S0010417523000087.

Esra Akcan, Paula Diehl, Margit Feischmidt, Krisztina Fehervary, Mischa Gabowitsch, János Mátyás Kovács, Cynthia Miller-Idriss, Agnieszka Pasieka, and Geneviève Zubrzycki invited me to various workshops, talks, and conferences where they not only gave me a chance to share work in progress, thereby aiding the development of the book, but allowed me to learn from their and other scholars' latest research in the field. I also owe extra thanks to Margit Feischmidt for putting me in touch with the Kiss-Pál sisters, Anna and Hanga, who transcribed many of my interviews. The interviewees' willingness to take the time to meet me and share their thoughts is, of course, a precondition without which this book would not have been possible.

Recurring, and always memorable, conversations with Mabel Berezin and Kim Scheppele about the rise and fall of democracies in Europe (East and West) over many years seeped into this book through osmosis. I presented early versions of the chapters on fashion and heritage tourism in the sociology department at the University of Amsterdam during an extended stay and am grateful to members of the culture group for genuine engagement with my research and insightful remarks, and especially to Olav Velthuis, Pamela Prickett, Olga Sezneva, and Ladan Rahbari for making this tough Covid year more bearable.

Iddo Tavory and Paul DiMaggio were the first to offer this project a stage at the NYU culture workshop, and I am immensely grateful to them as well as to Michèle Lamont and Viviana Zelizer for encouraging my work on this book and suggesting that I submit the manuscript to the culture series at Princeton University Press. The anonymous reviewers' careful and sympathetic reading of the manuscript helped enormously with refining the framing of the book's argument, and remarks from the editorial board pushed me to sharpen important details. Working with PUP editors Rachael Levay and Tara Dugan and with Theresa Liu and Anita O'Brien from the production team has been an absolute delight.

No matter whether carefully preplanned or impromptu, meetings with Gabriella Lukács, Julia Sonnevend, Márton Dornbach, and Michel Anteby always offered a pleasant mix of professional and personal ruminations on all things, including academia and the messiness of writing books.

I would be remiss not to thank Mónika Baár for her camaraderie and friendship throughout the ups and downs of our rocky international academic careers, for providing me with an abode in The Hague during my Covid exile in the Netherlands, and for allowing me to unwind in Florence when I needed some respite from laboring on the book. Piroska Tóth and Zoltán Szabó welcomed me in their Princeton home when I was a fellow at IAS and continue to surprise me with their outsize generosity and down-to-earth friendliness. Irina Reyn and Adam Loewenstein have helped me maintain a home in Brooklyn, where I wrote much of the book, by always being partners in navigating the complicated logistics of summer travel, research leaves, and Covid disruptions.

As with my first book, my brother proved indispensable as an unpaid research assistant. I am terribly grateful to him for chauffeuring me to various horseback archery events over the years. My longtime companion Tibor Beke is probably the only person who is even happier than I am that this book is finally out, so he will not be asked again to read the umpteenth draft of a chapter, entertain more lame theories about populism, and cope with the emotional rollercoaster of writing a book and finding a publisher. I will, nevertheless, continue to be dependent on his always sharp and candid advice.

MARKETING RADICALISM

1

Introduction

The very first interview I conducted for this book, with the owner of a small fashion label, turned out to be an unexpected epiphany. It brought into sharp relief a host of challenges—methodological, logistical, and ethical—that I would be facing in this research and was apparently oblivious to. After a long back-and-forth trying to organize a meeting, the owner asked me to go to see her in her home in Esztergom, an old historical city on the Danube, the seat of the Catholic archbishop in Hungary. The city is located northwest of Budapest, literally a stone's throw across the river from Slovakia, as this section of the Danube doubles as Hungary's border. I started out on a brutally hot summer day taking the train from Budapest's Western Railway station. I was relieved that my train was one of the neat, modern, air-conditioned Siemens railcars—not the gritty 1980s wagons with Canadian geese-poop-colored, faux leather seats that you literally stick to in the summer heat. This gave me hope that I wouldn't be completely drenched in sweat by the time I reached my interviewee's home. There were other surprises along the way, though.

I arrived in Esztergom roughly an hour later. The train station—a typical turn-of-the-twentieth-century building one can still find in cities across Central Europe that were once part of the Austro-Hungarian Empire—was being demolished. I found myself in a desolate construction site among makeshift containers for construction workers sweltering in the sun. Uber and other car-sharing services were banned in Hungary at the time, so it took me considerable trouble to get hold of a taxi. I also learned from the driver that the place I had to go to was quite a distance away, on the fringes of the city, somewhere near the hills that used to be an area for vacationers and summer cottages beyond official city boundaries. We drove through the historic city center, which looked surprisingly dilapidated: boarded up buildings covered with graffiti; even some graffiti in runic script, an important radical nationalist symbol. As we turned from the river toward the hills after a twenty-minute ride and were nearing the address, the driver casually told me that he knew one family, the Ambrus family, who lived around here. And last week there was even a TV crew from Budapest that came to interview them, he added. I replied, baffled, that this was quite a coincidence because I was coming to see the same family—the wife, Réka, more precisely. I ignored the comment about the TV crew. I was just happy that we had finally arrived and I wasn't late for the interview.

In fact, Réka was not quite ready yet and asked me to take a seat on the porch, leaving me temporarily in her husband Attila's care. The place was a small but friendly summer cottage converted into a year-around home. The porch was refreshingly cool. Attila offered me some water and a savagely strong espresso, and he entertained me until his wife became available. He was a short, muscular, middle-aged man with closely cropped hair and a horseshoe moustache that Hungarian men smitten by mystic nationalism often seem to sport. He looked strangely familiar, but I chalked this up to his facial hairstyle. He asked me about my project but soon began to talk eagerly about himself: how he was a potter working in a traditional Transylvanian style, and how nowadays even Transylvania—which is still widely considered a heaven of authentic craftsmanship—was flooded with fake craft products. He himself was fooled by buying a large "traditional" vase that turned out to be a useless knockoff and, most annoyingly, not waterproof. But, he continued, the vase in the end did immense service to him when he hid a large sum of money in it that the police failed to locate upon searching his apartment. He also explained how he had learned pottery in prison because he spent a fair portion of his life on the "dark side." I only half listened to these outlandish stories, thinking that he was either a genuine nutcase or just pulling my leg. I smiled and nodded politely, trying to concentrate on what I wanted to cover in the interview, stressing over whether I had enough cash for the taxi back to the station, and fantasizing about how, if I survived this trip without a heatstroke and made it back to Budapest, I would go to my favorite Vietnamese restaurant straight from the station and gulp down a full pitcher of their cucumber water, possibly with a shot of vodka, just to punctuate the end of a bizarre day.

Finally, Réka came, and we could start the interview. She was an unexpectedly young, intelligent, soft-spoken, but clearly strong-willed woman. I was animated by how well the interview was going and how she expanded my knowledge of the fashion brands that were part of a Hungarian folk-revivalist trend. My first interviews for new projects tended to be more forgettable. Réka also loosened up by the end and even kept me company outside her home while I was waiting for the taxi, passionately telling me about the bogusness of the Finno-Ugric theory about Hungarians' ethnic origins, which is a popular revisionist trope on the populist right that I will explore in chapter 5.

It was only when I got into the taxi to head back to the train station that it finally dawned on me who the husband was: the "Whiskey Robber," Hungary's number one celebrity criminal![1] The only criminal everyone in Hungary knows. A criminal whose life was being turned into a Hollywood-style gangster movie, slated to open in cinemas across Hungary that fall.[2] I had even watched the first trailer that came out just a week earlier. I almost laughed out loud in the taxi about how colossally dumb I was not to pay attention to his anecdotes and connect the dots. And now I understood why Attila seemed so amused by me. He probably couldn't honestly believe that I did not know who he was. The Whiskey Robber was a Robin Hood–type figure of the 1990s, an iconic character of the postcommunist transition, the first quintessentially capitalist criminal, a bank robber, a concept utterly useless under communism, as almost nobody would have bothered to rob a bank because money had surprisingly little value in life. The Whiskey Robber was a "gentleman robber" who brought flowers to the tellers, sent bottles of wine to the police, and acquired his nickname because he always downed a couple of shots of whiskey in a bar near the bank before embarking on his business. He was eventually caught after a long cat-and-mouse game with the police in 1999 but then escaped from prison using a rope cobbled together out of shredded sheets, electric cords, and shoelaces. After his recapture a couple of months later, he was sentenced to seventeen years in a maximum-security prison for thirty robberies. He was released early in 2012 for good behavior to start his life anew as a potter and an unlikely folk hero.[3]

By dwelling on this story, I am not trying to insinuate that today's radical nationalists are all somehow outlaws, even in the literal sense of the word. But an outlaw outlook on life is an important undercurrent to grassroots populist politics that is energized by anti-elite, anti-establishment, and anti-system sentiments. This encounter was also important because it was during this first interview trip that it became apparent to me the extent to which I would be out of my comfort zone during this research.[4] For instance, I would have to interact with people and a milieu that I always painstakingly tried to avoid both in Hungary and in the United States, where the Hungarian diaspora has a reputation for being "quite right-wing"—often likened to Cuban Americans in Florida—as the last significant wave of Hungarian émigrés settled in the United States after the anticommunist revolution of 1956. I would also have to present myself to interviewees in a way I feel ambivalent about, not because I deliberately misrepresented myself and my intentions but because I would not reveal to them fully where I am coming from and what my political convictions are. And I would have to be prepared for awkward situations like when Réka offered me a small gift, a handbag with a Transylvanian pattern (of the famous Torockó region) from her new summer collection. I profusely protested but realized that I would deeply offend her and undermine my credibility if I didn't take the gift. Likewise, as an urbanist, I was used to conducting research in large urban centers, but here it soon became clear that I would have to roam around the countryside to carry out my fieldwork. This really should not have struck me as a surprise because the return of radical nationalism in Hungary, like in many other countries, feeds on an urban-rural rift.[5] The Hungarian manifestation of this is a deep social and cultural divide between Budapest and the rest of the country, between the (West-oriented, cosmopolitan and prosperous) metropolis and the (inward-looking and economically precarious) provinces.[6]

But it also became clear that talking to people like Réka in person in their familiar environments would be immensely informative and offer a unique perspective into why so many people welcomed the populist turn in Hungary after Viktor Orbán's return to power in 2010. My experience in Esztergom immediately reminded me of Arlie Hochschild's highly acclaimed book *Strangers in Their Own Land* (2016). In it, through in-depth interviews and focus groups, Hochschild managed to capture the deep resentment about the perceived denial of the American Dream that animated Tea Party supporters in rural Louisiana and drove them to support Donald Trump in the 2016 elections.[7] Her work underscored the importance of directly engaging with supporters of the populist right to discern their worldviews even when social scientists often feel reluctant to immerse themselves in such milieus and are generally more inclined to study progressive activists who tend to be more like them.[8] The first interview for this book reassured me that a ground-up approach that took the views of populist sympathizers seriously would yield novel insights into the rise of popular support for the far-right even if it promised to be a bumpy ride.

Developing a better understanding of why more and more people across the world turn to far-right populist politics for answers to societal (and personal) problems seems particularly pressing, as we are witnessing a pronounced rightward shift in a growing number of countries. Far-right populist parties are not simply capturing an ever-larger share of the votes in general elections but have managed to form governments in such well-established liberal democracies as the United States, Italy, and the Netherlands. Far-right forces have come—and are projected to come—alarmingly close to capturing the government in a range of other countries, including France, Germany, Sweden, and Austria, while important democracies in the Global South such as in India or Argentina have also elected populist leaders.

Research on populism has prioritized the study of political parties, electoral politics, eroding democratic institutions, media, and political propaganda.[9] By contrast, this book takes a different approach by examining populism as a cultural—not just a political—process that aims to reshape cultural identities through reimagining the nation and the meanings of cultural citizenship.[10] It therefore emphasizes the role of cultural production, culture wars, consumer markets, and popular culture in accounting for the rise of far-right populism. It shows, in particular, how popular consumer culture can serve as a crucial vehicle for promoting new interpretations of national identity and circulating nationalist symbols, thereby fostering popular support for far-right radicalization.

Hungary is the focus of the book because this country has emerged as one of the most interesting and important cases to elucidate the dynamics and resilience of far-right populism, for three reasons. First, it has followed a dramatic backsliding trajectory, from being likely the most open and liberal state of the former Eastern Bloc in the 1990s to becoming the most firmly entrenched right-wing populist regime in the European Union. Second, the Hungarian case epitomizes a larger international trend: It demonstrates how radical nationalist discourse penetrates the public sphere and reconstitutes mainstream politics. This is a gradual process that has been affecting a broad range of countries, not just those that elected a far-right populist government. Hungary provides an ideological blueprint in this regard that has inspired populist political forces in many countries, from the United States to Israel. Finally, even though the far-right government was ousted in 2026, Hungary is still the country with the longest-serving democratically elected populist government in the world: Viktor Orbán's Fidesz won a landslide victory in the general elections in 2010 and a supermajority in this and three consecutive elections in 2014,

2018, and 2022. Its long reign offers important lessons about populism's deeper impact on political systems. The book traces key processes behind these seismic shifts in political culture while also offering more general lessons regarding the links between nationalism and far-right populism.

The rapid commodification of nationalist sentiments and the parallel growth of a vigorous cultural industry that supplies props for expressing and enacting radical nationalist identities were particularly salient developments in a postcommunist context. This book suggests that the emergence of cultural niche economies that rework the symbolic lexicon and material culture of national and ethnic identification has been an overlooked aspect of the rise of far-right populism. Cultural production and lifestyle practices, for instance, have provided a powerful instrument to revive and spread mythical history by making it attractive, tangible, accessible, and easy to circulate. This is why the book focuses on the intersections between markets and new forms of nationalism by looking at the manufacturing, design, and branding of radical nationalist products and lifestyle concepts. It argues that the increasing right-wing radicalization of politics and the expansion of "uncivil" publics have been aided by an expanding culture industry that effectively turns these attitudes into cultural commodities.

"Restoring the Nation to Greatness"

America's greatness, for instance, remained the dominant recurring theme in Donald Trump's 2024 election victory speech. He pledged to "restore America to greatness," to "unlock America's glorious destiny," "make America safe, strong, prosperous, powerful, and free again," "start by putting America first," which also means that "we wanna have borders" and "a strong and powerful military." Finally, he called on Americans "because together we can truly make America great again for all Americans."[11] Historically, such unabashed centering of the nation (and its superiority) in political discourse has been more of a trademark of European than of US politics. And this wasn't just Trump's sales pitch. The *New York Times* appeared on the day after the elections with an all-caps front-page headline that also spotlighted anxiety about America's self-image as a nation: "'Trump's America'—Victory Changes Nation's Sense of Itself."

America's growing preoccupation with its national destiny also confirms what has been a more general feature of far-right politics: the return of the nation as a powerful source of collective identity.[12] Far-right populist movements have in fact reinstated the nation as the ultimate symbol of political unity and mobilization, vowing "to restore its greatness." In his revealing book, *Empire of Resentment: Populism's Toxic Embrace of Nationalism*, Lawrence Rosenthal contends that Trump's election victory in 2016 was a watershed moment because it convinced "America's right-wing populists to migrate ideologically—from the Tea Party's free market fundamentalism to Trump's anti-immigrant, America-First nationalism."[13] With this move, the Republican Party began to resemble the right-wing anti-immigrant parties of Europe, which have been wedded to an exclusionary doctrine of nationalism—an "othering nationalism"[14]—that scapegoats immigrants and refugees as the main obstacle to national prosperity, the harmful Other.[15] These developments question American exceptionalism and imply increasing transatlantic convergence when it comes to the political repertoire of far-right populism. Hence, European experiences with far-right populist challenges offer clues that can shed light on populism's prospects and everyday dynamics in the United States too. In fact, political scientists have singled out Hungary and its far-right leader, Viktor Orbán, as offering particularly instructive lessons for America.[16]

Nationalism seemed to decline in the United States and Europe after World War II, leading to waning scholarly interest in the topic.[17] Even after 1989 the sudden resurgence of nationalism, triggered by the collapse of communism, was associated primarily with the dissolution of multiethnic communist states like Yugoslavia or the USSR.[18] These flare-ups of ethnic nationalism were also believed to be contained to the "more backward" regions of Eastern Europe, the Balkans, and Central Asia that hadn't quite moved beyond primordial understandings of nationalism. The post-1989 Zeitgeist was dominated instead by projections about "the end of history": the untrammeled progression of liberal democracy and global multiculturalism, an interconnected and interdependent world where nationalism would remain an anomaly and be surpassed by transnationalism.[19] The expansion of the European Union was a model project in this regard, although the tide began to turn after the 2004 accession of ten new countries. Soon, new forms of "toxic" and "othering" nationalism started making inroads into the public sphere and politics. The 2008 financial crisis exposed the shaky neoliberal underpinnings of globalization and sowed distrust in unfettered markets. But, ultimately, "it was the triple crises of 2015 (terror, financial, and refugee)—the attacks in France ranging from the attack on Charlie Hebdo to the Bataclan, the Greek debt crisis and the refugee crisis—that paved the way for the nationalist surge."[20] As liberal political forces fully embraced cultural globalization and neoliberal markets, dismissing nation-states as anachronistic or even pathological,[21] the opportunity to "reimagine" the nation for the twenty-first century was left entirely to the emerging populist right.

Nationalism research has also been split into two main camps along theoretical lines. The "political" approach, on the one hand, focuses primarily on elites' political projects and discursive practices. The "quotidian" approach, on the other hand, explores mundane lived experiences and sentiments of nonelites.[22] The latter camp, probing "everyday" or "banal" nationalism, infused new vigor into nationalism studies in the past decades.[23] But, as it was established in reaction, and to some extent in opposition, to the political approach, it has remained largely disconnected from it.

This book is launched from a ground-up perspective informed by "banal" nationalism, but it also aims to bridge the binary conceptual division of the field by showing that elite and popular visions of the nation are dynamically interconnected. The Hungarian case demonstrates particularly forcefully how "political" and "quotidian" practices constantly intersect. Hungary's far-right populist government recognized early on the political power of banal nationalism and made it its mission to enable, embrace, and legitimate (selected) vernacular histories and popular practices of nationalism. In chapter 4, for instance, I will elaborate how a state-sponsored extracurricular heritage tourism program for public school students becomes a vessel to channel popular radical nationalist symbols into public education. In chapter 5 I will discuss how amateur archeologists are facilitated by public funding and new institutions set up by the government to promote their revisionist histories of Hungarian ethnogenesis.

Reimagining the Nation Through Cultural Production in Populist Regimes

In his paradigm-shifting book that ushered in the "cultural turn" in nationalism research, Benedict Anderson proposed a constructivist notion of the nation as an "imagined political community."[24] He posited that citizens of a nation-state could simply not rely on face-to-face interactions with most of their compatriots to affirm their commonality. Instead, they had to symbolically construct, that is, "imagine," this national community. Cultural products played a crucial role in this process, most importantly, printed matter such as books and newspapers, maps, and museums, but also poetry, prose fiction, music, and plastic arts. And the new national communities became imaginable through a "half-fortuitous, but explosive, interaction between a system of production and productive relations (capitalism), a technology of communication (print), and the fatality of human linguistic diversity."[25]

In other words, the rise of capitalism expanded markets where cultural products were exchanged and circulated. The book was in fact the "first modern style mass-produced industrial commodity" and together with newspapers (just an "extreme" form of a book) was instrumental in consolidating vernacular languages and creating unified fields of exchange and communication.[26] Print capitalism was thus largely responsible for generating the fundamental material forms and circuits of communication through which the national community could be effectively imagined.

Anderson's principal aim was to explain the rise of nations and nationalism, so how national communities were sustained over time and how they continually needed to be reimagined received little notice in his work. Imagining and reimagining the nation is, nevertheless, a complex, historically contingent and multilayered process that takes place at different scales, with varying intensity, and through evolving technologies (e.g., social media). For instance, whereas the political and emotional sway of national communities diminished during the post-1989 spread of globalization, now a key objective of far-right populist regimes is to bring back a narrowly defined, anti-immigrant nation as the definitive foundation of collective belonging.

Cultural products and markets are central to imagining a national political community, as pointed out by Anderson, which makes cultural production a useful starting point for investigating how far-right populism strives to reimagine the nation. Sociological research on cultural production has revolved mainly around the study of classification and its links to social stratification, valuation and evaluation, representations, or cultural capital, and not so much around national identity and nationalism.[27] Studies that did examine the nexus between cultural production and nation building tended to prioritize the role of the state and cultural elites,[28] and this was emphatically true in the postcommunist context.[29]

The sociology of culture has also long maintained a sharp split between a cultural production and a consumption perspective.[30] My aim, however, is to follow a more integrated approach that recognizes the inherent interconnectedness of cultural production, consumption, and reception.[31] While cultural producers are my key informants in this book, the conversations I conducted with them always reinforced how cultural production is intertwined with consumption: Cultural objects like fashion are often coproduced with customers, especially for small brands with a cultural mission. Furthermore, cultural producers are themselves often consumers of their own and similar products and invest significant effort in understanding and responding to their customers' needs.[32] The insights of scholarship on subcultures that I build on similarly stress that participants frequently act as both producers and consumers of their subcultures. As I flesh out in chapter 3, the reason I draw predominantly on cultural producers' views is not that I consider consumers' perspective less relevant but that, in this work, I am more interested in cultural producers' agency in manufacturing and circulating identity narratives via consumer markets than in the ways in which consumers appropriate them.

But cultural production also highlights how cultural objects and markets intersect, which is especially important for capturing popular forms of nationalism. And cultural producers themselves are not always part of the cultural elite, as will be shown in the case of the owners and designers of small fashion labels featured in chapter 3, or the case of horseback archery aficionados who promote revisionist histories of Hungarians' ethnic origins in chapter 5. Their careers were often rooted in countercultural scenes and were motivated by strong antiestablishment, and specifically antistate, attitudes, which continued to influence their outlook and everyday practices even after they attained more mainstream recognition following the populist turn in 2010.

This is why the focus on cultural production helps to demonstrate that contemporary far-right populism is not a well-codified political ideology but a more fluid subculture in which expressive symbols, material objects, rituals, everyday consumption, and lifestyle patterns are essential carriers of political convictions and markers of group boundaries.[33] These symbolic economies also contribute to reconfiguring the boundaries between politics and the public sphere, allowing radical nationalist themes to penetrate mainstream political discourse. This occurs, for instance, because markets often successfully circulate radical nationalist symbols and narratives that are suppressed from official political vocabulary. These can include symbols that are not legally banned (unlike, for instance, the swastika in most European countries) but are nevertheless closely associated with radical nationalist politics, such as the irredentist Greater Hungary image in Hungary, or the tsar's portrait in Russia.[34] The visibility and legitimacy accorded to these symbols through their broad circulation on mundane consumer goods gradually helps to break down the barriers to the political mainstream and shift the boundaries of political acceptability. I also argue that this popular consumer culture has been eagerly mobilized by far-right populist governments in the culture wars in their efforts to establish an illiberal national cultural canon.

By taking the study of cultural production in this direction, I want to underline that the national is not confined to the political realm but increasingly extends into the economic. The imprint of nationalism and ethnicity on economic processes has been explored in a scattered manner across a range of disciplines, from international political economy to media and communications, addressing topics such as economic nationalism, ethnic enclaves, or nation branding. An extensive literature in international political economy originally defined economic nationalism through a set of economic policies, including trade protectionism, statism, and autarky, that were employed—and are about to be resurrected in many countries—to champion the economic interests of individual nations.[35]

More recently, attention has been expanded to policy efforts that seek to protect and reassert distinct national cultures feared to be undermined by globalization and neoliberal free trade. For instance, the elaborate system of geographical indications that give producers of artisanal foodstuffs exclusive rights to product names in Europe (e.g., Roquefort cheese, Prosciutto di Parma, Scotch whiskey) serves to recognize and ensure "cultural sovereignty" by safeguarding national cultures and local traditions.[36] Sociologists and anthropologists have primarily focused on the economic significance of ethnicity: on the role of ethnic enclaves and ethnic niche economies as a vehicle for immigrant incorporation,[37] and on the turning of ethnic groups into business ventures.[38] Interest has also surged in the practice of nation branding, the commercialization of national distinctiveness and heritage in the context of globalization and neoliberal corporatization, usually involving state-led efforts to boost the national economy.[39]

But these lines of inquiry do not quite capture the dynamics of cultural production that is driven by radical nationalism. Radical nationalist consumer culture has not emerged as a consequence of economic policy measures that sought to protect and promote the production and consumption of locally made national commodities.[40] It is also not a case of nation branding or corporatization of ethnicity as described, for instance, in *Ethnicity Inc*,[41] because national identity is not commodified chiefly for outsiders—tourists, foreign investors, or European Union bureaucrats—and for simulating national economic development. Instead, it relies on commodification and material culture to draw hard ethnic boundaries around national identity—even everyday clothing should display visible markers of Hungarianness. It is seen to offer tools for the cultural and political reimagining of the nation, which is part of a nation-building and sovereignty-affirming project that targets and mobilizes co-ethnics of the nation-state and ethnic diaspora communities beyond state borders. Radical nationalist consumer tastes and consumption practices still operate as an exclusionary mechanism, not just against immigrants and minority ethnic groups such as the Roma or Jews, but also against liberals and social progressives who embrace "faceless" global multiculturalism and gender-inclusiveness while rejecting ethnic and national markers as anachronistic and politically retrograde.

The study of far-right populism's cultural production conceptually benefits more from research on subcultures and "circuits of commerce."[42] Scholarship on subcultures emphasizes the significance of commodities and material culture as means of symbolic communication for social groups.[43] Clothing, language choice, music preferences, or leisure activities are politically meaningful. Consumer goods are mobilized as everyday material objects to define a "politics of style," to express and perform group identity in opposition to mainstream society.

The grassroots and countercultural nature of subcultures carries important implications for contemporary radical nationalist consumer culture. The general assumption about far-right populist regimes is that their preferred cultural expressions are determined in a top-down manner by the state and a politically anointed cultural elite in line with their pronounced authoritarian outlook. In the following chapters, however, I will show how crucial the countercultural origins of radical nationalist cultural production are, and how it is this antiestablishment attitude that populist governments hope to embrace to bolster their popular appeal.

Although subcultural studies effectively capture the political power of mundane cultural objects, they were not much interested in nationalism, as they were searching instead for manifestations of class-based resistance.[44] Even right-wing and extremist youth cultures such as skinhead and neo-Nazi groups and their appropriation of fashion and clothing brands were mostly explained as forms of class resistance.[45] Similarly, youth cultures remain the analytical focus in this field,[46] even though, as the case study chapters will elaborate, radical nationalist subcultures cut across age, gender, and class affiliation.[47] My book moves away from the tendency to spotlight only the most radical and extreme fringe groups that signal right-wing political shifts and pursues the seemingly more moderate but potentially deeper transformations that also engulf the societal middle.

In a similar vein, research on "circuits of commerce" helps to illuminate the loosely connected social networks of radical nationalist consumerism while this example simultaneously helps to expand the theoretical scope of this work. Viviana Zelizer coined the concept to describe how symbolic meanings that emerge through thick webs of social relations organize economic exchanges.[48] Economic circuits thus constitute a distinctive and widespread form of interaction. Producers and consumers of radical nationalism make up such an economic circuit because, for them, specialized commodities constitute a material culture that effectively carries shared understandings of national belonging and moral value.

Communities that emerge around radical nationalist consumer products and lifestyle practices thus indicate how political attitudes and commitments can also become the organizing principle of specialized economic transactions. This line of reasoning will be developed most fully in chapter 3, which looks at Hungarian folk-revivalist fashion brands. The other chapters will not only reinforce this argument but go a step further by showing how "circuits of commerce" in different fields—fashion, book publishing, horseback archery—are interconnected. They do not completely overlap but intersect in important ways, which contributes to scaling up radical nationalist cultural production and consumer communities. This scaling up intensifies after the formation of a far-right populist government that starts steering various forms of public support (e.g., financial subsidies, institutional recognition, increased visibility) toward their maintenance. The case studies in the following chapters will depict in detail how radical nationalist "cultural circuits" are integrated into mainstream cultural production with the aim of building a new national cultural canon, a key political aspiration of the far-right.[49]

Struggle for a Right-Wing Cultural Hegemony and an Illiberal Cultural Canon

In a Tanner lecture delivered at the University of Michigan in 1988, Toni Morrison spoke about the "Afro-American Presence in American Literature" in the evolving culture wars at the time.[50] She sharply summarized the enormous stakes involved in canon debates: "Canon building is empire building. Canon defense is national defense. Canon debate, whatever the terrain, nature, and range (of criticism, of history, of the history of knowledge, of the definition of language, the universality of aesthetic principles, the sociology of art, the humanistic imagination), is the clash of cultures. And *all* of the interests are vested."[51] Her views convey the intensity of the debate about literary canons in the 1980s and 1990s, when a rising conservative movement began to vehemently question what was taught in the humanities at US universities. They were particularly outraged by how feminism and multiculturalism criticized the classic Western canon in literature, art, and history for its racial, sexual, and political biases, urging revisions to the canon.[52]

But culture wars were not limited to the humanities or universities. They encompassed a much wider array of US culture and politics, revealing a deepening fissure between traditionalists/conservatives and progressives/liberals over the fundamental cultural and moral values that were supposed to provide a compass to American society. Political battles erupted over cultural issues such as abortion, gun laws, separation of church and state, sexuality, family values, or privacy.[53] And, as noted by James Davison Hunter, a prominent theorist of the culture wars, at heart they were about the mobilization of political resources around competing positions on cultural issues, that is, about how culture underwrites politics. Culture wars thus usually expose how politics is rooted in deeper cultural dispositions beyond attitudes and values.[54] Yet, they have often been dismissed in political discourse, predominantly by the left, as just smoke and mirrors, as a mere distraction deflecting attention from "real" issues—as conflicts are always seen to boil down to "it's the economy, stupid." The contemporary populist far right has, however, taken culture very seriously and ascribed to it a central place in its political playbook.

The latest resurgence of culture wars in the United States echoes many of the themes and underlying tensions that were manifest in its previous incarnations: the questioning of progressive university curricula, now targeting critical race theory and LGBTQ+ content;[55] identity politics revolving around wokeness and diversity, equity, and inclusion (DEI) policies; book bans over portrayals of sexual and racial identity in high schools and public libraries; or the high-profile Republican attacks on—and continuing threats to—universities in the wake of the Israeli-Hamas war. The current debates also highlight how political differences become increasingly entrenched and essentialized when they are defined around cultural and moral beliefs, exacerbating political polarization. Culture has clearly served as an important political battleground for the populist far right, which has fueled culture wars with the intention of disrupting the liberal cultural canon.

Culture wars have also played an important role for far-right populist movements in Europe. They are considered a means of working toward a right-wing cultural hegemony that is believed to be integral to solidifying and deepening political rule. The idea that culture is vital to a right-wing political breakthrough was formulated in the 1960s by one of the key thinkers of the French New Right (*Nouvelle Droite*), Alan de Benoist. He introduced the concept of metapolitics to argue that to gain political influence, one had to move beyond conventional political strategies and recognize the primacy of culture over politics.[56] De Benoist derived this lesson from observing the events of 1968 and the ways in which they contributed to the emergence of the New Left. He noted how the countercultural fervor of leftist student radicals inspired by Marxist cultural theories spread to broader social strata, generating a deeper cultural shift that eventually enabled political mobilization and opened the way for political changes.[57]

This conclusion led de Benoist to call for a right-wing reinterpretation of leftist cultural theorists, most importantly of Antonio Gramsci and his idea of cultural hegemony. In theorizing why communism failed to stop fascism in the interwar period, Gramsci developed his theory of cultural hegemony. He proposed that social order was maintained primarily through cultural domination and not coercion. Each political order is bolstered by a hegemonic ideology, "that is, a hegemonic system of ideologies that provide a common language, discourse, and normative visions shared by the contestants in struggle."[58] Class struggle for Gramsci thus also takes place in the cultural realm where competing classes (labor and capital) vie for attaining hegemony. The dominated class, while mostly willingly consenting to the reigning cultural hegemony, has some insight into the nature of their domination, and "organic intellectuals" can devise ways to break the status quo.[59]

So, even though the New Right started as an antileftist backlash against the cultural revolution of the 1960s, it was so impressed by the latter's effectiveness that it vowed to mimic its tactics and "reconquer the cultural and intellectual terrain occupied by the left."[60] Metapolitics in this scheme then becomes essentially synonymous with culture wars.[61] This modus operandi is evident in the contemporary context when the far-right populist agenda frequently just involves "flipping the script" of the radical left. For instance, de Benoist introduced the notion of "ethnopluralism" as a response to multiculturalism, advocating a "differentialist anti-racism" that aims to uphold the irreducible ethnic and racial plurality of the human species.[62] He maintains that racism should not be fought by negating the concept of race or by blending "all races into an undifferentiated whole," but by respecting and preserving ethnic and racial distinctiveness.[63] His "ethnopluralism" therefore basically stands for "an upside-down multiculturalism that amounts to a coded nativism, translating xenophobia and intolerance into liberal-democratic universalist language."[64]

Identity politics is similarly turned on its head. Far-right populists have criticized leftist identity politics for a myriad of reasons: for fragmenting society in the name of an ever-increasing number of subgroup identities; for emphasizing victimhood; for rejecting Enlightenment universalism in the name of individualist politics, for favoring a "pseudo-politics of recognition" over redistribution.[65] Yet, they appropriate the language of identity by turning it into a metaconcept of itself, which they call "identitarianism." For far-right populists, identity is "a bulwark against globalism, multiculturalism, and what they label the 'great replacement' (an anti-immigrant conspiracy theory)."[66] It is mobilized against pluralism and difference, and it aims to reroot the "people" in an essentialist and ethnically homogeneous—in German often denoted as *völkisch*—community that embraces white supremacy and, in the case of the United States, also a white Christian nationalism.[67] The ideological mirroring used in the case of ethnopluralism and identity politics is one of the far right's underlying strategies to undermine the cultural hegemony of liberalism.

The French New Right grew into the European New Right and has exerted considerable influence over the development of far-right populism across Europe since the 1990s, most significantly in Italy, Germany, and Belgium, but also in Russia (through the work of Alexander Dugin). The American Alt-Right and the pan-European "Identitarian" movement also claim to have been inspired by the ideas of the New Right.[68] In Hungary, too, the European New Right left an important mark. De Benoist's ideas about right-wing Gramscism and metapolitics have been the most influential in shaping Hungarian thinking about the role of culture in far-right populist rule. They have been adapted to Hungarian circumstances and further developed into a "metapolitical" plan of action for the Orbán regime.

The most important local interpreter of the New Right's ideological framework is a young historian, Márton Békés, who is the research director of The House of Terror Museum in Budapest—dedicated to commemorating the crimes of both fascist and communist regimes in Hungary—and the director of the XXIst Century Institute—a conservative think tank that is made up of "a community of thinkers committed to national sovereignty, democracy, freedom, market economy and Christian values."[69] He is also an important protégé of Mária Schmidt, director-general of the museum, a Holocaust historian, but also one of the richest Hungarians.[70] Schmidt has been part of Viktor Orbán's inner circle for decades and served as Orbán's main adviser during the first Fidesz government from 1998 to 2002.

Consequently, the Hungarian interpretation of the New Right's vision of culture as a political resource was synthetized by Békés in *Cultural Warfare: The Theory and Practice of Cultural Power*, published in 2020. This book has served as a written manifesto that makes explicit the Orbán regime's political objectives in the field of culture, and for this reason it warrants closer examination here.[71] As the title suggests, it promises to lay not only the ideological foundations but also a strategic roadmap for establishing a right-wing cultural hegemony in Hungary. It asserts that replacing the liberal with an illiberal cultural canon was an absolute necessity because even though Hungary had a supermajority right-wing government since 2010, in the cultural sphere this government could not even get 10 percent of the votes.[72] Dismantling the liberal cultural hegemony is particularly challenging because it still represents the global Zeitgeist, which means that the (re)production of local culture has to compete with the vast arsenal of tools and resources available for the production of global culture. Therefore, the state had to assume an active role in compensating for this power differential between the conditions of local and global cultural production in the interest of protecting national sovereignty.

An illiberal cultural hegemony is also portrayed as indispensable because the Orbán government's political aspiration went beyond building just a new political system; it wanted to define an entire era (*korszak*). This was a central idea that debuted in one of Viktor Orbán's (in)famous speeches delivered each year at a summer free university in Transylvania, Romania.[73] In his 2018 speech, Orbán announced that Fidesz's third supermajority election win could be understood as a mandate for his government "to build a new era." He explained that "an era, however, is more than a political order. An era is a distinctive and representative cultural milieu. An era is a kind of intellectual order, a shared mood, possibly a characteristic taste and mode of conduct. A system, a political system is usually defined by rules and political decisions, but an era is more than this. An era, instead, is defined by cultural trends, collective beliefs, and societal customs. Our task now is to embed the political system in a cultural era."[74] In other words, an epochal transformation requires something deeper than just political change, it needs to shift society's shared cultural and cognitive frames. And without an all-embracing cultural change, a political regime change remains incomplete and can be easily reversed.[75] In this context, culture wars become the key (metapolitical) tool in the struggle for cultural hegemony, which is in fact a war for cultural power.

The objective is a "conservative cultural decolonization," which requires the deconstruction of the deeply ingrained and globally backed liberal cultural canon.[76] In the Hungarian case, this is presented as uniquely difficult because from a cultural standpoint, the far right sees the postcommunist period until 2010 as the extension of the communist era. According to this position, the leftist political and economic elite of late communism struck an alliance with the liberal intelligentsia that grew out of the democratic opposition to secure their control over the postcommunist transition. Even though political power slipped from their hands a couple of times when they lost the elections (1990–1994, 1998–2002), they firmly held onto cultural power during the entire period. By this right-wing theorists mean that the post-1989 continuity in the individuals and families that made up the country's power and economic elite enabled these groups to maintain their cultural monopoly not just over cultural production but also over cognitive and discursive frames, structures of thought, and language use.[77] And, as mentioned earlier, they were also facilitated in this process by adapting and confirming to the expectations of global (neoliberal) power structures.

How to crack this deeply entrenched cultural monopoly became a major dilemma for Fidesz after its 2010 landslide election victory. The proposed action plan was not as elaborate as the diagnosis of the intricacies of liberal domination, but Békés put forward a bundle of suggestions for practical intervention in his capacity as an aspiring ideologue. He contends that Gramscian consent to power is achieved through culture embodied in myths, symbols, narratives, shared history, canon and legitimation, which circulate via institutions of public life (civic associations, forums, events, media, and organizations).[78]

On a more operational level, Békés emphasizes the importance of establishing new institutions that incubate illiberal cultural production and organizing them into close-knit networks. Fidesz's strategy has in fact involved setting up so-called parallel institutions, that is, duplicating existing public research institutes by opening a conservative version—a trend that will be explored further in chapter 2. This again illustrates the ideological mirroring that is a general feature of the far right's cultural strategy. Békés takes stock of this strategy a few years after the publication of his manifesto, noting that by 2023 eight new institutes were set up in the field of historical research and memory politics, seven conservative think tanks, three policy research institutes in support of governmental agencies, a journal, half a dozen quality publishers, and two or three nonprofit foundations that function as umbrella organizations.[79] New institutions have mushroomed hand in hand with sustained attacks on existing ones, most notably on the Central European University, which was pressured to leave Hungary, on the research network of the Hungarian Academy of Sciences, and on major Hungarian universities, whose autonomy was severely curbed by being coerced into a new governance model that reduces public funding while simultaneously increasing direct government control.[80]

In conjunction with the institutional strategy, a "three-level counter-hegemony machinery" is proposed. Level 1 involves "direct combat" on a day-to-day basis through daily and weekly papers, television and radio programs, and various internet platforms. Level 2 is responsible for "mid-term cultural work" with the help of monthly and quarterly journals, books, research institutes, and think tanks. Books, for instance, are described as a "weapon" and reading as a "military act." Level 3 deals with articulating the theoretical and philosophical foundations of the right-wing worldview through university lectures, book publishers, and film distributors, among others.[81] The important role these tools have played in Germany in the rise of the far-right political party Alternative für Deutschland (AfD) is frequently highlighted.[82] These three levels provide the institutional infrastructure for the circulation of political discourse, which is essentially "made up of an intricate web of myths, tales, stories, testimonials, i.e., narratives and the grand narratives (that we call metanarratives)."[83] Discursive strategies and the politics of language are crucial because they can eventually lead to discursive domination, the ability to define the terms and the language of political discourse, which is the first step toward cultural hegemony.

It's also true, however, that narratives are given special attention as the basis of metapolitical strategies for the right. Narratives are seen as a "collective, cognitive resource" that creates a strong emotional pull and can take many forms, including legends, myths, traditions, and oral histories. Political conflicts then often unfold as a clash of narratives between warring political groups, and narrative advantage can be converted into political advantage.[84] The centrality of narratives resonates with Arlie Hochschild's findings about "deep stories" in the right-wing communities she studied in the United States.[85] These "deep stories" are deep because they have been told and retold over many times across generations, tweaked and updated to contemporary circumstances. In the Hungarian case, many of these narratives revolve around mythical histories about the nation, which will be scrutinized more closely in the remaining chapters.

I also argue, however, that how narratives circulate and are reproduced in the process is as crucial as their periodic retelling. The following chapters will therefore trace how the same narrative (e.g., mythical national origin stories) can be re-created and disseminated simultaneously in multiple forms as cultural objects (e.g., books, clothing, traditional sport, heritage tours) and how this multiplicity amplifies their prevalence.

Most theorists of the New Right clearly write from the perspective of the cultural and intellectual elite and say precious little about the role of popular culture in the struggle for illiberal cultural hegemony. My book in turn will also shed light on how popular culture is mobilized in this process—for instance, by promoting a grassroots revisionist historiography (chapter 2), folk-revival in fashion (chapter 3), vernacular histories in public education (chapter 4), and amateur archeology and anti-Westernism (chapter 5)—and is embraced by the state in various ways to boost the regime's popular legitimacy. Popular culture also underscores the importance of consumer markets—overlooked in the elitist view—as important infrastructure for the circulation of identity narratives.

It is crucial to stress the countercultural attitude that continues to characterize both the elite and popular cultural producers of the populist far right. As, for example, the interviews in chapter 2 on book publishing will reveal, even cultural producers who have assumed powerful positions since the populist turn in 2010 persistently see themselves under the shadow of a lingering liberal cultural hegemony as marginalized actors in the cultural field. Therefore, their strategies and self-understandings are still very much driven by countercultural, counter-establishment narratives and frames of mind.

The Conceptual Minefield of Populism

"Populism" has become a ubiquitous yet slippery term, tangled up with a range of heavyweight concepts like nationalism, extremism, radicalism, fascism, or illiberalism.[86] There is some academic consensus that populism denotes a type of politics that is organized around the antagonism between "the elite" and the "people," claiming to redefine political rule in the name of the "people."[87] It can characterize both left- and right-wing politics, although most recently it has been primarily used to describe illiberal, antidemocratic, and antipluralist political trends. Populism is also no longer a fringe phenomenon of liberal democracies but has become mainstream, increasingly giving way to a "populist Zeitgeist."[88]

The question is still, nevertheless, whether it can be considered a well-defined ideology like other major "isms," such as communism, liberalism, nationalism, and capitalism, or rather a political movement, or simply a political style. An influential theorist of populism, political scientist Cas Mudde, defines populism as a "thin-centered ideology" that "considers society to be ultimately separated into two homogeneous and antagonistic groups, 'the pure people' versus 'the corrupt elite,' and which argues that politics should be an expression of the volonté générale (general will) of the people."[89] Populism's core revolves around the notion of "the people," and its "thin-centeredness" means, for instance, that it can be readily combined with other ideologies, from communism to nationalism to ecologism.[90] The combination of populism with nationalism has certainly been on the rise, seeking to reroot "the will of the people" in a narrowly defined, ethnically homogeneous community, and will be the focus of this book as well.

Additional perplexity arises from the proliferation of qualifiers and synonyms associated with populist politics, including far right, hard right, extreme right, radical right, as well as national conservative, nativist, anti-immigrant, neofascist, authoritarian, and any possible combinations of these (and some other) terms.[91] There is even a large-scale, international research project, The PopuList, that follows the changing evolution and use of these terms to identify political parties in thirty-one countries over a roughly thirty-year period, from 1989 to 2022. According to this classification, radical right parties, for instance, are distinguished by two core ideologies: nativism (a strong anti-immigrant stance espousing that only members of the "native group" should inhabit the state) and authoritarianism (a centralized, hierarchical rule focusing on the maintenance of order). Extreme-right parties share these ideological foundations but also question and want to overthrow the existing democratic order while approving the use of violence, like Greece's neo-Nazi Golden Dawn.

The far right, in turn, is more of an umbrella label that encompasses both radical and extreme-right parties.[92] "Hard right" has come into vogue recently and is used predominantly by media outlets. These criteria can help differentiate the ideological platforms of specific parties. Marine Le Pen's National Rally (RN) in France classifies as a far-right, populist party, the German AfD is a far-right, populist party that has an extremist element, while Hungary's Fidesz is also a far-right, populist party with strong anti-LGBTQ+ views.[93] This lexicon, nevertheless, still focuses narrowly on categorizing political parties rather than capturing the broader societal implications of populism as an emergent political order.

Simultaneously, there are strong voices insisting that populism is just a euphemistic label to sugarcoat the contemporary resurgence of fascism.[94] They contend that populist politics employs many of the same tactics and rhetorical techniques that fascist movements turned to in the interwar period, such as directing hatred against immigrants and minorities (e.g., LGBTQ+ individuals), undermining the independence of the judicial system, suggesting that violent vigilante justice against political opponents is acceptable, banning books, and "using education to indoctrinate the young in the narrative of national greatness, rooted in a glorious past."[95]

Erasing a pluralist history that includes the perspectives of marginalized groups—reflected in attacks on critical race theory or in denials of slavery's central role in the United States—and replacing it with a single version of the past that preaches national greatness, purity, and innocence while reinforcing strict gender roles and demonizing the left are as essential to contemporary populist representations and practices as they were to their fascist counterparts. The political purpose of this erasure is to justify the reproduction of social and cultural hierarchies that place one group above others based on arbitrary factors like race, ethnicity, and gender.[96] Education then serves as a key site where these distorted histories are disseminated in the form of mythic representations that create and sustain an emotionally charged sense of victimhood and resentment. Sources of victimhood and resentment can vary greatly across countries—resentment over the perceived denial of the American Dream in the United States,[97] or over unjust treatment by foreign powers in the case of Hungary—but they are as much a key mover of populist politics as they were during fascism.[98] Any critical scholarship that questions these one-dimensional narratives is seen as a political threat, hence the repeated assaults on universities in populist regimes from Trump's America and Orbán's Hungary to Modi's India.

There are certainly eerie similarities in the political goals and tactical repertoire of fascism and today's populism, as highlighted by the examples in the previous paragraph. But creating a simple equivalence between interwar fascist and contemporary populist movements not only would be ahistorical but would not necessarily enhance our understanding of current developments. Authors who warn against the ominous dangers of populism by invoking the specter of fascism often do this to maximize indignation and moral repugnance. They tend to write more from an engaged activist than from a scholarly perspective.[99] As a result, they often slip into generalizations that turn "fascist" into a catch-all term, a synonym for authoritarian, extremist, repressive, xenophobic, ethnocentric, nationalist—that is, virtually any manifestation of antidemocratic politics.[100] This becomes especially problematic in a postcommunist context because many of the practices ascribed to fascist politics (e.g., propagation of distorted histories in public education, censorship, book bans, use of state violence against dissenters) were also routinely employed by communist regimes, and thus not specific to fascism. They also tend to downplay important differences, for instance, the centrality of organized militia violence under the aegis of an electoral party that was at the heart of fascist politics.[101] Hence, in this book I prefer to follow a strategy that does not assume some inherent link between fascism and populism but focuses instead on empirically tracing links to the fascist era and its contemporary implications (e.g., the interwar fascist cooptation of folk symbolism in Hungarian fashion, or the lifting of interwar authors that advocated fascist views into the National Core Curriculum in literature after 2010).

Illiberalism is yet another term that has a firm place in the thick web of concepts closely interrelated with populism. It has also been an emergent and fluid concept that academia has for long evaded using while it rose to prevalence in media and political discourse.[102] It generally signifies the broad backlash against liberal principles such as pluralism, individual freedoms, universalism, and equality that entailed support, for instance, for human rights, protection of minorities, or ethnic, gender, and religious diversity. Illiberalism, by contrast, promotes intolerance, fear of difference, discipline, respect for hierarchy, authority, traditions, and "organic" collectives such as the family.[103] It was introduced by Fareed Zakaria in a *Foreign Affairs* piece that described illiberal democracies as regimes that have free elections but lack liberal institutions.[104] But its career as a concept tied to populism was really launched by Viktor Orbán in his "illiberal state" speech in 2014. Orbán lambasted liberalism for fostering "individual selfishness and rootless cosmopolitanism, creating a society of atomized and multicultural citizens who claim rights without accepting any duties to the national community and state."[105] Instead, he envisioned a "work-based" society governed by majoritarianism and strong conservative values. He also pointed to the "Asian model," predominantly Singapore and China besides Turkey and Russia, to note that liberal democracy is not the only political system that can generate economic growth.[106] This is an important theme whose popular cultural underpinnings will be examined in chapter 5.

Against this overview of the terminologically overladen terrain of populism research that aimed to clarify fundamental concepts, I want to explain the terminological choices I made for this book. I will primarily use three terms to denote different aspects of populist politics: radical nationalism, far-right populism, and illiberalism. I use radical nationalism when I want to emphasize the countercultural roots of right-wing populism. In a postcommunist setting, nationalism and its radical expressions were seen as a form of political resistance to the internationalism of the communist and the global multiculturalism of post-1989 liberal democratic regimes. In fact, Hungarian right-wing movements in the 2000s, before the 2010 populist turn, often called themselves *nemzeti radikálisok*, which is difficult to precisely translate into English but would be closest in meaning to "national radicals," recalling nineteenth-century political movements fighting for national self-determination.[107] By using far-right populism, I draw on Cas Mudde's classification discussed earlier, opting for this umbrella term that includes both radical and extreme right-wing political movements to situate Hungarian right-wing actors and developments vis-à-vis larger international trends.[108] Finally, illiberalism and illiberal refer to the cultural content, the cultural products and practices that promote illiberal values (e.g., intolerance, traditional values, heteronormative gender norms, majoritarianism), as outlined earlier.

Organization of the Book

The ensuing chapters explore four crucial and representative sites of radical nationalist consumer culture that have significantly shaped far-right populist cultural production in Hungary since the early 2000s: *book publishing* that has been central to today's culture wars, a defining element of far-right populist politics in and of itself; *fashion brands* that design and market explicitly national fashion items rooted in folk traditions; *heritage tourism* to neighboring countries (especially to Transylvania, Romania) to show how cross-border tourism strives to symbolically transgress current national borders and sustain the idea of a "Greater Hungary"; and *martial arts*, exemplified by horseback archery, that claim to recover "ancient" nomadic traditions embedded in a mythic Orientalism and a broader ideological mission of anti-Westernism.

These four case studies each illuminate different but fundamental aspects of far-right cultural production: book publishing focuses on culture wars, fashion zooms in on the formation of political "circuits of commerce," heritage tourism reveals how mythical historical narratives are propagated in public schools, and horseback archery exposes the deep roots of anti-Westernism as integral to populist illiberalism in Hungary. The analysis employs mixed-methods qualitative research building on a combination of interviews with various cultural professionals (e.g., fashion designers, craftspeople, curators, design consultants, book publishers); ethnographic observations at festivals, fairs, exhibitions, fashion shows, horseback archery camps; and the content analysis of documents, company websites, and social media platforms of key cultural producers (e.g., fashion brands, book publishers).

Chapter 2 examines the political weaponization of books and book publishing through the so-called national book publishers and bookstores and the spread of book bans. In the age of social media, books are believed to have lost their relevance in political discourse. But the striking proliferation of book bans—in the United States in 2024 there were over ten thousand instances of banned books in public schools[109]—reminds us of the unabating political influence of books and enduring censorship. Book publishing has also been identified as a strategic field by the European New Right, which affirms the precedence of culture over politics in achieving a right-wing breakthrough, urging the building of a right-wing cultural hegemony in the spirit of a "right-wing Gramscism."[110]

A group of boutique publishing houses and independent bookstores make up a significant niche market in the Hungarian publishing industry, specializing in nationalist fiction and nonfiction. Incidentally, the world's largest English-language publisher of far-right authors, Arktos, is also headquartered in Budapest. Chapter 2 maps how the mainstreaming of these right-wing publishers and normalization of far-right literature have proceeded hand in hand with the banning of books that contain LGBTQ+ content to mark out the contours of a new illiberal cultural canon.

Some "national" publishing houses, such as the family-owned Püski, trace their origins to interwar era fascist politics. Püski also operated in exile in New York City for nearly three decades after World War II, serving the Hungarian diaspora in the United States before returning to Hungary after 1989. These publishers were essential in keeping in circulation nationalist and far-right authors and literature that were banned under communism. Samizdat literature also included conservative and far-right writers who were compromised during interwar fascism and were outlawed by communist governments. Demand for these works grew exponentially after the fall of communism, which these publishers were quick to meet while extending their lists to new genres, including esoteric nationalism, speculative and mythical Hungarian origin histories, "traditional" martial arts such as horseback archery, and translations of the work of Western European far-right ideologues (e.g., Jean Raspail, Alan de Benoist).

Formerly blacklisted far-right Hungarian authors (e.g., Albert Wass, Cécile Tormay[111]) have been lifted into the national public-school curriculum, while contemporary progressive fiction that engages with the complexities of gender and sexual identity has been banned and declared harmful for children. I draw on interviews with owners of publishing houses, recurring visits to specialized bookstores, debates over the national curriculum and LGBTQ+ books for children, as well as company websites and social media materials to explain how books and book publishing shape far-right politics.

Chapter 3 focuses on fashion, which has historically been an important tool for expressing, enacting, and promoting national distinctiveness in Hungary. Similar to other countries, whose political independence was repeatedly challenged, political causes like national self-determination were often fought by cultural means, such as fashion.[112] Recent international examples—ranging from niqab and burkini bans in France and several other European Union states to the infamous burka vs. bikini ads of Germany's AfD party in the 2017 election campaign—similarly expose how dress and fashion constitute a crucial site where intense political conflicts over cultural belonging play out today.[113]

Chapter 3 highlights how, in Hungary, cultural heritage defined around ethnonational identity becomes politically instrumentalized, and how the communist regime's treatment of folk culture has facilitated its exploitation by far-right populist politics. I build primarily on interviews with fashion designers and owners of small labels (almost exclusively women), whose mission consists of incorporating "traditional" Hungarian motifs into contemporary everyday wear. Interviews with museum textile curators and fashion experts and ethnographic observations from numerous market fairs, exhibitions, and fashion shows complement the data.

These fashion producers, in addition to their commitment to local production and a craftsman ethic, promote the recovery of cultural heritage that emphasizes the reach of Hungarian ethnic culture beyond current state borders. They aim to revive and symbolically reclaim the aesthetic vocabulary of regions and territories that were detached from Hungary in 1920 because of the Treaty of Trianon and ceded to neighboring countries.[114] They also build on the countercultural legacies of dissident popular social movements like the Dance House movement, a grassroots folk revival movement that began openly challenging official communist cultural policies in the 1970s.[115] This movement was instrumental in creating demand for nationally inspired clothing that was not simply a traditional folk costume but incorporated folk culture into modern, urban everyday wear. Members of these movements—describing themselves as the "nomadic generation"—upheld national and ethnic folk heritage against what they saw as bogus communist internationalism propagated within the Eastern Block and strictly enforced by the communist Hungarian government. These countercultural roots continue to endow these fashion brands with a subcultural, antiestablishment edginess.

Chapter 4 delves into heritage tourism as a means to question existing national borders and restore an imperial vision of the nation. It examines a large-scale, state-sponsored student travel program that the Hungarian government launched in 2010, the year that marked the start of a brisk populist turn in Hungarian politics. The program, named "Without Borders" (*Határtalanul*), sponsors organized class trips of middle school students to areas of neighboring countries (Romania, Slovakia, Serbia, Croatia, and Ukraine) that belonged to the Hungarian state before World War I. The program's objective is to have thirteen-year-old school students visit Hungarian heritage sites in these countries to make them aware of the "real," pre–World War I borders of a "Greater Hungary." I obtained extensive and unique data about the travel scheme from the Hungarian Ministry of Human Resources through an extremely arduous Freedom of Information Act request.[116] The content analysis of these textual and visual materials offers insight into how ethnic diaspora communities become the cornerstone of a new populist understanding of the nation.

The chapter shows that the ultimate political goal of the program is to foster a chauvinistic and exclusionary ethnic definition of national belonging while symbolically reappropriating the former territories of imperial Hungary. It aims to instill the idea in public school students that ethnic Hungarian minorities beyond the state border should be viewed as part of an ethnically homogeneous Hungarian nation, and their habitat as part of Hungary's past and present. Additionally, the Hungarian government views state subsidies for heritage tourism as an important way to support Hungarian ethnic enclave economies in neighboring countries, as they contribute to the economic security and overall stability of these minority communities. The analysis sheds light on how the government exploits heritage tourism's informal and experiential character as well as its performative and affective power to institutionally validate vernacular histories of radical nationalism.

Chapter 5 investigates a martial art form, horseback archery that has been invented as a competitive sport in the past decades. Its objective is to recover a horseback archery tradition rooted in the classic warfare of Hungarian nomadic tribes that settled in the Carpathian Basin (encompassing today's Hungary) in the ninth century and brought this warfare with them on their long migratory journey from Central Asia. This chapter asserts that modern-day horseback archery successfully taps into the popular culture of mythic Orientalism, which has a long tradition in Hungary and is a key source of anti-Westernism. It has been embraced by the far-right populist government after 2010 because it provides popular backing to its crusade against Western liberalism and the European Union and its opening to Eastern autocratic regimes like Russia and Turkey.

Horseback archery has a long mythical history: It is described as warfare that provoked intensive fear in Western Europeans in the early Middle Ages and is often used to "prove" Hungarians' kinship with the Huns. This new martial art form has spawned a large following, while horseback archery shows have become a staple in local and national public holiday celebrations. Horseback archery requires lengthy training, extensive special equipment (bows, arrows, arrow quivers, special saddles, and other accessories), and handcrafted attire, while membership in sports clubs and competitions is fee based. There are also different strands emphasizing the sport, cultural heritage, or lifestyle aspects of horseback archery. Additionally, it has inspired an amateur archeology movement that aims to rewrite the history of Hungarian ethnogenesis.

The chapter is based on ethnographic data I collected by attending open days, competitions, trainings, and horse shows at the largest horseback archery camps in Hungary, as well as by visiting festivals like *Kurultáj*, a tribal assembly of the Hun-Turkic nations that takes place in eastern Hungary in the Hungarian *Puszta*, a steppe landscape with some of the largest sand dunes in Europe. Kurultáj is a high-profile, international three-day event—advertised as the largest cultural heritage festival in Europe—organized every two years in which horseback archery competitions and reenactment battles take center stage while the event also hosts a large market fair. My ethnographic observations are combined with interviews with horseback archers and craftsmen who manufacture horseback archery equipment and are partially gleaned from the social media feeds of key sports clubs. Horseback archery promotes deeply conservative views of masculinity, discipline, and community through stylized violence. But, above all, it locates Hungarians in a geopolitical kinship discourse, which asserts that Hungarians' true cultural kin are not to be found in Western Europe but in Central Asia, and that Hungary must look to the East for cultural and spiritual values as opposed to clinging to a decadent and morally declining West.

This book tries to carefully situate Hungary in international developments and current theoretical debates by incorporating multiple comparative examples throughout the text. Yet, it is ultimately an intensive fieldwork-based, in-depth case study of a single country, and its strengths lie in drawing out some of the sociological configurations that are particular to Hungary. As such, its broader objective is not to pinpoint causal regularities that can be readily generalized to other countries but to offer a more nuanced picture, an insider's view, of the dynamics between cultural production and far-right populism that complicates existing representations of far-right populist rule that often fall back on clichéd and one-dimensional accounts.

At the same time, the book does more than just argue that everything is "more complicated" when it comes to the culture of far-right populism on the ground. Most important, it calls for a wider and more systematic scrutiny of cultural producers as agents of spreading far-right populism. But it also identifies some general mechanisms that point beyond the Hungarian case. First, it captures the interplay between grassroots popular cultural advocacy and mainstream political embrace of far-right populism. Second, it delineates how far-right cultural production is scaled up and amplified through intersecting "circuits of commerce" and multiple channels of circulation. Third, it highlights how far-right populism presents an opportunity for geopolitical reorientation fueled by anti-Westernism. How these mechanisms evolve and apply to other cases will be spelled out in the conclusion.

2

Books as Weapons of Culture Wars

Journalist Árpád Szakács writes the following in the opening of his bestselling provocation of a book titled *The Dictatorship of Culture*:

> Society's destruction almost always begins through culture. Culture can be deployed as a strategic tool to demolish the state's traditional pillars, undermine its strength, obliterate its morality just like any other military warfare tactic. Culture is one of many methods: it prepares society for social change, it makes us get accustomed to the idea that bad is actually good, that the degenerate is beautiful, the bizarre is wonderful, deviance is welcome, and gender identity is harmful. In the West culture has already successfully fulfilled its mission as a Trojan horse to beget a new race: a new type of human being stripped of his national, religious and gender identity and devoid of any other ties. . . . Today wars are waged primarily with ideological weapons. Our culture is also bombarded with foreign ideas and not without success.[1]

Szakács and his coauthor Zsolt Bayer, another journalist, are key players in the culture wars that have been integral to the populist political repertoire following Fidesz's return to power in 2010 and intensified since 2018 after Fidesz's third supermajority election win.

The far right's main thesis is that even though Fidesz has been firmly in power since 2010 with a parliamentary supermajority, recapturing political institutions and control over the economy and the legal system, the cultural field remains hopelessly dominated by "a leftist-liberal hegemony that tries to influence society through its cultural clout."[2] Chief cultural warriors aim to expose the left's continuing cultural hegemony, debunking the widespread "liberal myth" that Hungary's far-right government curbs freedom of speech and sanctions leftist artists and intellectuals. They also assert, however, that this cultural hegemony needs to be laid bare to urge society to finally put an end to it. In their view, this is essential because "our culture no longer contains any Hungarian character, Hungarian distinctiveness, or Hungarian identity, not even in traces. Our theater and literary worlds that were once the breeding ground of ideas that inspired our glorious revolutions in the past today produce only cosmopolitan trivialities, our fine arts are the playground of the most deviant exhibitionists, our film industry is a cheap imitation of its U.S. counterpart."[3] The next task then, as sketched out in chapter 1, is to build a right-wing cultural hegemony partly by learning from the left about how to use culture effectively as political warfare.[4]

This assessment implies that culture is the last frontier, and apparently the most challenging one, that a far-right political restructuring has yet to overcome. The culture wars that are meant to achieve this objective take place in multiple sites through various techniques. They involve, for instance, the removal of universities' autonomy, the harassment of the George Soros–founded Central European University into leaving the country, direct political attacks on institutions such as the research institutes of the Hungarian Academy of Sciences, the takeover of the University of Theater and Film Arts, or the political appointment of far-right influencers to leadership positions at key museums, such as the Petőfi Museum for Literature.[5]

Books seem to occupy a privileged place in this political struggle. Influential thinkers of the New Right, most prominently Alain de Benoist, pointed out the importance of books in the fight for a right-wing cultural breakthrough. The significance of bookstores and publishers has been well-documented in the rise of the AfD in Germany, and book bans have been used as a political tool by far-right activists in the United States.[6] As noted in chapter 1, one of Hungary's main culture war promoters, Márton Békés, called books a "weapon" and reading as a "military act," assigning them a privileged place in the far right's "counter-hegemony machinery" to dislodge the liberal canon.[7] Books remain a potent vessel through which political discourse and identity narratives are circulated in ways that cannot be made obsolete by social media and digital technology. For instance, what should be taught in public schools is still fought around the books students should and should not read in every country. The national cultural canon is also defined through books when it comes to public education, as will be illustrated in the fierce debates over the required reading list of the National Core Curriculum.

The chapter begins by delineating how the structure of the book market, as it evolved after the end of communism, exacerbated political polarization and generated deep resentment in right-wing cultural producers. By drawing on interviews with publishers, visits to bookstores and events, the content analysis of publishers' book lists and signature publications, as well as social media sources, I identify the three main strategies that far-right book publishers have employed to challenge the liberal cultural hegemony in the publishing industry. First, right-leaning book companies were often established to publish authors and topics that the dominant liberal presses ignored and disapproved. Second, politically tainted authors and topics have been selected for publication to rehabilitate them while normalizing racism and anti-Semitism in the process. Third, books are used to directly attack (and cancel) liberal cultural producers and simultaneously pressure the government to legally sanction them.

The second half of the chapter shifts attention to the government's responses to grassroots pressures from the far right. It zooms in on a series of fierce public controversies over books that erupted under the populist government's reign since 2010, including the selection of books that make up required readings in the National Core Curriculum for public schools, and over children's books that deal with LGBTQ+ themes. These controversies demonstrate how books and book publishing are central in constructing a national cultural canon and how the far right relentlessly strives to rewrite this canon along illiberal lines.[8]

Origins of a Politically Polarized Book Market: Liberal Domination and Its Discontents

Book publishers on the political right tend to be small and try to survive by carving out distinctive thematic niches for themselves in a harsh market environment. They have deeply resented the extreme concentration of the Hungarian book publishing industry with two politically liberal book chains, Libri and Líra, controlling over 90 percent of the market.[9] Right-wing publishers' grievances about their cultural marginalization that poured out in all my interviews thus feel so real because they have been inscribed into the structure of the market. The populist far right views the deeply asymmetric power structure of the publishing industry as the product of postcommunist liberal politics—the handling of privatization in particular—that wiped out small publishers that were burgeoning after the fall of communism.

The emergence of small publishing companies in postcommunist Hungary was intimately tied to the reorganization of the book publishing industry during the market transition after 1989. Book publishing under communism was centralized and clustered around a few large, state-owned firms. These were privatized, broken up into smaller pieces, or completely dissolved in the 1990s. At the same time, new players could enter relatively easily as barriers to entry were low in this market. For instance, as the owner of the Anima bookstores recalled, "There was some regulation in the early 1990s that enabled publishers to sell their own publications freely without any permit."[10] Her husband's workplace decided to publish an adventure novel by popular interwar pulp fiction writer and journalist Jenő Rejtő, and they asked her to sell the book from a camping table repurposed as a book stand in the underground passageway of the subway by the Western Railway station in Budapest, underneath the square that was still named after Karl Marx at the time. She was a public school teacher by training, but because of an accident she became permanently disabled and could not continue with teaching. Over time other small publishers approached her to see if she could sell their books as well, so she was gradually expanding her inventory. "And then some relatives and friends showed up to help out with the work and this is how selling books from a camping table eventually grew into a family business."

I distinctly remember from my university years in the early 1990s that one really had the impression that books were sold everywhere across Budapest. Makeshift book stands mushroomed, not only in underground passageways but also on subway platforms, offering a bewilderingly eclectic mix of new books and newly founded, mostly political and literary magazines. This cornucopia of printed matter was an apt reflection of the craving Hungarians felt during the transition for freedom of expression in every medium after long years of communist censorship and ideological bans.

The way new publishers were set up was often ad hoc and unplanned. It was indeed quite common to end up in book publishing by accident. György Bedő, owner of Kairosz, used to work for the State Book Distribution Company (Állami Könyvterjesztő Vállalat), the central book distributor under communism. He founded his own company somewhat reluctantly after he retired, and his efforts to establish a major book distributor that would have united "Christian-national" book publishers dwindled. He started Kairosz in 1996 and was quite critical of the ways in which privatization transformed the book trade, describing the privatization of his former workplace as an instance of "robber privatization" that helped to jumpstart the rise of a "left-liberal cartel" in the book trade.[11] Kinga Erős, president of the Hungarian Writers' Association (Magyar Írószövetség), is also the owner of a small press, Orpheusz. She told me she had become the owner of the press largely by chance, inheriting it from a poet, László Deák, after he passed away. Deák had somehow ended up with it in the anarchic privatization process of the two state-owned fiction publishing houses. His mission to publish contemporary Hungarian poetry was noble but economically utterly unviable, and Erős struggled for quite some time after taking over the press to clear the considerable debt amassed by the former owner.

While publishing a few books and even starting a publishing house were relatively easy, challenges began to mount when it came to distribution and sales, as Géza Morcsányi, doyen of Hungarian quality fiction publishing, explained to me.[12] At the time of our conversation, he was the director of Líra, one of the two main book distributors on the market that, according to the right, exercise the left-liberal control over the book publishing industry. Clearly a liberal himself, he interested me not because he was part of the far-right corners of book publishing but because of his encyclopedic knowledge of the book trade in which he worked for over three decades. Morcsányi highlighted that book publishing was among the most quickly privatized industries and basically the only cultural industry that was privatized almost completely.[13] There was also a short transitory period around 1989 when copyright laws and royalties were handled quite casually, turning book trade into a blackish gray market, in which resourceful entrepreneurs could make a lot of money. But this era was soon over, with the privatization of book distribution and retail a few years later.

Two main companies, Libri and Líra, emerged through the privatization of the State Book Distribution Company mentioned earlier, which inherited and divided up the state-owned company's countrywide retail infrastructure as well. For a while there was a third important player, Alexandra, whose owner emerged from the gray market milieu of the transition years and also began his sales career as a street vendor on a camping table. But his company grew too large too quickly through risky—and, according to some, shady—credit financing, spectacularly crashing in 2016. Following Alexandra's insolvency, the concentration of bookselling became even more pronounced, with Libri and Líra basically controlling the entire market. Their grip on the book trade was further cemented by their establishing of flagship bookstores in shopping malls, developing of online stores, and acquiring book publishers. Libri also owns the largest Hungarian online book retailer, bookline.hu. All these developments were palpably stifling the prospects of small publishers and independent bookstores. Moreover, the consignment system that underlies payment between publishers and booksellers strongly favors the distributors. Booksellers take the books from the publishers on consignment and pay them at the end of the month based on the actual sales, keeping 60 percent of the sales price. They can return unsold copies to the publisher for no extra charge. Book sales are also characterized by stark seasonality, with most books sold around Christmas.

All these structural features of the market—most important, the extreme concentration of booksellers—make the life of small publishers extremely precarious, creating constant liquidity problems. The scarcity of bank loans and lack of opportunity for foreign investment given the linguistic isolation of the Hungarian book market further add to the hardships of small independent actors.[14] But in Hungary, this market environment is invested with political significance, and right-wing publishers believe that they are disproportionately and intentionally disadvantaged by the system. The CEO of Kairosz told me that when Alexandra, the third largest book distributor, was still around and aggressively growing, "they wouldn't order any books from us (or other publishers) that had God, or religion . . . or Bible in their title. That's how it went, that they would have nothing to do with religious books, no way." She also commented, though, that this type of explicit censorship was less common with the other two distributors, who would take any book that sells. With them, politics was coded more into the stark power inequality between publishers and distributors who own the bookstore chains and control the market.

Árpád Szakács, who is also the owner of Kárpátia Stúdió, the press that published his book manifesto, *Dictatorship of Culture*, complained profusely about the 60 percent cut booksellers keep and the consignment system. Our interview took place in a large shopping mall with a Libri bookstore. Szakács believes that "this high margin suffocates the system" and contributes to "crushing the publisher network of the conservative side. 60% . . . that is, for me to be able to get into the bookstore beneath us, they would keep 60 percent of the original price." He added that this situation was exacerbated by both distributors, Libri and Líra, buying up existing publishers: "They each own at least 10–15 publishers. They fill up their bookstores with their own publishers' products, thereby generating extra profit."

He also lashed out against the oldest and largest professional trade organization, the Association of Hungarian Publishers and Booksellers

(Magyar Könyvkiadók és Könyvterjesztők Egyesülése, MKKE). He emphasized that this organization was "made up of a circle of tradesmen who represent almost 100 percent a left-liberal ideology and who have enormous influence over the book trade. And . . . I saw this with my own eyes, they said it in front of me how conservative publishers should be swept out, finished: We take their books and put them into storage, we won't display any of them in the store, etc. . . . That is, there are techniques available for blocking [conservative publishers]."

Other right-wing publishers also complained about the lack of visibility in the chain stores. Libri and Líra would carry their books, but it would be hard to find them in the store. Often, they would only be available online. Books published by Libri- and Líra-owned presses would always take center stage in the stores: they would be featured in the central displays, "the pyramids," while other presses would be relegated to the shelves or to the online shop altogether. This practice fills right-wing publishers with resentment and reinforces a political interpretation of their perceived marginality.

Kinga Erős from Orpheusz tried to situate the ideological polarization of book publishing in a broader cultural context, stressing that it closely mirrors the deep political division of the cultural field at large, which has a long history in Hungary. She used writers as an example to illustrate how entrenched binary divisions have shaped the field at least as far back as the interwar era. Today writers are split into two opposing professional associations, the right-wing-conservative Hungarian Writers' Association (Magyar Írószövetség) and the left-liberal Fiction Writers' Society (Szépírók Társasága). The rift between them is so great, she said, that "I could show you people—I will obviously not name them—who will die with the firm conviction that anyone who is a member of the Writers' Association is a lousy writer, bereft of any talent etc. . . . and vice versa with members of the Fiction Writers' Society." But writers were similarly split in the interwar era, for instance, between two literary magazines, the pro-Western, leftist-liberal *West* (*Nyugat*) and the conservative, nationalist *East/Orient* (*Napkelet*).[15] The former was funded by a wealthy donor from a Jewish industrialist family, while the latter was subsidized by the government—the Ministry of Culture, led by Kunó Klebelsberg. Regrettably, Erős added, it continues to be impossible for anyone to escape this binary categorization:

> You should imagine this as a trench war, with a big swamp in the middle. There was a time when I was convinced it would pass with the old generations. But in the past 3–4 years I have come to believe that instead

> it is passed down from generation to generation. I can already see it among the twentysomethings. . . . Anyone who describes himself as an independent intellectual in Hungary is either lying or lacks self-awareness. There is no such thing, you cannot be independent; just by being, by taking a breath, you express, so to say, some priorities, some value preferences . . . and you find yourself put in a pigeonhole that you never picked for yourself.[16]

She confessed that she was not immune to this binary thinking either. She started her career during the height of socialist-liberal rule in postcommunist Hungary and was in a marginalized position as a conservative, right-wing writer. Now, she said, she could be seen as favored by the government's cultural policy, so she was supposed to feel empowered and flush with money. She noticed though that she was also holding grudges from the past but believed that it was justified to favor the right in cultural policy as compensation for past injustices: "I am in a similar situation but now on the other side of the potty, and I say damn, this is what you did to us for ten years, so where is the problem?"

I have to say that I was quite puzzled by how hurt, slighted, and marginalized these right-wing publishers felt. I expected them to be more triumphant now that they represented the government-supported mainstream, defined the dominant cultural trends, and had privileged access to state funding, which is always a game changer in cultural fields. Several of them were in significant positions of power: Erős was president of the Writer's Association, and Szakács was a high-ranking editor in the government-affiliated media empire. Between 2016 and 2020, he was the chief editor of the central editorial board of Mediaworks, the largest Hungarian media conglomerate that publishes all regional newspapers and many magazines.[17] But their outlook seemed more akin to what Szakács described in his book about cultural dictatorship: Despite having been in (or near) power over a decade, they continued to feel oppressed by the cultural power of the left. This deep resentment invested their publishing work with countercultural fervor.

But one also wonders why they bother to struggle on with their publishing companies if they continue to face such hardships and marginalization on the book market and barely scrape by economically. To this question, they all responded by downplaying the business aspect as a motivation—just like fashion designers will in chapter 3—and emphasizing the cultural mission for which the publisher was a vessel. Szakács, for instance, in response to my recurring questions about his press's marketing strategy and readership demographics, replied in a mildly irritated manner that he was not running the press on a traditional business model: "Let me say again that this is a hobby press. I don't care how many people buy the books and who they are. I don't really have the time and am not really interested to find out." He was convinced though that there was a core audience out there for the type of right-wing revisionist history that his press was so firmly committed to publishing.

Kinga Erős similarly told me that literary publishing in her case surpassed a simple market logic: "Look, this book market here . . . this is not a market story. I mean, there are people whose hobby is to collect stamps, and I publish books. These are two different stories [the book market and her motivations]. The way I do this, this is the only way it works, is that when the book comes off the press, its costs are already covered. So, even if I don't sell a single copy, I will not lose any money on it." Erős has developed a multipronged survival strategy: She applies for publication grants at public agencies and uses grants from foreign governments to publish Hungarian translations of literary works from their country, using the revenues to finance Orpheusz's book list. She also does all the work she can by herself with the help of her husband, who serves as the typesetter and graphic designer. She thinks even if she sells only a few copies and generates no profit, the books she publishes will make an impact. They will be reviewed in literary magazines and academic journals or receive media coverage, creating cultural visibility for the authors and their work.

Likewise, new generations of the Püski family, which has run its family press since the 1930s, feel bound by the founder's unwavering commitment. His son explained that "in some ways we were stuck with it [the press], we made a commitment that we will keep the press going at all costs until we can. This was meant so literally that when my father was already very ill, and passed away a week later, I had to take my two sons to see him, and he made them swear that they also will carry on." And the bar was set high by the founder, István Püski. His son recalled, for instance, how his parents auctioned off their furniture several times in the 1940s to be able to pay their authors and keep the publisher going. His father was dedicated not just to the authors but to the causes their work stood for: "My father was never thinking simply in terms of authors . . . but rather what the authors wanted to say. . . . The authors were not the primary concern but the topics. . . . The main thing was whether [the book] deals with Hungarianness (*magyarság*), with the problems, alternatives of the Hungarian people either in the form of a novel, politics, or any other form. It was never an option to consider the publication of a book that did not address these issues."

There is a larger political implication embedded in dismissing the business aspect of book publishing and foregrounding instead the cultural mission. Right-wing publishers' attitude implies that the left-liberal booksellers are only interested in commercial success, whereas the publishers follow a calling that transcends the materialistic drive that primarily defines liberals and the left. Right-wing actors constantly try to distance themselves from the capitalist underpinnings of the book trade and view books primarily as a cultural medium.

Illiberal Challenges to the "Left-Liberal" Canon

Right-wing publishers are devoted to their trade because they believe it will help to crack the cultural canon defined by the left and liberals, demonstrating close affinity with the New Right's vision and action plan presented in chapter 1.[18] They combine the three strategies outlined earlier—favoring authors and topics ignored by liberal presses; rehabilitating tainted authors and topics; attacking liberal cultural producers. I show how publishers combine and apply these strategies by examining representative examples from their publishing profile, book lists, signature publications, and personal interviews I conducted with the owners. These examples highlight some of the key narratives—the "deep stories"[19]—that make up the illiberal canon, demonstrating how books are one of the main carriers of these narratives. I also highlight the publishers' links, often through their authors, to various institutions, the government, and larger political circuits of commerce that elevate the visibility and potential impact of the published books.

As mentioned earlier, small right-wing publishers usually have a highly specialized thematic focus that reflects the cultural and political causes they deeply care about and see as unjustly dismissed by the liberal canon. Szakács's press, Kárpátia Stúdió, for instance, puts a lot of weight on publishing conspiracy theory–prone, right-wing revisionist history, while Kinga Erős's Orpheusz focuses on the publication of new talent in contemporary fiction and poetry from the ethnic Hungarian diaspora, as well as controversial works of literary history. Another principal area is religious writings, which had limited availability during the communist era but now constitute the core book titles, for instance, at Kairosz. The founder's goal was to establish a "Christian-national" (*keresztény-nemzeti*) publisher whose mission revolved around the preservation of the Christian roots of European culture, seen as increasingly forgotten in Western Europe. Among their most successful publications were two related pocketbook series, *Why Do I Have Faith?* (*Miért hiszek?*) and *To Be Hungarian* (*Magyarnak lenni*), that featured well-known right-wing intellectuals and public figures regarding their personal relationship with Christian faith and patriotism. Their all-time bestselling author was István Lovas, another well-known culture-warrior journalist who immigrated to Canada in the 1970s and worked as an editor for Radio Free Europe in Munich and New York from 1984 to 1990 before returning to Hungary to become one of the signature voices of far-right media.[20] The Püski family publishing house, which supplied the Hungarian diaspora in New York for several decades with Hungarian language books and samizdat literature, expanded its list in the area of mythical history after its return to Budapest, including revisionist works on the ethnogenesis of the Hungarian people.

Another publishing strategy involves outright attacks on liberal cultural products and producers. The best example for this is Szakács's bestselling *The Dictatorship of Culture*—the gift copy he gave me when I interviewed him was tied with a yellow band announcing in large print that the "First edition sold out in a week!" to emphasize the book's punch. His writings aim to aggressively unmask the enduring left-wing hegemony of the contemporary Hungarian cultural scene. He takes under scrutiny different fields of cultural production, from film to literature and book publishing. In muckraking style, he draws up lists of names of leftist-liberal artists and writers who have been critical of the Fidesz government for restricting freedom of speech and artistic autonomy. He exposes what a blatant lie it is that these people have been marginalized, enumerating how much financial support they each received from the government while claiming the opposite. He finds it particularly enraging that these cultural figures, fattened up with government subsidies, make a habit of publicly trashing the Hungarian government in the West at every possible opportunity. In the eyes of the far right, public criticism of the Hungarian government by liberal Hungarian intellectuals in Western media is an intensely sore point, a form of treason. Szakács's revelations read a lot like smear campaigns against specific individuals, though he is convinced—as he told me in the personal interview I conducted with him in the summer of 2019—that he simply pursues strictly investigative, evidence-based reporting.[21]

PROMOTING HISTORIC REVISIONISM, EXPOSING LIBERALS' "DOUBLE STANDARDS," AND NORMALIZING ANTI-SEMITISM

In the following paragraphs, I dive deeper into some of the defining topics and politically motivated business trajectories of the illiberal presses. When Szakács, for instance, told me that that he was not interested in turning a profit from his book publishing business, he added that Kárpátia Stúdió's book list primarily reflects his personal taste, his commitment to publishing books and authors he cares about, and represents views that contribute to shifting the balance of power in Hungarian culture. He explained that he founded the press in 2010 with two friends—who have since left the business—and has run it beside his day job as a journalist. The press started with publishing historical magazines. The flagship magazine was called *Greater Hungary* (*Nagy-Magyarország*), referring to pre-Trianon (pre-1920) Hungary, the image of which is widely used today as an irredentist and right-wing symbol that will be more closely examined in chapter 4. In fact, the Kárpátia Stúdió logo incorporates a simplified contour of Greater Hungary into its design.

The magazine was conceived as a high-end, glossy historical magazine similar in its graphics and layout to *National Geographic*. The idea for establishing a book publisher came from his conversations with friends, who also resented that "conservative culture can simply not be published. . . . There are plenty of authors and topics who cannot find an outlet because nobody is brave enough to publish them, and they just get dismissed." Szakács's insistence on calling the magazine *Greater Hungary* was a case in point, he added, because the term has been seen as shaky and carried a lot of stigma: "Even in more conservative circles when people heard it, they cringed." This is why he thought it was important to use the magazine to rehabilitate the concept and elucidate the "value system it stands for, the form of state it epitomized for over a thousand years, which created so much value."

Publishing a high-end magazine turned out to be quite costly, so the press decided to shift its attention to books instead. The magazine was still an important launchpad because it put Szakács, as chief editor, in contact with many like-minded historians and journalists whose writings he would then shepherd through publication by his press in book form. The press publishes about ten to fifteen books per year on average, mostly works of Hungarian history in areas that are overlooked or shunned by mainstream Hungarian (and Western) historiography. Some of these topics were also highlighted in *Dictatorship of Culture*, such as the exposure of communist terror during the Hungarian Soviet Republic's reign in 1919 and, especially, the role of Hungarian Jews in it. Related to this is an ambitious book series—with eight books published so far—on the history of freemasonry in Hungary, a passion project for Szakács. He traces most of the ills of Hungarian society to the Masonic lodges of the late nineteenth century, blaming them for incubating and spreading leftist-liberal ideology and for harboring Jewish political radicals. To illustrate their significance with a contemporary analogy, he suggested to me that we can think of them as "the Soros organizations of the times." He refers, unsurprisingly, to Hungarian-born US financier and philanthropist George Soros, whose name has become a trigger word for the right across the globe, deployed to vilify any progressive organization or public figure who received financial support from him, while portraying Soros as the ultimate (Jewish) enabler of radical left-wing ideas.

The freemason books are penned by Szakács's "star author," Ernő Raffay, a historian who also had an active political career in the early 1990s. He was a member of parliament and the political secretary of state of the Hungarian Ministry of Defense in Hungary's first freely elected government. He went on to become the director of the Institute and Museum of Military History, then switched to academia to teach as a professor at the Gáspár Károli University of the Reformed Church in Hungary. In 2019 he was appointed to the Advisory Board of the newly founded Institute of Hungarian Research (Magyarságkutató Intézet), set up by the Ministry of Human Resources that year "to conduct research into the past, language and origin of the Hungarian people, which has been impossible until now."[22]

The opening of this institute is part of the Fidesz government's effort to create a parallel network of new research institutes that are firmly under its control, unlike the research institutes of the Hungarian Academy of Sciences, which are still seen as more liberal and independent, even after the politically motivated massive institutional reorganization they were forced to undergo in 2019.[23] The new, "duplicate" institutes generally receive better funding in exchange for loyalty to the government's far-right populist agenda. The Institute of Hungarian Research has been subject to intense public attention and been quite savagely ridiculed in the remaining pockets of liberal media for its anachronistic, ethnocentric, and nationalist mission, the dubious credentials of many of its researchers, and the scientifically unsound theories it promulgates.

Raffay's name recognition stems largely from his political role in Hungary's first conservative government in the postcommunist era, benefitting the sales of his books and increasing the visibility of his publisher. Szakács told me that the freemasonry books cumulatively had sold nearly 120,000 copies. It's hard to verify these numbers for lack of consistent industry statistics, but if he is not embellishing the sales figures, then the books have indeed been quite a hit. Any book that sells over 10,000 copies is considered a successful publication in Hungary and qualifies as a bestseller with over 30,000 sold copies, given the tiny size of the market because of the country's linguistic insularity. A book that sells around 120,000 copies is a blockbuster, and it is mostly books that are required reading in public schools that can reliably generate sales numbers in this range.

The Masonic-Jewish conspiracy theories of the freemason books are also updated to the Cold War and contemporary era and are part of the far right's quest to normalize anti-Semitism. Books in this genre that focus on the present day examine the dirty secrets of the financial and capital markets and the centrality of Jewish bankers in them. The *Matrix of Money* (*A hálózat pénze*), for instance, depicts how informal networks of shady characters moved money across rival political systems in the postwar period, often instructed by Jewish Hungarian bankers from Switzerland, to financially exploit small countries like Hungary.[24] The author, Zsuzsanna Borvendég, is a historian at the new Institute of Hungarian Research who received one of the highest state awards, the Knight's Cross of the Hungarian Order of Merit, in 2022.

Other authors are even more blatant in their efforts to whitewash anti-Semitism. Half of *The Dictatorship of Culture* is devoted to coauthor Zsolt Bayer's chief mission, which tries to wrap anti-Semitism in high-brow intellectualization.[25] His essays also perfect one of the fundamental rhetorical tropes of the far right, the notion of "double standards." He consistently harps on how the logic of double standards is habitually applied to discredit the far right both locally and internationally. The broader argument that is implied here, beyond the normalization of anti-Semitism, is, of course, that the logic and practice of double standards have been key to maintaining the cultural dominance of the left.

Bayer uses, for instance, the example of the Hungarian *numerus clausus* law that was passed in 1920 to limit the number of Jewish students in higher education. He argues that even though the original text of the law never mentioned Jews—it referred to "minorities"—it is still routinely upheld as an example of Hungary's uniquely virulent anti-Semitism. By contrast, he continues, nobody talks about the restriction of Jews in terms of *numerus clausus* in the United States, although almost all private universities engaged in this practice between 1918 and 1950.[26] He also stresses that US universities were much more effective in excluding Jewish students thanks to these policies than Hungarian universities, but still the United States is not stigmatized in this regard to the same extent as Hungary.

Similarly, Bayer draws up a list of eminent Western writers, such as Ezra Pound, Louis-Férdinand Céline, Knut Hamsun, and Gerhart Hauptmann, to ask how it is acceptable in the West to celebrate the work of authors who openly entertained anti-Semitic, profascist and pro-Nazi sentiments. He cites the example of the Norwegian government that opened a memorial museum in 2009 in honor of Hamsun, a well-known Nazi sympathizer.[27] When the Israeli government protested, Norwegians responded by saying that "it is possible to appreciate a writer without accepting his political views and to separate his oeuvre from his political role."[28]

Bayer also scrupulously investigates the workings of political "double standards" in the local Hungarian context. He is puzzled by, for instance, why a right-wing, profascist historian and politician of the interwar era, Bálint Hóman, does not deserve a public statue while numerous Hungarian public figures who actively supported the Communist dictatorship remained officially recognized after 1989.[29] He compares Hóman with the Marxist philosopher Georg Lukacs to illustrate the "double standards" in this decision. In his view, Hóman's legislative backing of the annihilation of Hungarian Jews stemmed from the Zeitgeist; it was not directed at specific individuals—it wasn't, so to speak, "personal." As a private person, "as a humanist, he was quite sorry for what happened to the Jewry."[30]

By contrast, Bayer argues that Lukacs actively participated in the killing of people and was one of the masterminds behind the "red terror" of the Hungarian Soviet Republic. He claims that Lukacs directly ordered the killing of eight people during a military retreat while the Hungarian Red Army was fighting Romanian forces. He also goes as far as to make statements like "Lukacs is no different from Hitler. Or Goebbels."[31] And yet, he gripes, Lukacs is still part of the cultural canon despite having blood on his hands, while Hóman is denounced although he was not (specifically) responsible for anyone's death. Bayer's outrage against Lukacs was channeled into a broader campaign targeting Lukacs and his legacy, which led to the removal of his only statue from a Budapest park. The Lukacs Archive, which was set up in Lukacs's Budapest apartment shortly after his death in 1971 and was dedicated to preserving his library, manuscripts, and letters, was shut down in 2016 despite international protest.

This work is emblematic of the right's rhetorical strategy to relativize anti-Semitism and illustrates the lengths to which far-right ideologues are willing to go to make this look like an intellectual endeavor. The far right's general claim is that there should be no difference between judging race or class-based violence: The crimes of communism should be treated on equal terms with the crimes of fascism. Instead, in Hungary, "crimes committed against Jews are still considered unparalleled and unforgiveable while crimes committed against non-Jews are not even worth a mention."[32]

Another canonical topic for far-right publishers is, predictably, Trianon, the trauma and injustices of the large-scale territorial and population losses Hungary suffered in the aftermath of World War I with the dissolution of the Austro-Hungarian Monarchy.[33] Trianon is a foundational historical moment for the far right, which remains steeped in resentment and victimhood over this event and its erasure under communism—its centrality is underscored in the other chapters of this book too. Szakács publishes a broad range of revisionist authors on Trianon, including Raffay, who was also the founder and copresident of the Hungarian Trianon Society and cofounder of the Trianon Research Institute. A curious book recently published in this area is a reprint of the work of an interwar author, Ferenc Olay, who argued that an important reason for the unjust punishment that the Treaty of Trianon inflicted on Hungary had to do with how the West developed a distorted image of Hungarians and their treatment of ethnic minorities long before World War I. He demonstrated his thesis by analyzing the portrayal of Hungary in the history textbooks of various Western European countries, highlighting how "they tried to manipulate public opinion in the West to despise Hungarians." These history textbooks instructed generations to think about Hungarians as "primitive, barbaric murderers, semi-nomadic herdsmen who work during the day but go plundering at night."[34] The far right widely shares the argument that the West's Orientalism is to blame for Hungary's continued mistreatment in international politics.

While the main geographical focus of the book lists is Hungary, there are also books published every year by foreign authors on topics that neatly align with the far-right political orientation of the press. Recent examples include the Hungarian translation of *The Eurasian Mission* by Alexander Dugin, the chief theorist (political philosopher, analyst, strategist) of the Russian far right.[35] Dugin's books are originally published by Arktos Media, the largest international far-right press that has been headquartered in Budapest since 2015.[36] The ideology of neo-Eurasianism is one of the centerpieces of his work.[37] It promotes the idea of Russian-Asian greatness, suggesting that a "Euro-Asian empire" that unites all Russian-speaking people can successfully fight the U.S.-led Western world. Dugin was thrust to the center of media attention in August 2022 when his daughter was killed by a car bomb in connection with the Russian-Ukrainian war. He is widely assumed to have been the intended target of the attack.

INTERWAR LEGACIES AND THE RENAISSANCE OF MYTHICAL HISTORY

A few publishers, such as the Püski publishing house, build on a longer history that goes back to the interwar era.[38] Püski was the main publisher of the so-called populist (*népies*) writers in the 1930s, who came from the peasantry and brought the everyday experience and plight of this group to the public through their writings, introducing a new voice into Hungarian literature. They envisioned a "third way" between capitalism and communism whose leading force would be the peasantry and the populist intellectuals growing out of their ranks. The anti-Semitic overtones of how they saw the role of Jews in Hungarian society and more overt coquetry with fascism discredited this group and pushed it to the literary margins after World War II.[39]

Püski resumed its operations as the war ended, but the press was nationalized after the communist takeover in 1950 and became increasingly suspicious in the eyes of communist cultural policy makers. István Püski was eventually imprisoned in 1962. A few years after his release, he immigrated to the United States with his family and settled in New York. They carried on with their publishing business, operating out of their apartment. They also started organizing lecture and performance tours by Hungarian writers and artists for the Hungarian diaspora in the United States. They bought a small, dilapidated bookstore on Second Avenue in Manhattan, an area still at the center of Hungarian immigrant life in New York at the time, and opened the Püski Publishing House, through which they continued to publish the authors that made up their core list in the interwar period. They also began publishing authors who were banned in communist Hungary and disseminated samizdat literature. The Corvin Hungarian Bookstore on 82nd street became a focal point of Hungarian culture among Hungarian immigrants as well as political dissidents. Once communism fell, the Püski family returned to Hungary, reopened its flagship bookstore in Budapest's first district, and restarted its publishing business. The checkered history of this family publishing house draws attention to the countercultural cachet that radical nationalism derives today from the oppositional role it played during the communist era.

As the founder's son told me on a sweltering summer morning in their bookstore in Budapest, there was never any doubt that they would return to Hungary as soon as it was politically possible: "The first moment when my father could, and this was in 1989, he moved the press back home [to Hungary]." He added that they returned also "because the function that the press fulfilled until 1989, supplying Hungarian émigrés with books published in Hungary and Hungarian books, newspapers published in the Carpathian Basin and the entire continent [Europe], was over. It was no longer necessary because everyone could now simply return home." Today the bookstore and the press are run by the third generation of the family. Its publishing profile remains surprisingly consistent, although they have also added new titles by contemporary authors and expanded into more politically radical intellectual territory. They continue to publish the interwar populist writers, some of whom, like Dezső Szabó and István Sinka, have long been the subject of stern criticism because of their open anti-Semitism.

The press, however, has made forays into new thematic areas that are among the principal intellectual preoccupations of the far right. One such area explores Hungarians' origin histories, going back to "preconquest" and "prehistoric" times,[40] concocting theories and discovering evidence that lend support to mythic histories about the geographical and cultural origins of Hungarians as an ethnic group, which will be further developed in chapter 5. There is also fiction delving into these topics, thematizing especially the early period of settlement in the Carpathian Basin, involving epic battles with the "West" in which Hungarians miraculously triumphed over their mighty enemies. Püski has a best-selling author in this field, Róbert Gyula Cey-Bert, whose historical novels have been widely popular. These works generally espouse popular versions of ancient national history, with the explicit aim of questioning the official historiography of the period. This antiestablishment, antiscience stance is what infuses these writings with political meaning and intentionality while turning their publication into a political-cultural statement. They also raise the even larger question of "whether investigating the distant past is a matter of science or a subject of faith."[41]

A distinctly arcane but cult-inducing example of these popular mythical histories is called *Arvisura* and is published by Püski. The *Arvisura* series is a modern reconstruction of the founding myth of Hungarians, rooted in Shamanistic spiritualism.[42] It propagates the kinship theory between Hungarians and Huns, which has been firmly rejected by mainstream historical science. It is essentially a mythopoetic work that contains the literary works and traditional customs of the shamans of the twenty-four Hun confederated tribes.[43] It was recorded over three decades in the postwar period by a steelworker, Zoltán Paál, from the northern Hungarian city of Ózd. His writings were discovered after his death in the late 1990s and have generated a large following since their publication. Together with another similar spiritualist compilation called *Yotengrit*, also published by *Püski*, they serve as holy scriptures for some ethno-pagan movements.[44] They also promote the Turanic ethnogenesis of the Hungarian nation that questions the established understanding that Hungarians come from Europe, tracing the group's original homeland to Central Asia instead. Turanism as a cornerstone of right-wing mythic history will be investigated in detail in chapter 5 on horseback archery. As the treatment of ethnic prehistory is central in neo-pagan circles, the *Arvisura* and *Yotengrit* series already pivot toward esoteric nationalism, another important turf of the far right.

As Szakács's Kárpátia Studió is linked to authors who hold positions at the newly minted, government-affiliated research institutes (e.g., Institute of Hungarian Research), Püski is also informally linked with one of these institutes, Retörki (Research Institute and Archive for the History of the Transition; Rendszerváltás Történetét Kutató Intézet és Levéltár). It publishes books by the institute's members and carries their books in its store. Püski is also linked to the horseback archery scene, as it is the exclusive publisher of the writings of Lajos Kassai, the founder of the modern horseback archery movement in Hungary.

Some of these right-wing publishers, like Kairosz and Püski, still have their own bookstores, which host book talks by authors and have served as important spaces of community building for a right-wing audience.[45] But the increasing concentration of book sales, the migration of bookstores into shopping malls, and the rise of online retailers caused a steep decline in independent bookstores, including the ones that specialized in far-right literature. This was, nevertheless, a distinctive niche in Budapest in the world of independent bookstores until the 2010s. But otherwise, only those stores survived in this niche that at least partially moved into shopping malls, like the small local chain store, Anima, which eventually also had to shutter. The vanishing of these niche stores significantly deepened the upset about the liberal control of the book market.

Required Reading: What Should Students Be Reading in Public Schools?

While far-right publishers pursue their trade as cultural missionaries in hope of eroding the left-liberal canon, the government aids this cause by fostering a sharp rightward shift in the types of books children read in public schools. Hungary's new National Core Curriculum (*Nemzeti Alaptanterv*, NAT) was passed on January 31, 2020, introducing a major overhaul for the list of books students in middle and high schools are required to read to successfully complete their education. Moreover, the new curriculum did not merely bring about significant changes to the book list but ushered in increasing centralization and significant curbs in teachers' autonomy. In many countries, such as the United States, very few if any books are mandatory in public schools, although there are still intense struggles over what books should be excluded from school curricula and public libraries.[46] In Hungary, by contrast, there is a fairly long list of books that all students are obliged to read in each grade, as stipulated by the National Core Curriculum. These books are also a constant matter of public debate, as they are meant to represent the quintessence of Hungarian culture, the national cultural canon.

Revamping public education was high on Fidesz's agenda after their return to power in 2010 because they believed it had been progressively undermined by excessive decentralization and liberalization dictated by liberal politicians from the party of Free Democrats who mostly controlled educational policy under socialist-liberal governments after 1989. The first set of amendments to the National Core Curriculum was passed in 2012, but the real paradigm shift arrived with the 2020 revision. As Hungarian media scholar Péter György emphasized, "using the National Core Curriculum as a tool of redress is a radical move, but there is undoubtedly no faster or cheaper way to make somebody culturally acceptable than by making their works required readings."[47] In the following I examine key controversies that ensued around the canon-shifting efforts set forth by the National Core Curriculum.

THE RIGHT-WING TURN OF THE NATIONAL CORE CURRICULUM

The preparation of the new National Core Curriculum started in 2017 and was surrounded by controversy from the start, but the uproar from public school teachers, professional organizations, and liberal media that followed the publication of the new NAT took the government by surprise. The NAT concerns the basic content, learning outcomes, and methodology of public education.[48] It is organized into ten areas of literacy (*műveltségi terület*), including Hungarian language and literature, the arts, man and society, man and nature, and mathematics, among others. It also formulates nine key competencies (e.g., linguistic competence, digital competence, social and citizen competence) that were originally developed at a European Union summit in Lisbon in 2000. The ultimate objective of NAT is to ensure that students acquire the same core content and competencies in each school across the country. This not only lays the foundations of shared knowledge but enables students to easily transfer between schools if necessary and establishes clear pathways to high school graduation or university admission.

Changes to the Hungarian literature and history curriculum were heavily criticized upon NAT's publication, but it was undoubtedly the required reading list that struck a nerve with different constituencies. While the required readings may not even have been the most problematic feature of the new NAT overall, they resonated most with a broader public, as they epitomize the national cultural canon espoused by the government's educational policy. The new NAT removed from the required list, for instance, the work of Hungary's only Nobel laureate in literature at the time, Imre Kertész. Kertész's writings revolve around the Holocaust, and his best-known novel, *Fateless* (*Sorstalanság*), which portrays the experience of the Holocaust from a child's perspective, had for long been a required text. Simultaneously, added to the mandatory reading list were conservative and far-right authors from the interwar period, such as Albert Wass, whom I will also discuss in chapter 4; József Nyírő, whose books were also banned before 1989 because of his involvement in the pro-Nazi puppet government of the Arrow Cross party during World War II; or Ferenc Herczeg, the interwar bestseller author who was a key figure in the revisionist movement that rejected the Treaty of Trianon. Most of these newly incorporated authors had previously been printed and promoted only by right-wing niche presses.

Authors from the revisionist far-right canon were already introduced to NAT in 2012, provoking widespread outrage, but the 2020 NAT lifted them to new heights while simultaneously downgrading or fully erasing other perspectives. As noted on the largest (at the time) liberal online news platform, Index: "our only Nobel-prize winner in literature, Imre Kertész, is not even mentioned in NAT. And it is evident that mediocre, conservative writers who collaborated with the [pro-Nazi] Arrow Cross party have undeservingly received disproportionate weight to counterbalance liberal, pro-Western authors."[49] The 2020 NAT tried to justify this by highlighting Hungarian literature as an essential instrument of national identity formation, rectifying earlier versions of the National Core Curriculum that were criticized for not being "national enough." And the concept of the nation it promotes reaches well beyond current territorial borders to include diaspora authors, as the NAT equates the mission of Hungarian literature with "acquainting [students] with the most distinguished works of Hungarian linguistic and literary culture that were created by Hungarians in the Carpathian Basin."[50]

The term "Carpathian Basin" refers here to the territories of pre-Trianon Hungary. The right often uses this geographic name in official parlance as a substitute for the more provocative, openly irredentist "Greater Hungary" designation.

Discontent with the new NAT was instant and widespread. Professional associations such as the Teachers' Democratic Trade Union (Pedagógusok Demokratikus Szakszervezete, PDSZ) or the Association of Hungarian Language and Literature Teachers (Magyartanárok Egyesülete) vehemently protested. In one of their protest initiatives, PDSZ asked teachers who didn't agree with the new NAT to post photos of themselves on the organization's Facebook page. Protesting teachers frequently posted their photos with signs saying that they would refuse to teach fascist writers. Individual schools publicly expressed their disapproval, while several parliamentary opposition parties (e.g., DK, Párbeszéd) demanded the immediate withdrawal of NAT.

Many notable contemporary writers also expressed their consternation. Pál Závada, for instance, decried the omission of contemporary Hungarian writers, as well as the anachronistic conceptual and methodological approach to literature education. But he was also disappointed in parents because he felt they were indifferent to the government's efforts "to raise zombies from their kids who lack competitive knowledge, are nationalist, chauvinist, and unable to think for themselves."[51] In a similar vein, others remarked how out of touch the required books were with students' experiences, considering that the youngest authors included were of their grandparents' age.[52]

Professional teachers' organizations were especially flabbergasted by the blatant ideological instrumentalization of the national curriculum. In their official statement, the Association of Hungarian Language and Literature Teachers lamented:

> This core curriculum turns literary education again into a servant of politics and ideology. . . . It contains ideological starting points that cannot lead to a valid teaching plan. The literature curriculum puts at its center the concept of Hungarian victimhood, the importance of mourning over Trianon, and the declaration of unity with the cross-border Hungarian ethnic diaspora. While not denying the legitimacy of the pain felt over this historic trauma or the fact that Hungarian literature transcends state borders, we believe that making this pain serve as the main thrust of literary history is a deeply antiliterary posture.[53]

But the backlash to the protests from the far right was equally fierce. In recent years, several new teachers' associations have sprung up, besides the established organizations quoted earlier, that have staunchly supported the government and its initiatives. These developments mirror the trend described earlier about the duplication of key civic and research organizations with the intention of establishing government friendly versions of existing critical institutions. One of these new associations, The Cultural Association of Hungarian Language and Literature Teachers of the Carpathian Basin (Kárpát-medencei Magyartanárok Kulturális Egyesülete, KMKE) greeted the new NAT, expressing its confidence that "it can bring about real quality improvement in teaching Hungarian language and literature."[54] The association's president, poet and literary historian Mihály Takaró, was also part of the expert committee that developed the new National Core Curriculum. The inclusion of the most controversial interwar writers is widely attributed to him. Professional organizations repeatedly questioned his involvement in the committee because of his far-right views.[55] He saw as NAT's key positive feature that it drew no line between Hungarian diaspora and mainland authors, and "finally, after several decades, there is once again a shared cultural code, which enables every Hungarian student from Brassó [Brasov] to Pozsony [Bratislava] to be educated in the same spirit."[56]

Others fervently attacked NAT's critics. A security expert from the Center for Fundamental Rights (Alapjogokért Központ), another government-friendly new research institute, warned that those who question the normative values on which NAT is built become unwitting supporters of a new type of hybrid war that wants to weaken Europe, erase its Judeo-Christian roots, and dissolve its nations into a "Brave New World" without values and identity.[57] The National Theatre's director, Attila Vidnyánszky, added that "the liberal alternative to the government's curriculum plan envisions Hungarians in this country who are petty, wrecked by constant pangs of guilt, longing to be submissive and given direction."[58] Far-right media also played the hackneyed Soros card, alleging that some of the critical teachers' organizations (e.g., the History Teachers' Association [Történelem Tanárok Egylete]) are funded by Soros's Open Society Foundation, insinuating that they acted as paid provocateurs.[59]

The previously featured trendsetting cultural warriors, journalists Árpád Szakács and Zsolt Bayer, lambasted NAT critics, repeating many of the arguments they made in their book about the left's cultural dictatorship. Szakács recycled one of his pet theories about the long-term detrimental influence of freemasonry, suggesting that current NAT critics just continue in the footsteps of the early twentieth-century freemasons, upholding the principles of "atheist-materialistic history and literature education." Left-wing media mocked his "tinfoil hat theory" and called him "the shaman of the culture wars," but he remained unfazed by the mockery.[60] Bayer reached again for the double-standards trope, arguing that criticism of Wass or Nyírő for their anti-Semitism was hypocritical given that several Hungarian and foreign authors (e.g., Ezra Pound) who have espoused anti-Semitism have been part of the core curriculum for a long time. He also derided teachers protesting with the "I won't teach any fascist writer" sign: "Has the 'lady pedagogue' ever read a line by the 'fascist' writers, Wass, Nyírő, or Herczeg? Or is she just burping up the liberal (*libsi*) canon?"[61]

CRITICS BEWARE: DOG POOP IN THE MAILBOX

Tensions and emotions around NAT flared up again in 2021, almost exactly a year after it became law. The second act was sparked by an unassuming episode: an interview with Krisztina Tóth, an internationally accomplished contemporary woman writer in her fifties. In a lighthearted conversation published in *Könyves Magazin*, the online magazine of the Libri-owned online bookseller bookline, Tóth was quizzed about her reading habits as a child, the book she was currently reading, and the one she would never lend to anyone.[62] The interviewer also dropped two questions about the National Core Curriculum, asking Tóth which book she would include among required readings in literature and which one she would remove if she had the power to do so. It was her answer to the second question that started the avalanche.

She named Mór Jókai's *The Man with the Golden Touch* (*Az arany ember*) as the novel she would strike off the required list. She said she was particularly weary of how gender roles for women were depicted in this book. The novel, a Hungarian classic from the nineteenth century, centers on the double life of the protagonist, Mihály Tímár, a successful businessman in search of happiness. The more successful he becomes as a capitalist entrepreneur, the less he can find love in his relationships. He is trapped in an unhappy marriage with the daughter of a Turkish dignitary, whose wealth and death propelled him onto the path of enrichment. He then strikes up a secret, long-term relationship with a young woman he accidentally meets on a remote island in the river marshland of the Danube in Serbia. The book focuses on how he navigates the pressing moral and practical dilemmas of this double life. The author, Mór Jókai, was one of the most distinguished and prolific Hungarian writers of the late nineteenth century, and *The Man with the Golden Touch* is his best-known and most widely read novel. A star-studded film adaptation in the 1960s cemented the book even further in the Hungarian cultural canon.

In the bookline interview, Tóth criticized the novel for the outdated, conservative female role models it was projecting to middle school students.[63] The interview progressed as a casual conversation and was published in a niche online magazine, so neither the interviewer nor the interviewee felt that there was much political stake in the voiced opinions. But then a liberal weekly, *HVG*—an economic and current affairs magazine modeled on *The Economist*—sampled the interview in its online edition, spotlighting Tóth's take on required readings, which went viral on social media.

The ensuing attack on Tóth from the right was vicious and relentless. In many ways she embodied the perfect target for this type of political bullying. She is an openly liberal poet and fiction writer whose work frequently addresses women's issues from a feminist perspective. She is also the adoptive mother of a Roma girl. Her views on the patriarchal streak of nineteenth-century literary romanticism were interpreted against her contemporary politics in the larger context of increasing right-wing hysteria over gender issues. Critics depicted her as the mouthpiece of "Western wokism" who wants to undermine traditional heteronormative values, not sparing even such eminent classics of Hungarian literature as Jókai's most popular work.

An opinion piece in the right-wing daily paper *Hungarian Nation* (*Magyar Nemzet*) was titled "Ban the *Man with the Golden Touch* because it is not gender conform!," implying that this was Tóth's original intention and illustrating how her comments on the National Core Curriculum were distorted as they went viral. The piece described how Tóth "put on a Europhilic yoga pose, shaking her head in condescension, mocking the antiquated thinking of the Hungarian people because 'they' got upset over the noble and holy ideals she collected from the cultural drains of the West." It continued by suggesting that "she enlisted as a servant of cultural leftist ideology" and her "thinking is retrograde and boring, she only regurgitates the current formulas of Western cultural discourse."[64] A few months after the debate peaked, Tóth gave an interview to an Austrian left-liberal magazine, *Falter*, about the attack against her in which she called Hungary a toxic country.[65] This added fuel to the fire and confirmed Tóth as an "agent of the West" because, for the far right, denouncing Hungary in Western media is the ultimate treason that left-liberal intellectuals routinely commit.[66]

Right-wing media also mobilized women authors and conservative feminists to lend female authority to their criticism of Tóth. One of the most politically influential right-wing female writers, Katalin Mezey, also penned an opinion in the *Hungarian Nation* questioning Tóth about why she did not criticize the male protagonist for his moral failures and the flawed role model he offers for young men instead of just criticizing the female leads, who in fact represent commendable virtues such as loyalty, solidarity, honesty, diligence, discipline, and patience.[67] Similarly, an interview with a conservative writer and gender scholar appraised Tóth's reasoning as symptomatic of "an overzealous political correctness," an act of "literary statue-demolishing" while also patronizing for teachers and parents because she assumes that they are unable to separate the past from the present.[68]

The onslaught on social media escalated the feud even further. The far-right online portal 888.hu accused Tóth of hypocrisy and double standards, alleging that she would never criticize Roma women for identifying with traditional women's roles even though this was common among them. The author pointed to Mónika Lakatos, an internationally famed Roma singer, who spoke about Roma traditions in a magazine interview for *Hungarian Cuisine* (*Magyar Konyha*). She recounted how women in her family never ate at the same table with the men—they always ate together with the children. According to 888.hu, this example exposes Tóth's advocacy of the Roma as purely abstract and detached from everyday realities and customs. Online comments on articles and Facebook posts were the most savage and the least fit to print, at times racist and certainly misogynist, degrading her as a writer and as a woman. They warned that "she was infected by the rainbow mania," called her a "whore," a retard—using a Hungarian phrase, *agyatlan liba*, reserved specifically for women—a "neogenderist," a "liberalcannibal-intellectual," "a stinky communist," and a "literary inquisitor," among other names.[69] They claimed she couldn't even cook and told her to work in the fields rather than write books.[70] Someone added for dramatic effect that "Hitler was a boy scout compared with today's neoliberalist Bolsheviks" like her.[71]

Cancel-culture arguments were fired on both sides, the right accusing Tóth of trying to cancel Jókai, one of Hungarian fiction's giants, while the left accused right-wing media of trying to cancel Tóth, or anyone who dares critique the traditional cultural canon.[72] She was lambasted for wanting to introduce censorship to schools at a time when "already everything was about LGBTQ issues."[73] But some commentators went even further and claimed that her take on required readings was a premeditated provocation to "test the boundaries of the nation's natural ability to defend itself" to "see how the health of this institution [the nation], which has repeatedly recuperated itself in the past thousand years, could be effectively undermined" when "the only treasure and support of this sorely tested nation are its mother tongue and the apostles thereof like Jókai who cultivate it with humility and not through the veil of silly gender theories."[74]

The fervor around Tóth's interview might seem puzzling, but it demonstrates the outsize importance of the books that get consecrated in the National Core Curriculum as required readings, constituting an important cornerstone of Hungary's literary canon. The debate also highlights how gender issues have increasingly occupied center stage in culture wars, as the next section will also illustrate. The severity of the personal attacks on Tóth and the vulgarity of the comments had to do both with her being a progressive female writer and her criticism of how gender roles are taught in schools. In her Facebook post, Tóth also noted the shocking lack of civility in the reactions and pleaded that "even the most ardent Jókai fans should refrain from putting dog poop in her mailbox [again]" as an act of revenge—which apparently happened to her in real life.[75]

Grinding Children's Books: Moral Panic Over LGBTQ+ Fairy Tales Paving the Way to Legal Restrictions

In September 2020, Dóra Dúró, deputy leader of the far-right party the *Our Homeland Movement* (*Mi Hazánk Mozgalom*), pulled a publicity stunt in which she shredded a children's book, *A Fairy Tale for Everyone* (*Meseország mindenkié*).[76] She claimed she did this because the book, a collection of fairy tales including queer retellings of some Hungarian classics, amounted to homosexual propaganda that was harmful to children.[77] The controversy that followed was one of the most politically consequential episodes of the culture wars in populist Hungary, culminating in the passing of anti-LGBTQ+ legislation that served as the model for Ron DeSantis's "Don't Say Gay" law in Florida while paralleling similar LGBTQ+ restrictions in Poland and Russia.

Dúró and her husband, Előd Novák, have been fixtures of the far-right scene in Hungary for nearly two decades and somewhat of a political power couple, first active in Jobbik, the first far-right parliamentary party in post-communist Hungary, and then as founding members of the *Our Homeland Movement*, a successor party to Jobbik's radical agenda. The book-shredding—called "book-grinding" (*könyvdarálás*) in Hungarian—was a carefully choreographed public performance, which Dúró also posted on YouTube, though the video was soon removed from the platform because of its hate speech content.

Centering a homophobic and transphobic campaign on a children's book revealed how the far right began framing anti-LGBTQ+ attacks as justified in the name of child protection, which was a novel strategy at the time. This is now a tactic we see across various countries, including the United States, with book bans and legislation against gender-affirming care for teenagers, often because of grassroots far-right civil activism by groups like Moms for Liberty.[78] In Hungary this shift coincided with LGBTQ+ organizations' efforts to combat growing hostility and restrictions in the wake of the populist turn in 2010 by reaching out to children and adolescents with educational initiatives.[79] The children's book *A Fairy Tale for Everyone* was the product of such an initiative by the Labrisz Lesbian Association.

The volume contains seventeen stories that were written by professional authors commissioned by Labrisz and by amateurs whose stories were selected from an open writing competition. It is the first Hungarian children's book that deals with LGBTQ+ experiences. The stories feature characters who are gender diverse while also representing ethnic, religious, and socioeconomic minorities. Several of them rework well-known fairy tales from Hans Christian Andersen, for instance, by replacing traditional with culturally more diverse characters, including a gay prince who ends up marrying not a princess but her brother, a three-eared rabbit, a giant-fighting young girl, and a Roma Thumbelina. The Network of Human Rights Educators (Emberi Jogi Nevelők Hálózata, EJHA) also prepared teaching materials to accompany the book, to be used in teaching sessions in kindergartens and elementary schools. This became an especially controversial aspect of the book project.

The book-grinding stunt snapped the public out of the numbness of pandemic lockdowns and reignited the culture wars over LGBTQ+ communities and other stigmatized groups. Professional book trade organizations like the Association of Hungarian Publishers and Booksellers (MKKE) immediately condemned Dúró's act and likened it to book-burning by the Nazis. One of the book's authors I interviewed added that "it's not simply the book burning, which has a terrible history, but the fact that the characters in the tales embody lots of different identities [and] made me feel that my own personal family model [being the adoptive mother of a Roma boy] was shredded in this act." Psychologists issued an open letter protesting the book-grinding and the pseudo-scientific claims Dúró drew on to deem the fairy tales detrimental to children. But the far right also jumped on the opportunity to deploy the full discursive repertoire of homophobic attacks. Some local mayors tried to ban the book, although these promises were either not fulfilled or quickly overturned as illegal. Those who vehemently defended the book-grinding argued that the problem was the very existence of the book, not its public shredding. And it was not fair to call a mother of four—referring to Dúró—who is only concerned about the well-being of her children a Nazi.[80] A Facebook comment on Dúró's page contended that it is surely right that "books cannot be ground, but what she ground was rubbish."[81]

Building a set of arguments around child welfare became the defining strategy of the right in the ensuing controversy. First, the far-right press insisted that the issue at stake was not a human rights concern as the left claimed but required scientific expertise. And whereas the book's right-wing critics tried to approach LGBTQ+ content aimed at children with scientific objectivity, the left-liberal "gender lobby's" approach was purely ideological. A contribution by a right-wing commentator in the *Hungarian Nation*, a sociologist-economist by profession, illustrates the elaborate conspiratorial framing of the argument: "Let's try to treat this as if we were looking for answers to a specific policy question and not searching for a way to capture political power by establishing Gramscian cultural hegemony through ideological struggles waged by an LGBTQ proxy party backed by foreign powers and woke multinational corporations."[82] Another right-wing columnist added that for the LGBTQ+ movement, science itself was the subject of a power struggle, and whoever disagreed with them was labeled unscientific. Thus, LGBTQ+ activists called, for instance, the work of Paul Sullins, a sociologist at the American Catholic University, about the developmental problems of children raised by gay couples "bad science." They also dismissed the research of a wide range of similar conservative scholars, including Robert P. George, Pierre Manent, Patrick Lee, and John Finnis, on the same grounds, hoping to enforce a kind of "Jacobin terror," ostracizing dissenters and stifling free debate, an integral part of academic life, putting an end to the pluralism of opinions.[83] Related to this argument about scientific objectivity, there was a verbal fistfight among Hungarian psychologists, most of the profession condemning a conservative psychologist, Emőke Bagdy, who frequently appeared in public media and was wholeheartedly endorsed by far-right groups as a "prominent expert," and who capitalized on her media access to support the position that exposure to LGBTQ+ content at an early age may harm children.

Second, critics clamored that targeting children with LGBTQ+ materials "crosses a line." They think it is incredibly treacherous to use children's books as a vessel for this type of content because "unsuspecting" parents can "accidentally" purchase it without knowing that it contains "homosexual propaganda" and end up "unwittingly" harming their children. As an op-ed publishing librarian put it: "The liberals (*libernyákok*) are provoking us again. They slap us in the face with tinfoil-wrapped human rights revealing that they couldn't care less about any of the values that are important to us. They don't care about what we believe in to be natural; they demand equal treatment for their aberrations in every sphere of life. Until now they have left our children alone, but now with *Fairy Tale for Everyone* they have crossed a line."[84]

Third, the fact that the NGOs involved in the book project specifically prepared lesson plans and workbooks to be used in sensitivity training for children in kindergarten and elementary school was portrayed as intentionally insidious. When LGBTQ+-themed activities are introduced to unformed children—such as "when a small boy's homework in kindergarten is to imagine what it would feel like to turn into a girl"[85]—it becomes clear that "this is a war, and the recently published LGBTQ children's book is a manifestation of the enemy's diversion warfare"[86] and "they want to raise LGBTQ soldiers."[87] This is why LGBTQ+ children's books were declared to be a "Trojan horse" and more dangerous than Pride. They amount to a "mental hormone therapy" (*szellemi hormonkezelés*), according to an interview with a "renown education researcher."[88] And while elaborating these arguments, right-wing media sources never failed to note that the nongovernmental organization (NGO) behind the book project received financial support from George Soros through the Open Society Foundation.

But the controversy was more than just a war of words: It did translate into action on various levels. There were protests organized in front of Labrisz's office, the NGO that launched the book project, several members received threats, and the Consumer Protection Agency started harassing them for providing misleading information about their products to their customers.[89] The Hungarian branch of the Madrid-based ultraconservative and ultra-Catholic CitizenGO civil society organization, which mobilizes primarily around anti-abortion and "antigender lobby" causes, issued a petition to protest the book and allegedly collected nearly seventy thousand signatures.[90] The Our Homeland Movement called for a boycott of the stores that sold the book, and the far-right Sixty-Four Counties Youth Movement (Hatvannégy Vármegye Ifjúsági Mozgalom) posted a red warning sign with the organization's logo on some of these bookstores that read "Attention! In this store homosexual propaganda materials that are dangerous for children are being sold."[91]

Several contributors to far-right media also accused the government of sponsoring the book, as its production received some funds from the National Cultural Fund (NKA). Consequently, they demanded that the government intervene and pass legislation that would prevent LGBTQ+ groups from targeting children "with their propaganda."[92] It is unclear whether the government felt pressured by far-right activists for fear of losing supporters or whether the controversy simply presented a window of opportunity to make a move it always intended. Regardless, shortly after the book-grinding incident, Orbán commented on the case, agreeing with the critics that LGBTQ+ groups should "stay away from our children!" Predictably, soon afterward, the government decided to draft and pass legislation that put in place significant limitations on LGBTQ+ rights. The Child Protection Act (colloquially referred to as the "homophobe" or "pedophile" law) that was passed in June 2021 stiffened penalties for pedophilia but also intentionally conflated pedophilia with membership in LGBTQ+ communities. Last-minute amendments to the law, largely in response to the controversy around *A Fairy Tale for Everyone*, introduced the banning of the promotion and portrayal of LGBTQ+ themes in education and media to minors. Additional amendments in 2022 further restricted the adoption rights of LGBTQ+ parents and their access to fertility treatments. The European Union criticized the Child Protection Act and launched legal challenges against Hungary and Poland for similar measures (e.g., "LGBT-free zones").[93]

Just as I was finishing this chapter in early June 2023 came the shock announcement that Libri, the largest book trading and publishing firm in Hungary, was sold by its owner to the Mathias Corvinus Collegium (MCC), a government-affiliated educational NGO.[94] The news took the public and the book world by surprise, triggering both instant anxiety and consternation among authors and publishers on the left while prompting loud cheers on the right. A few years earlier there were speculations that the government might forcefully try to break up the left-liberal dominance of the book market, but these fears waned and gradually gave rise to hope that it would be spared from a drastic remake. Libri's takeover came so suddenly and unexpectedly that rumors instantly started spreading about the majority owner, one of the company's founders, being pressured to sell his shares. Some high-profile authors immediately announced their departure from Libri, while others were hanging on to the new owners' public proclamations that editorial decisions would not be affected by the change of ownership.

The case of Libri and the book market in general epitomizes the intrinsic power mechanisms of populist rule in post-2010 Hungary. The playbook is deceptively standard and simple. After years of rumors, periodic media attacks, mounting pressures from grassroots far-right actors, uncertainty, mixed messages, including the sustenance of hope that an intervention might be averted, a government-friendly NGO or oligarch acquires control over a market, industry, or cultural field through a hostile but legal takeover. After initial pledges from the new owners that nothing will change and their decisions will not be driven by partisan politics, a gradual reshaping will commence and any resistance will be coopted, undermined, refracted, and, if necessary, openly suppressed.

The first signs of change since the acquisition involved tightening the enforcement of the measures introduced by the Child Protection Act in response to the children's book controversy: levying fines on bookstores for not properly distinguishing LGBTQ+ books—wrapping them in special transparent foil[95]—and not removing them from the children's section. Also, the cafés in Libri's flagship stores in the largest shopping malls had a makeover and joined the Scruton "café and community space" chain, creating a very visible link to MCC, whose headquarters hosted one of the first such cafés. They are named after Roger Scruton, the conservative British philosopher, a favorite theorist of Viktor Orbán, and a strong supporter of Orbánism. His library is on display in the cafés, and his books and extensive Scruton memorabilia, such as branded totes, water bottles, his bust, T-shirts with his quotes, and a scented candle "oikophilia" (meaning "love and feeling for home"—one of his key concepts), are now sold to accompany your cappuccino. But there are certainly more changes to come to Libri's book offerings, too.

This development again aptly highlights the importance of books in culture wars, explored in this chapter. The focus on books and publishing illuminates the indispensable role they play in delineating cultural canons around which culture wars are waged, and which serve as a political instrument in the toolkit of populist politics. When it comes to analyzing how cultural canons change, social science scholarship has focused primarily on progressive challenges, such as decolonizing social science curricula.[96] But as the Hungarian case illuminates, far-right actors also mount challenges to current cultural canons and want to shift them further to the right. In the first part of this chapter, I showed how cultural warriors on the right define culture as warfare, thereby raising its political stakes. Journalists and publishers see books as tools to break the cultural hegemony of the left, which in their eyes continues despite the right's control over politics and the economy and continues to be a "threat." This "threat," often defined broadly as liberalism, is also identified as something emanating from the "outside," from the "West," and being a source of foreign influence that will ultimately undermine national sovereignty unless contested.

Ironically, survey research on the Hungarian cultural field confirmed the reputational asymmetry of left-liberal cultural actors: Even right-wing cultural figures were found to be more likely to recognize the achievements of leftist rather than rightist cultural actors.[97] The onslaught on liberal cultural producers has clearly been ratcheted up to a new level to shift this longstanding status quo. The various controversies analyzed in the chapter underscore how school curricula, especially required reading lists, are key sites of culture wars over rewriting cultural canons, and children's books have been catapulted to the center of identity politics and the struggle over LGBTQ+ rights.

A faint sign of hope, nevertheless, is that the outcomes of these political struggles over culture are never straightforward. In the controversy over *Fairy Tale for Everyone*, LGBTQ+ communities have suffered real setbacks. But there has also been considerable backlash to the far-right attacks against them, and unexpected expressions and acts of solidarity. As the book's publishers explained to me, they were originally planning only a small print run (fifteen hundred copies) and distribution largely through informal networks. The controversy created the kind of visibility they never envisioned, enabling them to reach not just haters but a supportive audience as well. As a result, to date the book has had three print runs and sold thirty-four thousand copies, which makes it a bestseller in the Hungarian book market.[98] It has been translated into eleven languages, and its authors have been invited on international book tours. In 2021 Dorottya Rédai, one of the book's initiators, was named among the one hundred most influential people on the TIME 100 list. This is an interesting trend we see in other countries as well. Many authors in the United States whose books have recently been banned experienced rising sales afterward (e.g., Jodi Picoult's *Nineteen Minutes*, Art Spiegelman's graphic novel *Maus*), signaling how purchasing books can also become an expression of solidarity against far-right attacks. It is indeed useful to keep in mind that the power of books—banned books in particular—can cut both ways.

3

Reviving Folk Traditions to Refashion the Nation

Fashion has been enlisted to display, enact, and promote national distinctiveness in Hungary, as in many other countries whose political independence was often under attack. After suppressing the 1848 revolution, for instance, the Habsburgs banned the Hungarian national dress in the monarchy, which nevertheless only strengthened its political significance and symbolism of resistance.[1] These countries therefore often fought political causes like national self-determination by cultural means such as fashion as well.[2] Besides these historical legacies, there are numerous contemporary examples in the context of rising far-right populism that underscore the larger political significance of dress and fashion as an important site where political conflicts over cultural citizenship play out.[3]

There are cases when governments try to define the boundaries of cultural belonging by regulating forms of acceptable and unacceptable attire, almost always involving clothing worn by women. Burkinis (full-body swimsuits), for instance, continue to be banned in state-owned swimming pools across France despite legal challenges. Hijab and burka bans are in place or are being considered in several European countries.[4] Political parties also often formulate messages in their election campaigns about the symbolic boundaries of the nation through dress.[5] One of the main campaign billboards used by the far-right populist party AfD in the German parliamentary elections of 2017 pictured two blonde young, bikini-wearing women from the back, accompanied by the slogan: "Burkas? We prefer bikinis." Similarly, the Israeli culture minister, Miri Regev, sparked controversy at the Cannes Film Festival in 2017 for appearing in a dramatic dress printed with the Jerusalem skyline, which included East Jerusalem, the contested Palestinian area of the city. While far-right populism in Western Europe rallies around restricting Islamic dress in particular, in postcommunist Eastern Europe, far-right populist politics frequently embraces the revival of folk-inspired attire to project patriotism.[6]

When it comes to radical politics, the close association between some fashion labels and far-right groups has been widely covered in the media and scrutinized by some academic researchers.[7] Members of far-right extremist groups across Europe were known for informally appropriating clothing by brands like Lonsdale, Fred Perry, and New Balance. The brandscape of the far right has, however, undergone significant transformation since the early 2000s, as documented by Cynthia Miller-Idriss in her study of Germany.[8] She shows how neo-Nazi-friendly clothing brands have become specialized, professionalized, and increasingly normalized due to the intricately coded use of extremist symbols.

Against this larger international backdrop, this chapter focuses on the role of fashion in reimagining the nation in far-right populist regimes like Hungary. Ethnographic fieldwork led me to fashion brands that are centered on ethnic and national heritage, stressing the importance of incorporating "traditional" Hungarian motifs into contemporary everyday wear. I tried to map the full spectrum on which fashion producers imagine themselves as carriers of national and folk heritage, suppliers of national identity markers, and makers of meaningful "social skin."[9] One end of this spectrum is occupied by brands that are intimately tied to radical nationalist subcultures and their sympathizers. The middle range includes brands that try to adapt venerable folk traditions to meet contemporary clothing needs and infuse them with arts and crafts elements, and others that are propelled initially by nation-branding aspirations while catering, albeit not exclusively, to an international audience for cultural affirmation. The other end of the spectrum is defined by brands that experiment with how folk heritage can be harnessed to a socially progressive agenda, either by empowering discriminated Roma ethnic minorities or by emphasizing the ecological benefits (e.g., sustainability) of traditional craftsmanship.

While there is significant diversity across the brands, the overall spectrum is not evenly populated and clearly tilts toward the nationalist end, which this chapter centers on. The chapter also reveals that despite the apparent stylistic variety, owners and designers of these brands share some deeper cultural schemas that turn the making of fashion into an intensely political process around narratives of national belonging.[10] All these brands are small fashion labels organized around one person or a small family business, and the identity of the makers and owners themselves is often quite complex. They are dominantly women, although men also have a distinct place in this ecology.

Fashion producers cultivate various meanings of Hungarianness and Hungarian heritage through their work that contribute to populist reimaginings of the nation. They promote, for instance, the recovery of cultural heritage that emphasizes the reach of ethnic Hungarian culture beyond current state borders. They design fashion that aims to revive and reclaim the aesthetic vocabulary of regions and territories that were detached from Hungary in 1920 by the Treaty of Trianon and ceded to neighboring countries. Thereby they propagate an understanding of Hungarian heritage that is rooted in pre–World War I imperial nostalgia, symbolic irredentism, ethnic superiority, resentment, and victimization at the hands of foreign powers. These narratives have featured prominently in the populist Orbán regime's broader refashioning of Hungarian nationhood, as discussed in other chapters of this book and elsewhere.[11] Fashion producers also assert their commitment to small-scale, local production anchored in traditional values of nuclear family and ethnically homogeneous communities as a counterpoint to a profit-centered global fashion industry. Their brands similarly build on the countercultural legacies of dissident popular social movements, such as grassroots folk revival movements that demonstratively displayed Hungarian national markers, challenging the official antinationalist cultural ideology of the communist regime since the 1970s.[12]

This chapter places the heritage revivalist aspirations of contemporary Hungarian fashion in a broader scholarship on economic nationalism. Fashion inspired by folk revivalism offers insights into popular forms of nationalism, emphasizing a bottom-up, relational, and practice-oriented approach to understanding how the national extends into cultural markets in populist regimes. The analysis begins by drawing on current scholarship that theorizes the links between cultural production and nationalism. Subsequent sections review (1) how the search for Hungarian heritage has been fueled by a backlash to the communist repression of national culture; (2) how fashion brands form "circuits of commerce" and view themselves as close-knit cultural communities; and (3) how they profess to operate as value-driven businesses that are sustained by crafts ethics and shared cultural values centering on the revival of an ethnically defined cultural heritage rather than simply a profit motive. The chapter demonstrates how these fashion producers normalize radical nationalism and imagine an ethnically homogeneous nation through consumer communities, underlining the significance of cultural production for far-right populist rule.

Branding and Consuming the Nation

Nations have generally made a comeback as a powerful source of collective identity, and far-right populist regimes have defined the nation as the ultimate source of political unity, as outlined in chapter 1. The national now importantly encompasses not just the political but the economic realm as well, as exemplified by the increasing prevalence of nation-branding initiatives.[13] Various forms of economic nationalism have received some attention, but research on the interface of economic life and nationalism has been sporadic and scattered across different disciplinary fields.[14]

There has been a palpable surge of interest in nation branding in recent years, but this literature is defined by a relatively narrow focus on national representation that is outward facing and created in a top-down fashion by external consultants for an overwhelmingly international audience.[15] Less attention has been paid to economic nationalism that is linked to practices of everyday and "banal" nationalism[16] and diverse manifestations of ethnic commodification.[17]

Fashion and dress certainly constitute a domain of everyday life that can easily become a medium for displaying national sentiments and ethnic distinctiveness while being simultaneously exploited for political propaganda.[18] Some research in fashion studies has shown how sartorial practices can provide insight into everyday nationhood, especially its performative aspects. It has explored the role of fashion in the process of nineteenth-century "national awakenings,"[19] the emergence and changing use of specific garments as markers of the nation,[20] or the construction of national distinctiveness in the context of globalization.[21] These studies offer historically nuanced analyses of mostly individual country cases, such as the intertwined representations of race and nation in the evolving fashion of the nineteenth-century United States or the multiple interpretations of "Chinese style" across the global Chinese diaspora.[22]

But there is little research on the place of fashion in the recent return of right-wing ethnonationalism that accompanies the spread of populism.[23] Literature in this area is dominated largely by investigations of how fashion in

Russia is mobilized to coproduce patriotism as a tool of governmentality and a central ideological anchor of the Putin regime. Especially after the annexation of Crimea in 2014, Russian patriotism was also channeled into dress culture, and Russians became inclined to exchange foreign for local fashion brands and for clothes with Russian patriotic slogans and symbols. Drawing on Foucault's concepts of biopolitics and governmentality, Ekaterina Kalinina focuses on how Russian fashion brands position themselves vis-à-vis the patriotic and gender narratives that are propagated by the state.[24] Similarly, Olga Gurova examines how fashion designers as cultural intermediaries are encouraged to follow patriotic fashion, and how this shapes their interpretations of patriotism as well as their creative conduct.[25] By comparison, individual clothing choices—such as the kalpak, a traditional conical felt hat, or Muslim women wearing hijab—in the former Soviet Republic of Kyrgyzstan acquire political meanings when they are set against larger debates about authentic representations of Kyrgyzness.[26] Others explore the visual language conveyed by the revival of patriotic attire across postcommunist countries in Central and Eastern Europe, drawing on ethnic folk motifs, traditional embroidery, crafts festivals, historical reenactment events, and religious symbols, among others.[27]

But in Hungary, in sharp contrast to Russia, where patriotic fashion is a top-down initiative promoted by the state, fashion designers of small folk-revivalist labels associate themselves with a grassroots movement that now receives more mainstream recognition and political approval—which was long overdue, in their view. They emerged and operated as subcultures defined by a strong anticommunist stance. Research on subcultures has been crucial in exposing the political significance of cultural production and consumption, but because of its privileged focus on youth cultures and class resistance, nationalist subcultures that cut across class, gender and age have been largely left out of its purview, as noted in chapter 1.

The Hungarian folk-revivalist fashion designers I interviewed also see themselves as embedded in a close network of relationships with their customers, employees, subcontractors, and fellow brand owners, defined by their commitment to protecting and upholding ethnic cultural heritage and their origins in the pre-1989 countercultural movements that contributed to the fall of communism. Thus, they make up "commercial circuits" that arise from a shared political and cultural attitude.[28] Fashion producers view commodities as constitutive of a material culture that effectively carries shared understandings of national belonging and moral value. Their work fosters the emergence of consumer communities organized around radical nationalism, thereby extending the theoretical scope of commercial circuits. They highlight, namely, that political convictions can intersect with specialized economic transactions and consumer objects.

Tracing Folk Revivalist Fashion

This chapter combines the content analysis of interviews and exhibition catalogues and the visual analysis of the websites and social media feeds of fashion labels with ethnographic observations (direct and participant) in the workshops of fashion designers and at various events. The core of the empirical data comes from thirty interviews conducted between 2017 and 2022 with owners and designers (in most cases the same person) of small fashion labels that aim to incorporate traditional Hungarian ethnic motifs and/or craft-based techniques into their contemporary clothing collections.[29] In addition, I interviewed several experts, including the chief curator of the modern textile collection at the Hungarian National Museum; the co-curator of the largest and highest-profile exhibition featuring Hungarian folk-art heritage, held in Budapest in 2018 in the series of National Salons at the Hungarian Kunsthalle (Műcsarnok), the major exhibition venue for contemporary art in Hungary;[30] and the main organizer of a series of design competitions, called *Gombold Újra!* (*ReButton It!*), that were launched in 2010 and aimed to reinterpret Hungarian heritage in contemporary fashion.

I followed a multipronged strategy in selecting my interviewees. The initial set of interviewees were identified in research I pursued on right-wing civil society.[31] The websites of right-wing civil society organizations often contained advertisements for clothing and other consumer products associated with the right-wing scene. After preliminary interviews with some of these clothing brands, I decided to broaden the pool of interviewees to encompass a fuller spectrum of relevant brands. I combined snowball sampling with information about designers and brands I gathered at relevant exhibitions, festivals, and fairs. For comparative context, I also included a few small fashion labels that were local but did not make Hungarian folk heritage the chief source of inspiration for their designs. Another selection criterion I applied was the stability of the businesses behind the brands. They were all run as small businesses that have operated for seven to ten years, and one for over thirty years. Whenever possible, I conducted the interviews in the workshops or the retail stores of the designers, which offered important ethnographic background. In some cases, the workshops were set up in the private homes of the brand owners. The aforementioned exhibition held at the Hungarian Kunsthalle in 2018 included a room in which the most influential contemporary fashion brands that strive to revive folk art heritage were displayed. The roster of designers presented there confirmed that I managed to interview the most important actors in this field.[32]

I focus chiefly on the cultural producers' perspective (fashion designers, business owners) because this provides the most comprehensive insight into Zelizerian circuits of commerce: They have the most extensive and dense networks of relations with customers, employees, artisans, distributors, competitors, and the broader public. They, their family members, and close friends often wear their labels, and they also put a lot of effort and expertise into creating narratives around their products that resonate with customers. As small brands, they interact very closely with and actively seek out the needs of their customers. Therefore, even though I did not systematically interview consumers of the brands examined here, I could build on the fashion producers' intimate familiarity with their customers. And indeed, I devoted considerable time in my interviews with designers and brand owners to mining their knowledge about the social profile of their consumer base.

I also attended more than a dozen exhibitions, roundtable discussions, market fairs, and fashion shows in Hungary as well as in the United States, in the Hungarian House in New York City, that featured garments by the brands whose owners I interviewed.[33] I visited most exhibitions in the form of guided tours where the guides were key figures of the art and crafts scenes whose works were displayed in the exhibition. In some cases, I toured the same exhibition several times with different guides. Over the past five years I have also regularly attended Hungary's largest folk arts and crafts fair, the Festival of Folk Arts (Mesterségek Ünnepe), which is held annually in Budapest in the framework of the August 20 national holiday celebrating the founding of the Hungarian state. This four-day festival/fair always features relevant vendors as well as fashion shows as part of the program. The interviews were analyzed in Atlas.ti using an open coding strategy and triangulated with data from the other sources.[34] In the interviews I used the notions of heritage and tradition to elicit views about ethnic and national identity as opposed to directly prompting interviewees to talk about this topic. This way the connections my interviewees made between heritage, tradition, and national sentiments were spontaneous and not provoked by steering questions, which could have made them suspicious of my motivations and less forthcoming in their responses due to the explicit political angle.

Legacies of Communism: The Repression of National Culture and Folk Art Deemed Kitsch

A prominent theme that ran through the interviews detailed how Hungarian national culture did not receive due recognition in everyday life. It was overlooked and underappreciated, and this neglect was generally seen as a legacy of the political treatment of folk and traditional crafts under communism. On the one hand, communism turned traditional Hungarian craft products into kitsch to be sold to tourists in centralized and state-owned souvenir shops in downtown Budapest. On the other hand, it disapproved the open display of national cultural markers as tacky, backward, premodern, and overly nationalist, promoting instead more cosmopolitan tastes and aesthetics. Fashion producers examined in this study see it as their core mission to restore Hungarians' pride in wearing nationally explicit clothing and remove the cultural and political stigma that the communist regime inflicted on Hungarian national heritage.

The owners of the Igéző brand, two energetic young women in their thirties, explained that they had gotten into fashion design after they realized they wanted to do something about the general lack of appreciation of Hungarian folk art heritage, which they saw as a lasting effect of the repression of national culture under communism. They switched to fashion after a relatively brief stint in interior design. They recalled that, as interior designers, they were constantly asked to design Mediterranean homes in turn-of-the-millennium Hungary with lots of cast iron and antique-looking walls, or IKEA-style Swedish homes, or even African-style interiors. They were wondering what was going on in Hungary that "we emphasize the influence of all sorts of other cultures in our homes, in our dress, so even in things that are really intimate, albeit we might have no connection whatsoever to Africa or India, just because it's beautiful," but nobody ever asked them to design a home that "emphasized their Hungarianness." And the same was true for clothing where Hungarian folk art was dumbed down to kitsch and a few oversimplified embroidery motives in the communist era. The Kalocsa embroidery was probably the most widespread of these decorative patterns that the souvenir shops on Váci Street, once Budapest's premier shopping street, were bursting with. The phrase, "the kitsch of Váci Street" (*Váci utcai giccs*) cropped up in almost every interview and was used as a shorthand for the trivial commodification of folk art that began under communism with the primary aim of targeting foreign tourists.

Folk art as a stylized commodity marketed to foreigners was one of the few uses of folk art in fashion that the communist regime saw as legitimate. For Hungarians, however, this stamped Hungarian folk art as kitsch—trite and cheap—and encouraged people instead "to turn to foreign cultures because they perceived them as more sophisticated." The brand owners felt that this was in large part why ordinary Hungarians were simply not aware of how much richer and more diverse the repertoire of traditional Hungarian motifs was: "We sense," they continued,

> that many people do not know, they have no idea; this is probably another reason why they turn to other cultures, because they see that it's trendy, because it's more visible, it's more publicly known, and unfortunately, they don't know Hungarian heritage, that there are treasures here as well, which they can display in their homes or on their clothes. There is ignorance, or lack of knowledge; they [Hungarians] do not know their own culture and based on what they heard they were often full of prejudices.

This is why Igéző believes its mission is to familiarize their customers with the wealth of traditional Hungarian motifs on the clothes they make that are also reasonably priced and eminently wearable (figure 3.1). They have found clothing to be a much more effective medium than interior design to achieve this goal.

The status of folk and national dress traditions has also been contested and ambivalent in design education, reflecting another legacy of the communist disapproval of this heritage. After World War II the study of folk art–based dress and fashion was removed from the curriculum at Hungary's premier arts and design university—formerly the Iparművészeti Egyetem, now called MOME (the Moholy-Nagy University of Art and Design). This happened not only because folk traditions, closely associated with rural peasant lifestyles, were perceived as antimodern in a communist country undergoing rapid and forcible industrialization, but also, and especially, because its earlier applications were tainted by their links to right-wing political movements in the interwar era.[35]

The owner and designer of another brand, Meyke, described how this negative bias against folk art–inspired fashion shaped her career. She turned to this tradition in defiance, looking to Hungarian cultural icons from the turn of the twentieth century, such as the classical music composers Béla Bartók and Zoltán Kodály, who sought to incorporate folk traditions into modern high culture. But, in her view, drawing on folk art heritage for

FIGURE 3.1. Igéző dresses on sale at the Festival of Folk Arts. Photo by author.

contemporary fashion was still "totally taboo" at the time she graduated from MOME in 2003. She noted that she had a hard time at the university after she became interested in working with folk cultural patterns and techniques. Her professors strongly discouraged her from pursuing this route. Meyke told me that during her studies it was still "pretty taboo to openly display Hungarian national identity awareness" at the university. There was concern that the line between Hungarian folk heritage and kitsch was too easy to cross. It was also treated with suspicion as an example of "naïve art" and popular culture that became politically co-opted by the right in the 1930s.

Meyke thought it was ironic that while Hungarian designers were reluctant to use Hungarian folk motifs, prominent international fashion designers, like the Japanese Kenzo, had no reservations about experimenting with them. Kenzo used Kalocsa embroidery and Richelieu technique (a cutwork technique using eyelets and ladders), and even though his applications were not authentic, he was not afraid to use folk art. Folk heritage has a distinct lineage in other countries, too, but in Hungary there is always concern and anxiety that it will morph into kitsch. Meyke lamented, "But who else could carry on this Hungarian folk heritage if not those who have it in their guts, in their blood, that is, in their roots. Who could sustain it? Another nationality? I don't quite understand how."

The idea that Hungarians are somehow embarrassed by their own folk and national heritage and are basically ashamed to wear it in public came up regularly in the interviews and was contrasted with examples of other countries where this did not seem to create cultural tension. According to the interviewees, this unease was also the product of the cultural stigmatization of folk art–inspired fashion during communism. This is why they see their work as dedicated to removing this stigma. The owner-designer of the By Me brand, Tünde Hrivnák, recounted an example of how this deeply ingrained prejudice against folk art could, until recently, only be softened through external, Western cultural attention. She cited a Formula 1 race in 2011 in which the McLaren team's star drivers, Jenson Button and Lewis Hamilton, wore overalls and racing gloves covered in Kalocsa embroidery, generating positive coverage in international media. She underlined that "there was definitely a breakthrough in 2011 when Hamilton and Button put on overalls that were decorated in Kalocsa patterns. So, you needed two international celebrities to open the eyes of those who are no fans of folk art to see the enormous treasure of folk art in this country."[36] Others mentioned the media sensation that Nicole Kidman caused in Hungary when she was photographed wearing a summer dress in full Kalocsa embroidery on a family outing.[37]

In a related vein, several interviewees pointed to the marked contrast they sensed between Hungary and other countries regarding public approval for traditional wear being part of people's everyday wardrobe. As the Igéző designers put it: "Not to mention that in neighboring countries, in Austria or in others, it is perfectly natural to wear a dirndl,[38] to wear traditional national dresses, or in the case of Africans, you can see from afar that they often wear traditional dress, others wear turbans, etc.; it is natural that these things are part of their everyday life, whereas in Hungary this is all political." Her casual comparison with other countries is meant to lend weight to her argument that in Hungary the wearing of folk-inspired traditional dress became particularly stigmatized under communism because it signaled the social backwardness of rural peasantry as well as the right-wing political legacy of the 1930s.

The direct political nature behind public disdain for traditional dress was recognized and explained by other interviewees, like Katalin Hampel, who is undoubtedly the doyenne of Hungarian dress. She has been in this business for over thirty years, longer than anyone else active in the field. For her, first of all, it was important to draw a distinction between Hungarian national dress and Hungarian folk dress. "Folk dress" (*népviselet*) is from the provinces and was worn by peasants and poor people in rural villages. Hungary, according to Hampel, has at least 130 different types of folk dresses. By contrast, "national dress" (*nemzeti viselet*) comes from the Hungarian aristocracy and was worn by the Hungarian nobility until the mid-nineteenth century, the so-called Reform Age, before it also became a staple for the bourgeoisie and then trickled down to the popular classes by the 1930s. In the end, "everyone from the porters to the errand boys was wearing clothes adorned with the signature *passementerie* braid-work (*zsinóros-paszományos*) that had an anti-German edge at the time."[39]

The terms traditional, national, and folk are often conflated and used interchangeably today. Communism lumped these terms together under the umbrella of antimodern and anticommunist, that is, features of conservative regimes that came before it. In the nineteenth century "national dress" was an "invented tradition" that amalgamated ethnic motifs of regional (folk) dresses into a visual representation of the nation-building process.[40] Hungarian nobility originally started to wear a national dress in the royal Habsburg court as a form of political protest against imperial rule.[41] Even after Hungary formally became an equal partner in the Austro-Hungarian Monarchy in 1867, Hungarians continued to wear this attire, "as a symbol of national difference, ethnic pride, and aspirations for independence."[42] Its broad diffusion across social classes after World War I was coupled with the rise of nationalism and fascism.

Hampel's clothing line carries the aristocratic tradition to the present, producing modern variations of classic menswear pieces like the "Bocskai suit" and jackets,[43] and applying the same *passementerie* technique to exclusive ladies' fashion (figures 3.2 and 3.3). She herself claims venerable aristocratic forerunners in her family, which she also recounted in detail in a life history interview published as a book by Kairosz, an important right-wing publisher discussed in chapter 2.[44] Today she caters to the new conservative Hungarian political and social elite that no longer shuns this fashion but proudly sports this attire at national public events and holiday celebrations. Her regular clients include famous opera and operetta singers as well as high-ranking right-wing politicians and their spouses, including a former state president's wife.

Hampel also asserts that Hungarian national dress was strictly forbidden under communism because of its association with the aristocratic class and

FIGURE 3.2. Bocskai and *díszmagyar* (Hungarian dress) combination in the 1930s. Bálint Hóman, shown here, was an important interwar politician and cultural administrator who was well-known for his pro-Nazi sympathies. https://commons.wikimedia.org/wiki/File:H%C3%B3man_B%C3%Allint.jpg.

right-wing politics in the interwar era.[45] She recounted how "the communists hated everything that had to do with the nobility or the bourgeoisie; they chased away the aristocracy, and the haute bourgeoisie, and despised everything associated with them, the castles, the dresses, the silver candleholders and trays." Wearing these traditional dresses in public could provoke police action until the late 1980s: "If before the regime change [in 1989] someone decided to wear a Bocskai jacket on our national holiday on March 15, there was a good chance that the police would round him up."[46] Although this type of dress is no longer politically persecuted, the legacy of the communist repression continues into the present. Hampel confirmed that this traditional national dress was more accepted today, especially since Hungary's illiberal turn in 2010, "but there are still these liberal circles, which

FIGURE 3.3. *Passementerie*-braided dresses in Hampel's atelier. Photo by author.

include some of my friends and where I was questioned, 'so are you still making those fascist dresses'? Now, no fascist ever wore a *passementerie*-braided dress, so you hear this also because people are just misinformed, but there are people who are bothered by this, who do not like if something is 'too' Hungarian, who do not respect heritage."

Moving toward the radical end of the political spectrum on which I suggested to place the brands at the start of this chapter, one encounters an increasingly elaborate discussion of broader identity issues, not just strictly in relation to the making of clothes. These views reveal widespread resentment over the repression of national culture by foreign rulers, even before communism, which they blame for Hungary's failure to develop a "vigorous" nationhood. The owner of Szervető, for instance, repeatedly invoked the notion of a "healthy national consciousness" that is, in her view, sadly lacking in Hungary. She believes that people with a "healthy national consciousness" know where they come from, what their roots are, and where they are headed, and this helps them to set out their goals and keep their life together also at the personal level. The problem is that Hungarians have a conflicted relationship with their Hungarianness:

> I believe that Hungarians' back was broken by the Austro-Hungarian Monarchy, and by the Habsburg dynasty, and they were constantly deprived of a healthy national consciousness, of the opportunity to experience their Hungarianness as something to be proud of, to be a strong nation, to grow in a constructive way, without foreign help, without Austrian help, without anybody's help; to grow in an organic unity, like Switzerland. . . . But . . . I believe that if we had not sold the air space to the French, and the land, or the mines to the Canadians etc., then this country could endure; there was already evidence for this when the country managed to persist just on agriculture. And the Finno-Ugric theory didn't do any good to Hungarians either. I think just because there are 105–106 words in common with Finnish, this doesn't necessarily mean that there is a strong kinship; let's forget about this. We have at least as many words in common with the Turks as well, still no one speaks about a Turkish-Hungarian theory of kinship, right? Therefore, I think that for the young and for people in general this identity consciousness is very important so that they can be proud of being a Hungarian, of having been born here, that they can work here, sow their seeds, start a family, that they are Hungarians, and do not want to leave the country. I believe that there are a lot of gifted Hungarians who cannot grow because they lack this ambition, this force.

These historical examples are erratic and somewhat incoherent but highlight some of the important vernacular tropes of Hungarian historical identity narratives, underscoring the role of "foreign oppression" in blocking Hungarian progress. The criticism of Finno-Ugric theory—which puts Hungarians in this language family, implying ethnic kinship among groups (e.g., Finnish) in it—is a cornerstone of radical right-wing ideology that traces Hungarian ethnic genesis to Central Asian groups (e.g., Turks) instead. It is a theme that will be explored in greater detail in chapter 5.

FIGURE 3.4. Szervető's official logo, also displaying the brand's name in runic script. Photo by author.

Moreover, Szervető's owner sees her clothing brand as a tool to boost Hungarians' self-esteem and heal their "ailing national consciousness" (figure 3.4).

At the far end of the spectrum occupied by radical nationalists, the brands do not simply bemoan the repression of natural culture by communism or various foreign oppressors. They pledge to proactively reclaim Hungary's grandeur and mobilize fashion as a weapon in this quest. Harcos (Warrior), for instance, is a brand that draws on radical nationalist symbols such as runic script, the Greater Hungary image, or the mythic Turul bird rather than just folk motifs and traditions.[47] It was launched in 2004 by a former car locksmith in Balmazújváros, a small town in northeastern Hungary, an area with a strong support base for Jobbik, the most influential radical right-wing party at the time. Harcos is the most widely known and disseminated radical nationalist clothing brand, embraced also by key protagonists of the radical nationalist scene, such as members of "national rock bands" like Romantikus Erőszak (Romantic Violence).[48] The label that was purportedly affixed to each piece of garment included the following "warning" to unequivocally proclaim the political message of the brand:

> Warning: WARRIOR (HARCOS) is not only a fashion label, it is . . . a weapon against the system that is governed by the most harmful ideology ever, that of liberalism. We use HARCOS apparel to distinguish ourselves from the grey mediocrity, the slaves of the system who do not feel that the Hungarian people of the Carpathian Basin are one and indivisible regardless of the present borders. For us it is natural to express **love for our homeland** and appreciate our ancestors who made unforgettable sacrifices so that we can still raise our head with dignity **in the heart of Europe**. We who wear HARCOS apparel are fighting for a country in which the national interests of Hungary triumph above all. I recommend my clothing line, **THE RADICAL PATRIOTS' WEAR,** to everyone with no age limit, but only to those who identify with the above values [emphasis in original].[49]

The quote best illustrates how some hope to literally weaponize fashion in the interest of a nationalist cause.

Brand as Community

Cementing loyalty to a brand by strategically building a community around it has become a somewhat hackneyed marketing cliché. The term "brand community" was introduced in the early 2000s to describe "a specialized, non-geographically bound community, based on a structured set of social relations among admirers of a brand."[50] Since then, it has developed into a powerful marketing and advertising paradigm to reengineer customer relations by, for instance, harnessing the power of social media to leverage the brand. While carefully crafted brand communities can benefit large corporate brands as much as smaller boutique brands, they have been seen as uniquely important for smaller brands. A strong and loyal brand community can often turn a small brand into a lasting success.

Community is omnipresent in my interviews with small Hungarian fashion producers. Yet, the various ways in which community matters to them also move beyond the brand community concept of cutting-edge marketing theory in the United States. Community operates at multiple scales: It interweaves producers and consumers via intersecting communities organized around kinship, place, tradition, and ethnic identity. Fashion producers thus embrace a view of community that closely resonates with the rediscovery of the power of traditional communities—family, fatherland, church, nation—in far-right populist discourses.[51]

The dense and diverse web of these community relations provides the "circuits of commerce" that sustain these brands and their cultural mission.[52] The "circuits" of these brand communities are reinforced by their members' firm commitment to restoring and protecting Hungarian heritage. Historically, these small brands have also built on a long tradition of private dressmakers and small ateliers that persisted even throughout the communist era and on a thriving so-called boutique culture that grew out of the gradual softening of the centrally planned economy in the 1980s, giving way to the rise of private businesses even before the fall of communism.[53]

Family plays a pivotal role as a community anchor both in orienting the interviewees toward their careers in fashion and in the production process. Many of the women owner-designers learned to sew from their grandmothers and mothers, followed in their footsteps in studying industrial and fashion design, or were inspired by family lore about grandmothers who were the "naïve artists" of their peasant village communities. As Tünde Hrivnák from By Me recounts, both her grandmother and mother were seamstresses, and she always wore clothes that were handmade by them as opposed to the shoddy prêt-à-porter of the communist apparel industry. "Moreover," she says,

> my mother was into photography in addition to sewing and documented everything. Basically, from age one onwards, I went to the nursery and kindergarten in elaborate pantsuits and skirt suit sets that were richly embroidered by hand. . . . I learnt the most from my grandmother and mother, and by the time I was in grade school around the age of 10–12, I could pretty much sew anything and was helping my mother draw the circle diagrams for a plissé [for skirts]. So, I learnt this profession basically without noticing it because I liked it so much. I was always, like, this is so great that I can do these things with my grandmother and my mother.

She also underlined that this continuity across generations was really important to her because the passing down of skills, knowledge, and traditions from the older to the younger generations was also a way to connect these generational communities.

Family networks also figure significantly in production and in securing the operation of the businesses. Again, in the case of By Me, Tünde started her business with a personal loan from her father so that she would not be exposed to the vagaries of market-rate bank loans with often usury-level interest rates for small businesses. Her sister is the graphic designer behind the brand image and maintains the website. The girlfriends that run Igéző mention that they came close to quitting several times; they could only weather economically challenging times because they could fall back on their family's financial support. Ildikó, who designs and makes pearl jewelry using traditional folk craft techniques, describes how her husband's support made it possible for her to leave her day job as a teacher and organizer of children's programs at the Museum of Agriculture to devote herself full-time to her craft. For a long time, her jewelry was sold exclusively at folk arts and crafts fairs, imposing a grueling travel routine on her throughout the year, which she endured with her husband's and daughter's assistance. Similarly, the owner and designer of Aurora Folk Glamour, whose core business is also folk-art inspired jewelry, was deeply influenced by her travels as a child across Hungary with her art-dealer parents, who specialized in collecting and selling antique folk art. Her mother still regularly supplies her with the antique coins she uses for her most sought-after *lázsiás* necklaces.[54]

Parts of the production process, most typically garment design and business management, often takes place in a workshop in the owner's private home. Meyke works out of a cramped apartment in one of the grittier downtown districts of Budapest that doubles as a home she shares with her son and husband and triples as a temporary shelter for her down-and-out friends from her religious community. She is planning to move to a family house in one of the more affordable suburbs of Budapest to accommodate her expanding clothing line and corresponding need for more space. Aurora's apartment, located in a rapidly gentrifying part of Budapest's working-class eighth district, serves as a workshop and showroom for Aurora Folk Glamour. Her customers often prefer to pick up their online purchases in person instead of using mail delivery, even if they have to travel long distances, to experience the coziness of her workshop-showroom. These visits also enable Aurora to build lasting relationships with her customers.

Family and production are also entangled in place-based communities that are essential for the cultural identity of these brands. Tünde Hrivnák's family on her mother's side can be traced back to the eighteenth century when her ancestors were part of a Slovak community that was settled in the city of Tótkomlós in southern Hungary, a very long distance away from majority Slovak areas, as part of large-scale repopulation efforts, primarily by the Habsburgs, that followed the end of Ottoman rule in the eighteenth century.[55] To her, the folk motifs that she grew up with always defined this local community that was neither Hungarian nor Slovak but referenced this particular Slovak ethnic enclave in a majority Hungarian area.

Distinct repertoires of folk motifs are always tied to place. They originate from and denote specific geographic regions, and variations in the patterns reference smaller local communities within these regions. The brands discussed here define their authenticity in large part through preserving the regional integrity of folk motifs: They claim never to mix motifs from different regions. Simultaneously, they emphasize the use of regional motifs from areas in neighboring countries that used to be part of Hungary before World War I, especially from Transylvania (Romania), as integral part of Hungarian heritage and a way to include cross-border diaspora communities in the Hungarian nation (figure 3.5).

Katalin Hampel believes that folk motifs always marked out specific communities: "They were very closed communities, and they used the same motifs, the same colors for centuries; this is partly why these old, folk dresses are so beautiful, because one village never went [to the other], never emulated, and never mixed [its motifs] with those of another village." And again, Réka from Szervető scales up this theme to the level of national consciousness. She recounts how she founded the brand to try to do something for Hungarians (*magyarságért*), to do something about the lack of solidarity (*összetartozás*). "And then," she says, "I realized that [folk] motifs bind people together, they provide a common identity, a common drive for people; that is, a sense of belonging."

Moreover, some of the brands, like By Me and Piroshka, collaborated with local artisan collectives in producing some or all of their collections. By Me collections are all designed around well-known regional repertoires, such as the aforementioned Kalocsa embroidery, the Matyó pattern linked to the northeastern city of Mezőkövesd, and a special and intricate lace technique associated with the city of Kiskunhalas in southeastern Hungary.[56] In each case she worked together with local artisans, who produced the traditional embroidery or lace insets for the individual pieces she designed. These collaborations were often solicited and mediated by local politicians in these cities who hoped to support the heritage industries in the often struggling local economies while gaining visibility for their local cultural heritage. But the designers also stressed the importance of folk artists' moral integrity

FIGURE 3.5. *By Me* fashion show at the 2025 Festival of Folk Arts featuring the *Székely Land* (a region of Transylvania) collection, with St. Stephen's statue and the Fishermen's Bastion in the background. Photo by author.

and the almost familial connection they developed with them during their collaboration. Tünde Hrivnák talked in superlatives about the Folk Arts Association in Mezőkövesd: "And at the beginning, there was Bernadett Papp, the art director at the Folk Arts Association who is a fantastic folk artist. She is somebody who personifies to me discipline, respect, fairness, honesty and precision, that is everything I associated with my grandmother I see in her now."

Similarly, Piroshka worked together with one of the oldest family business in the Hungarian hand-dyed blueprinting (indigo) tradition for a contemporary indigo summer collection,[57] and with the "Folk Art and Domestic Industrial Cooperative" from Heves in northeastern Hungary for a collection that was inspired by the abstract geometric aesthetics and simple white-blue-red color scheme that characterizes the traditional embroidery of this region.

The communal feel of these brands is also reinforced by a touch of amateurism. This does not seem to be a strategically calculated marketing strategy but rather the product of the dense relational networks in which designers are embedded and are integral to their successful operation. Frequently, when these brands display their collections in fashion shows or on their websites, they work with amateur rather than professional fashion models. They enlist women and men who are part of their social, cultural, and customer networks to showcase their clothing lines at diverse events. Katalin Hampel always asks prominent customers, such as influential right-wing politicians' wives and her favorite opera singers, to join her fashion shows on the runway and even to perform a few arias or folk songs.

Several designers (e.g., Meyke, Réka Juhász, NHA) regularly enlist folk dancers from the Dance House Movement—a very important folk revival movement in Hungary—to wear their dresses in their shows.[58] They typically have close personal relationships with these dancers, who are also their regular customers. In fact, the Dance House Movement that started in the 1970s as a grassroots movement was instrumental in creating demand for nationally inspired clothing that was not a traditional folk costume but modern urban everyday wear.[59] Fashion producers' links to these folk revival movements underscore how traditional Hungarian arts and crafts practices were considered countercultural and politically critical of communist ideology before 1989.

Szervető's owner often scouts models among the visitors at the folk arts fairs and reenactment festivals where they sell their apparel, like the stunning young, blonde falconer who was featured in their online and print catalogue. She was spotted by chance at a fair wearing a T-shirt by Szervető and was asked to model for their upcoming catalogue. The Whiskey Robber, husband of Szervető's owner, also occasionally appeared in the company's online catalogues. By Me's owner also explained: "Everyone I invite to participate [in the show] knows exactly what kinds of clothes they will put on, what they are going to showcase, and what we represent with this." The main point is not that they are professionally trained but that they truly understand the symbolic meaning of the clothes and the value of national heritage.

Last, but most important, customers are seen and treated as part of a community. The owners and designers know the overwhelming majority of their regular customers in person. As Erika and Zsuzsa from Igéző described:

> Sooner or later, everyone feels like they are girlfriends of ours. Namely, there is an atmosphere here that is different from when you go into Zara and pick a blouse, and you're done and say goodbye, but here we get involved; many questions come up while processing an order that are often personal, and then we enter into a mutual conversation and basically get to know these people to some extent. This can be both good and bad; it can be a double-edged sword [they laugh], because we get to know a lot of interesting people and we learn about how they found us, apropos the clothes, but often we also learn stuff about them that we don't always want to know.

Albeit the clothes are not made to measure, customers often request alterations and actively participate in the remodeling of the clothes. Sometimes they even make demands regarding the range of motifs that brands use as part of their repertoire. Most designers told me that they had introduced certain pattern sets that were solicited by customers who either offered them their family heirloom collection of embroidery motifs or volunteered to do the ethnographic research on some regional pattern variation.

Customers still primarily find these brands through word of mouth, although social media has extended their reach internationally, often tapping into ethnic Hungarian diaspora communities abroad, in the United States in particular. The Hungarian House in New York has hosted several fashion shows that popularized these brands, and they have participated in events like the Sarasota Hungarian Festival in Florida. They also regularly appear in front of ethnic Hungarian audiences in neighboring countries, particularly in Transylvania (Romania). And some, like By Me, have been returning attendees at Central Asian cultural events, such as the "Women and Fashion of the Turcic World" organized by the International Organization of Turcic Cultures (TÜRKSOY), reinforcing the importance of the Central Asian cultural connection for right-wing populists that will be explored in chapter 5.[60]

Overall, the owners feel that their main customer base is drawn to their brand by more than just superficial aesthetic preferences. Erika from Igéző thinks that "first of all, people come who have some additional connection: They are into folk dance, or for some reason it is important to them to wear clothes that are marked by Hungarian motifs." The specific community reference group of the customers evidently varies across the brands. Hampel's key customer base, for instance, includes aristocrats. She claims that descendants of each and every prominent Hungarian aristocratic family (the Esterházys, the Zichys, the Andrássys, and so on) have frequented her store. Furthermore, she always hears from her customers about who else is wearing her clothes because they all take note of each other. So, when one of her friends attended a wedding in the castle of the French La Roche family and was sitting across from a countess, they looked at each other and simultaneously blurted out Hampel's name, realizing that they were both wearing a dress from her. In a similar vein, Tünde Hrivnák fell back on her Slovak roots in recruiting her first customers. The president of the Slovak minority council in Hungary, who comes from the same city as she does, ordered a suit from her. Then, the wife of the Slovak ambassador to Hungary saw her and fell in love with her dress, and through these connections Tünde gradually developed a clientele among foreign diplomats stationed in Hungary and high-ranking Hungarian politicians' wives. And she was also developing a capsule collection in special collaboration with a Hungarian aristocrat.

Szervető targets customers with a very different social and demographic profile—moderate income lower-to-middle class customers from the provinces—but is no less emotionally attached to them:

> Absolutely, Szervető is a community. People tell me that Szervető is tantamount to me, but I tell them that that's not true. I am the mother of Szervető at most, or its engine, or its clutch or something similar . . . but I really think that everybody is a Szervető who wears it. You can only understand this as an organic whole. The seamstress is part of Szervető, and so is the textile dyer, as well as those who wear the clothes. Everyone contributes to making this into something; the customers are spreading the brand as much as I or others from the production team do.

She also proudly recounts an anecdote she heard from a friend. The story involves a young woman who jumped on the train at the last minute and had no time to purchase a ticket. Then the conductor came around, and she was ready to pay the surcharge for purchasing the ticket on board, but the conductor told her that he noticed that she was wearing a Szervető T-shirt and that he was also a fan and owned several pieces by the brand, so not only did he not make her pay a surcharge, he did not charge her at all. Similarly, Réka was convinced that Szervető "connects people. If two people with a Szervető bag, or wearing a Szervető T-shirt, cross paths in Budapest, I am sure they will smile at each other . . . , they know that there is a connection between them, and this is wonderful."

Business Versus Craft: A Value-Driven Practice

The stories about the communal warmth of the brand could easily be dismissed as cleverly disguised marketing talk. But in this section, I explore further how these fashion producers consistently downplay the business aspect of their brand in favor of noneconomic returns and the cultural contribution they believe they make to the preservation and popularization of Hungarian heritage. This again extends Viviana Zelizer's framework on economic circuits because it shows that these brands are not just embedded in a dense web of social relations but engage in practices that privilege a socially meaningful, culturally committed, traditional craft logic versus a market logic of production.

It is hard to estimate how influential these small fashion brands are in terms of sales, profits, and market share relative to mainstream fashion brands. Instead, the criteria I used to select them included, most importantly, stability and continuity. The brands I studied have been in business continuously for an average of seven to ten years, with some, like Hampel, being around for thirty years, or By Me for seventeen at the time of the interview. For contrast, I also selected an unsuccessful brand, Piroshka, by a Berlin/Budapest-based young designer, which folded after a couple of years precisely because she could not generate the social networks necessary to maintain her venture. Her socially progressive message about the ecological value of folk traditions did not resonate with consumers, in sharp contrast to other brands that stress the revival of a proud national heritage that was ideologically repressed under communist rule.

The owner-designers all emphasized that although they were hoping to—and were happy to be able to—make a living out of their business, they were not in it for the money, and profit considerations were secondary. They reiterated their commitment to a craft ethics and the nonmaterial rewards they reaped from their work. Most interestingly, when asked about what they considered their biggest success, not one respondent mentioned typical business indicators of success (e.g., increasing sales or profits, growing number of employees, expanding business opportunities). I was surprised, for instance, not just by the content but also by the speed and spontaneity with which Igéző tackled this question:

> Hmm, this word "success," well, to us it is already considered a success that yesterday this little girl put on this dress and she was so sweet in it. . . . I mean this feeling. . . . And we are also proud of those who wear [our clothes]. I mean we are proud that certain people wear our clothes, that they appreciate our work, and then this feels like success, it feels like it all makes sense, and it feels good to do this. . . . These people represent certain values so that we say, "oh, we would give it to them for free as well," it is an honor that they feel that our clothes are worth wearing. . . . For instance, they express their Hungarianness in a way in which we think it should be expressed. They are the kind of people who are ready to stand by their Hungarianness.

When I followed up, asking them for an example of someone specific they had in mind, they mentioned the celebrity horseback archer, Lajos Kassai, who will be a central character in chapter 5. Likewise, Tünde Hrivnák from By Me notes that "to me success always means the same thing: to see the smile on the face of the person for whom we're making the dress as she pays and takes the dress." She adds, however, how touched she was when she received a Pro Urbe award from her home city, Tótkomlós, in recognition of her contribution to preserving and publicizing local cultural heritage. She was impressed by the size of the crowd that turned up for the award ceremony and all the encouragement she received. She felt that they exhibited strong support for "this entire way of thinking, the efforts to save the embroidery; the fact that they know that I'm doing this, and that this means a lot to them too, and I hope they will somehow benefit from it too . . . in any case, my take on success is always linked to people and goodwill."

Professional success is also measured by the frequency of invitations to folk-themed and juried design competitions and fashion shows, including some state-sponsored shows abroad, as well as to prominent festivals and fairs such as the largest and most prestigious folk arts fair, Mesterségek Ünnepe, which takes place annually in August in the courtyards of the Buda Castle in Budapest on a major national holiday commemorating the founding of the Hungarian state. But again, Réka from Szervető underscored that in addition to these strictly professional achievements, what is spiritually even more important to her is to bring her ware to ethnic Hungarians in Bratislava (Pozsony) in Slovakia or in Transylvania, Romania, "who fight each day to preserve their Hungarian identity, and they are indeed the true

Szervetős." She refers to the difficulties members of Hungary ethnic minorities face in neighboring countries when it comes to practicing their language and culture.[61] This example underscores again the importance of symbolic irredentism for these fashion producers by embracing ethnic motifs from regions detached from Hungary in 1920 and diaspora Hungarians as their special customers.

Some, like Katalin Hampel, see their main achievement in the overall integrity of their work and business: To Hampel, her success is "the whole thing because I am doing something that is my hobby, because I have colleagues that I like, that I like to work with, some I have been working with for thirty-one years, for instance, with an eight-five-year-old colleague who still regularly comes by [the atelier]. The fact that I created a workplace where people enjoy working; the fact that I can make dresses, we can make dresses, that make everyone look beautiful, that make everyone leave [the atelier] content."

Practicing fashion as craft and adhering to cultural authenticity are valued over economic gain and growth. This commitment to craft-based or craft-inspired production and nonmaterial benefits highlights how the brands see themselves as part of a value-driven economy, with the key values defined around tradition, national heritage, and community. They repeatedly described their work as centering on "rescuing"—not simply preserving—"traditions, heritage, motifs and values" (*értékmentés, hagyománymentés, motívummentés*). The owner of By Me, for instance, elaborated how important it was to her to get to know heritage activists, authentic folk art, and traditions linked to Kalocsa embroidery. That is, not just the embroidery technique itself but its broader context. She says she got to know a lot of people from Kalocsa before she embarked on the collection because she believed one can only bring the motifs to life if one is familiar with its authentic environment. In relation to a high-profile fashion show in the Smithsonian in Washington, DC, in 2013 in which she participated, she observes that she felt this show did an excellent job of using fashion to showcase the best of Hungarian culture. According to her, this is potentially something that can motivate a younger generation to see hand embroidery the way she sees it:

> As an incredible world that cannot be measured in money, because as Aunt Ica [a folk artist she worked with] used to say, "You can make a living out of handicraft work, honey, but you will never become rich." And, unfortunately, there is this strange thing with younger generations that

> they want to become instant celebrities and get rich, and they forget that there are things that cannot be acquired through celebrity status or with money. For instance, the fact that you can get to know people like the ones in Kalocsa and that you can live in an environment like that. And, yes you can make a nice living out of this work, but only if you are committed to the values that can be found exclusively in these [authentic] environments.

Each owner stressed that they would not compromise quality in the interest of profit or the reduction of production costs. Even the brands, like Igéző, that actually use machine printing technology as opposed to hand-embroidery, go to great lengths to explain how their manufacturing is still more akin to a craft technique than mass production because, even though it is machine printed, each piece is basically unique, and the application of the motifs still requires artisan skills. Others explain that they always educate their customers about how long it takes to produce the garments: that a button with a traditional *passementerie* technique is made of six hundred unique hand stitches, or that a Halasi lace inset in a dress takes about six months to prepare, and that these production schedules are not negotiable.

Many of the brands do not have their own production workshops but subcontract the manufacturing of the garments. Yet, they always emphasize how carefully they select the manufacturer, try to build a long-term relationship with them, and insist on keeping the production in Hungary. I tried to push the interviewees on the issue of growth and how even smaller brands can nowadays grow dynamically by outsourcing their production to foreign countries, including China. When, for instance, I mentioned this to Réka from Szervető, she just laughed. She said it was out of the question, and "the brand would just die then; I'm sure it would die. My soul would also die, that is, not just the brand would, but I definitely would."

The brands I examine here were generally aware of each other's existence. They frequently referred to one or the other brand during the interviews without my soliciting explicit comparisons. When I asked them if they were also competing for the same customers and a larger share of the market, they unanimously responded that this was not the case. They perceived the other brands as having a unique profile and occupying different niches. They maintained that they actually welcomed the diversity, tried to learn from each other, and were in principle supportive of other similar brands.

As Zsuzsa from Igéző put it: "We are so different from each other, we have no problems with the brands you listed, we know each of them in person, and I'm not saying that we are friends but we have a very good relationship" and "when we feel they contribute to this mission and represent a wellspring [of inspiration], we like that, even if it's different and I personally don't like it or would never wear it, but if there is a group that is attuned to this particular vibration and needs exactly this, that's fine with us. This is what makes the world round, we don't all have to be the same." As far as competition is concerned, she continued, "it is not in our blood, it is really alien to us to compete with anyone. If people don't want us, they don't want us, but if they do, that's great, then we'll be delighted." When these brands experience competition as a threat, this usually comes from cheaper knock-off products that copy elements of their designs without the use of quality materials and craft techniques. Almost all of them mention that they feel their designs have been emulated on global mass-produced garments, and Romani remarked that some of their designs were plagiarized by fast-fashion monolith Zara.

Fashion has long served as a powerful source of identity narratives and a material tool of national identity politics in Hungary.[62] But the Hungarian case illuminates more generally how cultural industries can objectify, reproduce, and provide effective conduits for the circulation of these narratives of national belonging. Hungarian fashion labels that are organized around reinvigorating nineteenth-century national dress styles such as the Hungarian dress or the Bocskai; rehabilitating folk-art heritage through ethnic motifs that symbolically question Hungary's current state borders; and dedicating craftsmanship to creating strong visual and material representations of Hungarian pride also reveal the deep cultural resentment that propels the engine of Hungarian national identity. This resentment feeds on vernacularized memories of centuries of foreign imperial rule, imagined and real social, political, and cultural deprivation inflicted by foreign powers—such as the devastating effects of the Treaty of Trianon after World War I—as well as the forced internationalism and bogus cosmopolitanism that governed the communist period. These historical legacies fuel deep distrust in a globalized world and compel some cultural producers, exemplified here by makers of fashion, to feel they have a mandate to redeem Hungarian culture, rectify its perceived marginalization, and restore a "healthy national consciousness."

The fashion producers examined here do this by offering a refuge in cozy cultural particularisms: familiar, affective, kinship-like, dominantly feminine brand communities that can also function as "imagined communities" of a political nature.[63] The owners and designers of the fashion brands rely on intersecting social circles—including family relations, place-based local communities, folk revival groups, and traditional craft networks sustained through fairs, festivals, and reenactment events—to build "circuits of commerce" that can then be extended to new consumers and become the bases of a meaningful community. But these consumption-oriented "imagined communities" do not necessarily require regular face-to-face interaction, formal membership in social movements, organizations, or tight-knit youth subcultures to elicit a sense of belonging.[64]

These fashion brands remind us that practices routinely associated with progressive politics, such as support for local economies, revival of craft techniques, community-based brand development, and female-owned entrepreneurship, can also be channeled for conservative political ends to cement cultural insularity and foster suspicion in the outside world.[65] It also extends the scope of understanding women's involvement in contemporary populist politics from a narrow emphasis on their voting behavior and a few high-profile political party leaders (e.g., Marine Le Pen in France, Alice Weidel in Germany, Giorgia Meloni in Italy) to their influence as cultural producers.[66] The Hungarian case thus shows how a relational and practice-oriented approach to economic nationalism can help us shed light on the role of cultural producers and everyday material culture in lending popular support to far-right populist rule and its provincial, illiberal visions of national belonging.

4

"Making Hungary Great Again"

HERITAGE TOURISM AND SYMBOLIC IRREDENTISM

In a protestant religious middle school in Mezőtúr, a small town in the center of the Great Plain in southeastern Hungary, students are sitting in a special literature class that prepares them for a four-day class trip to Romania. The teacher poses a question about what comes to their mind first when they hear the expression, "without borders" (*határtalanul*). One student responds that it makes her think of the free movement of people and the free circulation of ideas. Another notes that it reminds her of how they can now freely go to visit Hungarian relatives in areas of neighboring Romania that used to belong to Hungary. The teacher strongly reinforces this latter point, adding that those territories "used to be part of Hungary for much longer than the time since they have not been."[1]

Then she draws students' attention to a quote she has put on the board: "I want to feel boundless love for my homeland." The Hungarian word for boundless is the same as borderless (i.e., "without borders") and is often used in ways that exploit the double entendre. This is the case with this quote, which is a line from a 1970s pop song titled "Without Borders" by singer-songwriter József Dinnyés, a prominent member of the Hungarian beat generation, who is often referred to as the Hungarian Bob Dylan. The lyrics imply that the Hungarian homeland reaches beyond the country's borders to encompass Hungarian ethnic minorities in neighboring countries, and this is precisely why the song was censored during communism. Any mention of ethnic minorities outside Hungary, even the purely poetic questioning of borders, was politically controversial, a potential provocation to "socialist brother countries," given the historically contested nature of these borders and a long history of ethnic strife in the region. In the literature class, the teacher concludes the discussion by telling students that she hopes that they will also develop boundless-borderless love for their homeland during their trip to Transylvania, Romania. These thirteen-year-old seventh graders are embarking on this journey as part of an extensive government program, dubbed "Without Borders" (*Határtalanul*), to former territories of Hungary that the country lost after World War I.

This student mobility program offers unique insight into how public schools have become an ideological battleground for populist politics. It shows how cross-border heritage tourism serves to bolster an ethnonational identity by establishing strong cultural ties to ethnic diaspora communities that live beyond the nation-state's territorial borders. National borders in Central and Eastern Europe were repeatedly, and often violently, redrawn in the twentieth century and have remained disputed ever since. Various ethnic groups were also forcefully relocated across borders and subjected to discrimination and stringent assimilationist policies in their new home countries following both world wars.

European integration and the accession of ten formerly communist countries from Eastern Europe to the European Union in 2004 and 2007 were meant to dispel remaining tensions over borders and the incongruity between territorial borders and the boundaries of ethnic communities. But, ironically, fading national borders enabled the construction of new cultural and political practices that not only helped to reestablish relations with cross-border ethnic diasporas but also increasingly used these communities to reimagine the nation in the ethnic-majority country. In countries like Hungary, this process has been instrumental in eliciting a shift from a civic to a strongly ethnic definition of national identity, contributing significantly to the rise of far-right populism since 2010.[2] Heritage tourism remains a key cultural and economic practice—especially in Poland, Hungary, and Germany—that symbolically questions current national borders, emphasizes shared ethnicity as the chief source of national belonging, and aims to increase the viability of ethnic enclave economies in countries where the given ethnic group is a minority.[3]

Within this broader framework, this chapter demonstrates how Hungary's far-right populist government mobilizes heritage tourism in public schools to shift the national imagination for new generations. It also highlights how this objective is implemented through policies that are not entirely top-down and coercive but grant agency to participants, enabling the incorporation of grassroots nationalist and populist sentiments. At the center of the analysis is the large-scale *Határtalanul* program that the Hungarian government introduced in 2010, the year that marked a brisk populist turn in Hungarian politics. This program encourages and financially supports middle school and high school students to take organized class trips to areas of neighboring countries (Romania, Slovakia, Serbia, Croatia, and Ukraine) that belonged to the Hungarian state before the Treaty of Trianon was implemented in 1920 (figure 4.1). Between 2013 and 2019 about 300,000 students have participated in the program, nearly 30% of the targeted age cohort.

This program is significant because it exemplifies the elaborate propaganda toolkit of far-right populist governments that often exploits ground-up tactics and targets young, malleable minds. It elucidates how the Hungarian government utilizes the public education system to reengineer the meaning of the nation by promoting a narrow and exclusionary ethnic understanding of cultural membership and by selectively overemphasizing Hungarian heritage in regions that have had multiethnic, multireligious, and multicultural histories for centuries. The program illuminates how market practices such as tourism are embraced and mobilized for ideological purposes. The Hungarian government also views its subsidies for heritage tourism as economic support for Hungarian ethnic enclave economies in neighboring countries, which can contribute to their economic security and overall stability.

I acquired a unique data set from the Hungarian Ministry of Human Resources through a long and arduous Hungarian Freedom of Information Act Request (see further details about the process in the methodological appendix). The set contains detailed information about all the class trips (N = 2,374) that took place between 2013 and 2016, which were the decisive years for the institutional consolidation of the program. Schools need to submit a comprehensive application package to obtain funding from the program, which includes, among other things, a specific thematic focus, a detailed itinerary, and an agenda for preparatory meetings before and follow-up meetings after the trip. The summary of these items as well as data about the amount of funding the government awarded to each school make up the bulk of the information in the data set. Based on my initial analysis of this aggregate data, I took a random sample of thirty trips for each year

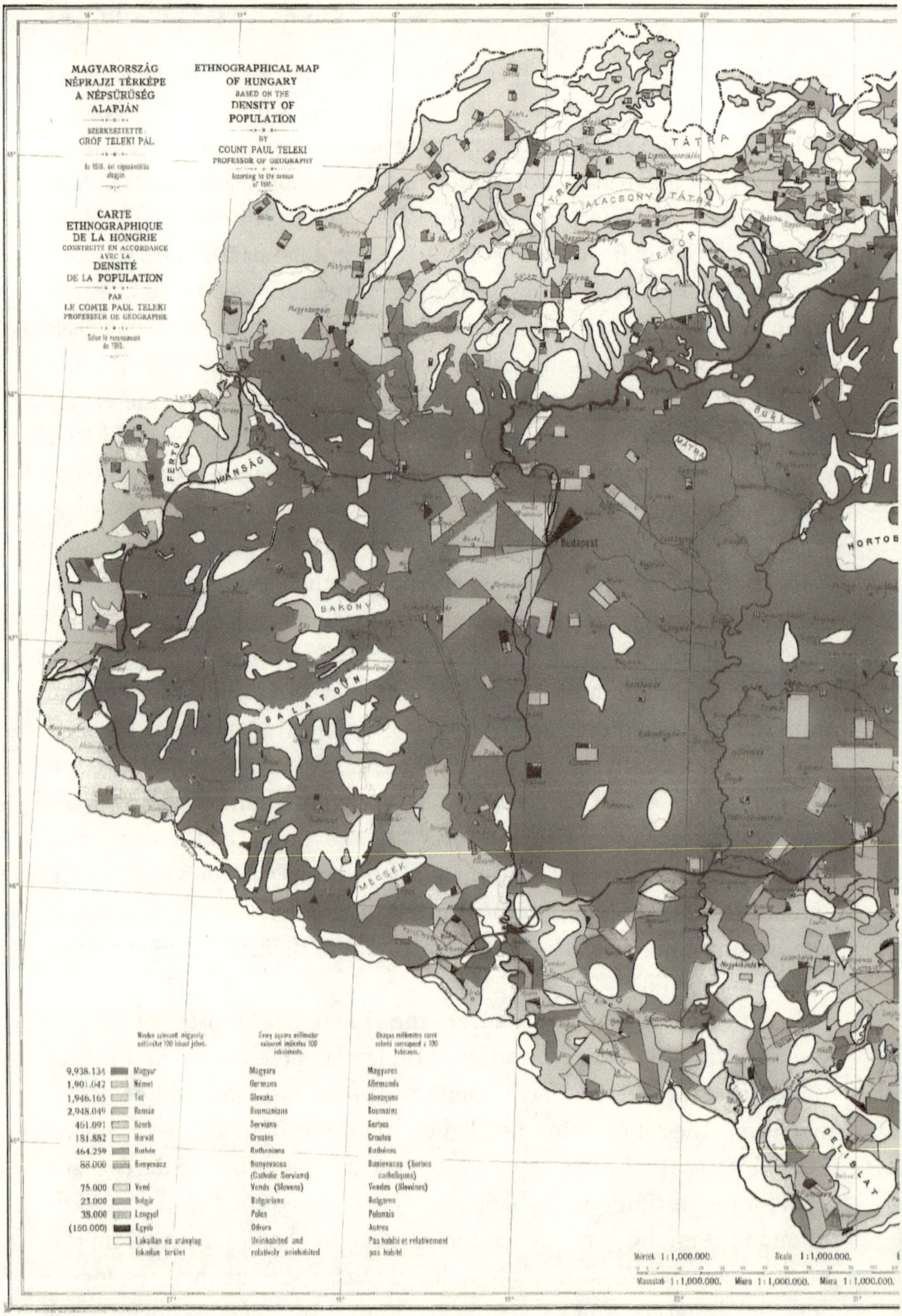

FIGURE 4.1. "Carte Rouge"—"Red Map" prepared by Hungary for the peace talks in Trianon. This ethnic map of Hungary is based on the population density of the various ethnic groups according to the 1910 census. In the original,

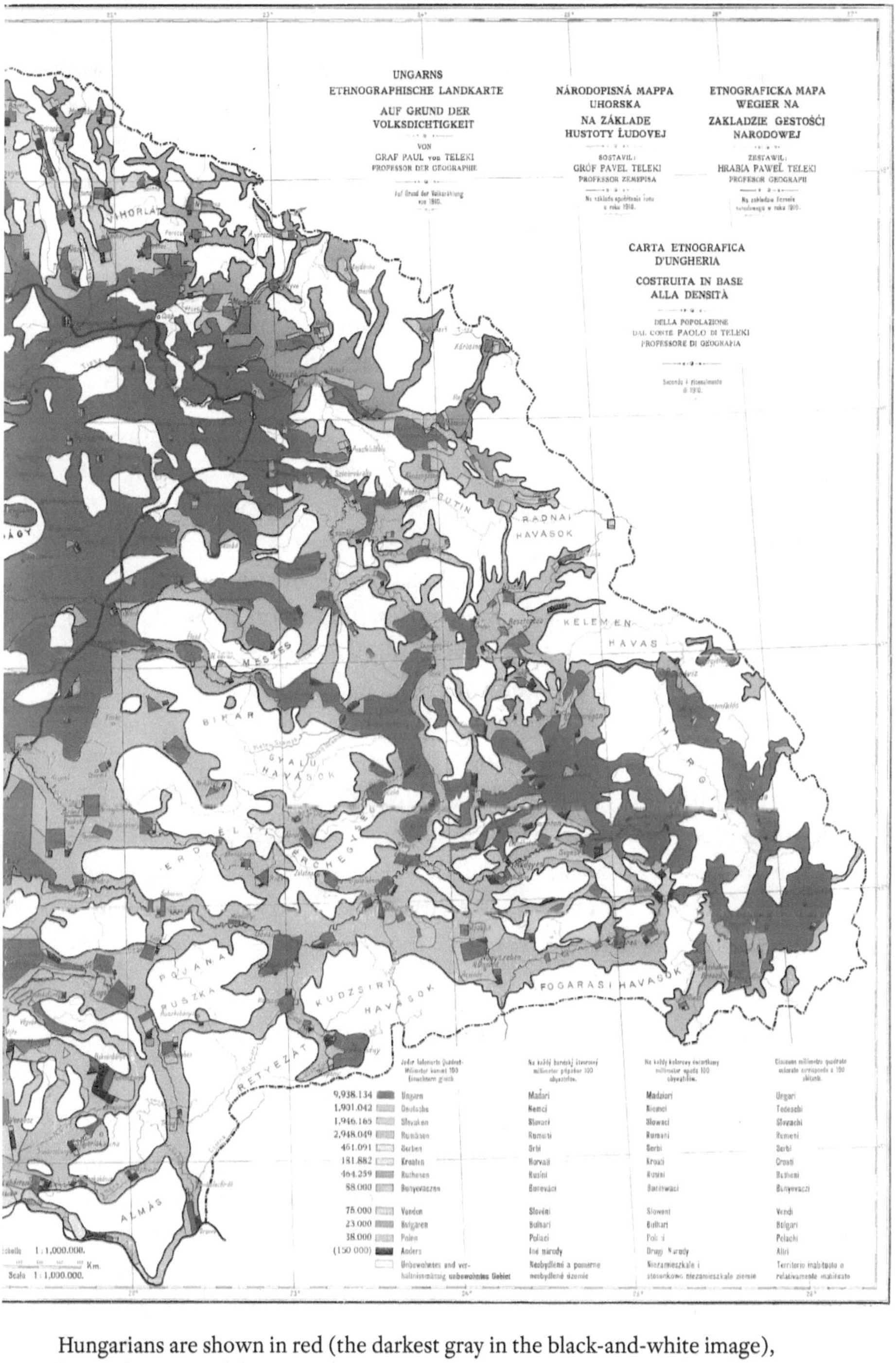

Hungarians are shown in red (the darkest gray in the black-and-white image), hence the name of the map.
https://commons.wikimedia.org/wiki/File:Ethnographic_map_of_hungary_1910_by_teleki_carte_rouge.jpg.

between 2013 and 2016, stratified by the destination country and the location of the applicant school (Budapest versus the countryside). I obtained the entire dossier of each of these trips, including the original application, the final report, and a wealth of supporting documents that constitute the empirical basis of my analysis here.

The chapter first offers a broader theoretical context to the role of public education in nation building while explaining how heritage tourism assumes an ideological purpose in Hungarian public schools. It then scrutinizes the government's main goal with the travel program—the promotion of a new national identity that is rooted in ethnic unity with cross-border Hungarian diaspora—and traces how this vision is translated into an institutional framework. The next section contrasts the government's perspective with the school's narratives, surveying how participants navigate and shape the program through three main narrative frames: a quest for ethnic kin beyond Hungary's current borders and the symbolic reappropriation of ethnic Hungarian heritage sites in neighboring countries; immersion in a mythical and distant past; and continuous flirting with radical nationalist symbols. These frames highlight how the government's framework leaves room for exploiting grassroots and popular nationalism present in schools to complement and enhance the program, pushing it into a more radical direction. The discussion that follows reflects also on how reliably students' and teachers' orientations toward the trips can be surmised from the reports. The chapter concludes by assessing student travel programs' importance as a political instrument for remaking a new generation's national imagination in Hungary and beyond.

Heritage Tourism, Nation Building, and Public Education

Public schools are one of the central institutions in which the social order is reproduced. They play an essential role in shaping students' habitus, their taken-for-granted life worlds.[4] They were also developed to support various political and economic projects, such as nation building, industrialization, and democratization.[5] Especially in the wake of the spread of universal, obligatory, and free-of-charge education, public schools became key instruments of nation building in modern states.[6] Public schools as political means of nationalization were particularly important in crumbling multiethnic empires that struggled to transform themselves into nation-states in the late nineteenth century. This was emphatically true in Central and Eastern Europe, where majority and minority ethnic groups often clashed over issues of language use and education. Hungary was among the countries that aggressively used the public school system to nationalize—to Hungarianize—ethnic minorities living under Hungarian rule in the late nineteenth and early twentieth centuries.[7]

Public schools have also been a place where the nation is imagined, and students are socialized into imagined national communities.[8] Even with the steady rise of globalization, national content has been preserved in school curricula, and textbooks continue to deploy nationalist narratives throughout the world.[9] Yet, research on how today's schools inculcate ideas of nationhood and national belonging into students has been confined to a few narrow areas: the study of history education and textbooks,[10] and to a lesser extent, school ceremonies and similar performances of nationhood in educational settings.[11] More recently, attention has shifted to civics classes and citizenship education, exploring how these are now conceptualized and designed as vehicles for immigrant incorporation.[12]

But broader pedagogical practices or extracurricular activities are rarely investigated within the framework of nation building. Field trips, for instance, which have for long been a staple in primary and secondary education, have received little notice from this perspective.[13] The only notable exception is Israel, where a "culture of trips" developed and has been understood as central to forming Israeli national identity. School trips and hiking tours are incorporated there into the educational system in both school and out-of-school settings.[14] They serve as a form of secular pilgrimage, reaffirming a sense of belonging and physically reconnecting participants to the land of Israel.[15]

Simultaneously, interest in ethnic tourism—often closely coupled with heritage tourism—has been on the rise. Studies explore how the politics of ethnicity was catapulted into the marketplace, turning ethnic groups into business ventures, or "ethnopreneurs."[16] As a result, we see the proliferation of ethnic products and ethnic marketing, and the rapid expansion of heritage industries and genealogical tourism. The significant growth of Jewish heritage tourism in postcommunist Central and Eastern Europe is part of this larger trend.[17] But genealogical tourism is also linked to ethnic diaspora populations who develop various forms of "homeland nationalism" through reconnecting with their ancestors' homeland.[18] A variant of this literature deals with the commercialization of national distinctiveness and heritage by focusing on the spread of nation branding and its entanglement with globalization and neoliberal corporatization, as also examined in chapter 3.[19]

The Hungarian case of state-sponsored heritage tourism is theoretically informative because it helps to connect and advance disparate lines of research. On the one hand, it shows how, in a neoliberal manner, the state harnesses cultural consumption like heritage tourism to promote a new understanding of the nation in public schools. While there is growing literature on how heritage tourism feeds various national identity narratives, these works focus primarily on mass tourism and rarely investigate the role it can play in educating public school students about national belonging. My main argument is that the informal and experiential character of tourist travel combined with heritage tourism's performative and affective power creates fertile ground for the incorporation and institutional validation of vernacular histories and popular forms of radical nationalism.[20] The analysis thereby contributes to developing perspectives that cross-pollinate dominant but divergent approaches to nation building: the macrohistorical strand focusing on state practices and microanalytical scholarship on everyday and banal nationalism.[21]

On the other hand, the Hungarian case expands our understanding of ethnic heritage tourism by highlighting that diaspora tourists are not necessarily gravitating only toward a nation-state, homeland, or sacred center. Diaspora tourism can also move in the opposite direction, as tourists travel from their nation-state to territories in other countries that are seen as home to their ethnic kin. This form of diaspora tourism maybe particularly common in former empires (e.g., Russia, Turkey) and nation-states that lost significant territories, which they feel resentful about and try to reappropriate through cultural practices like heritage tourism. Cross-border heritage tourism thus underscores the importance of ethnic diaspora communities in defining the symbolic value of national territories and the pliable boundaries of the nation-state.[22] The Hungarian case also directs attention to transborder diaspora populations that were created by shifting international borders rather than the much more frequently studied examples that emerged through migration.[23]

The *Határtalanul* student mobility program was formally established by a parliamentary decree on October 21, 2010.[24] This decree simultaneously mandated the introduction of a national public school Memorial Day on June 4 to celebrate a newly minted national holiday, the so-called National Unity Day (*Nemzeti Összetartozás Napja*) in commemoration of the 1920 Treaty of Trianon. It also called for a new cultural institution, "The House of Hungarians," to function as an information and cultural center showcasing the life of Hungarian transborder and diaspora communities while coordinating and providing curricular support for mobility and other educational programs. That the travel program was launched as part of a larger package of new legislation clearly signaled the government's intention to fundamentally rethink and retool its relationship to ethnic Hungarians beyond state borders. The measures of the decree contribute to what the government calls a new "politics of the nation" (*nemzetpolitika*), which requires a new vision for defining the relationship between polity and nation, and a long-term policy strategy (*nemzetpolitikai stratégia*) for determining how transborder and diaspora communities fit into this new concept of the nation.[25]

The status of ethnic Hungarian minorities in neighboring countries has played a central and divisive role in Hungarian politics in the post-1989 period regardless of the political orientation of ruling governments.[26] The new Fidesz government, however, brought a radical shift to this policy area after it returned to power in 2010 by defining these communities as an integral part of the Hungarian polity. New policies have moved from simply expressing solidarity and providing economic and cultural support to promoting closer incorporation of ethnic Hungarians into the nation. This led the state in 2011 to extend to them citizenship and voting rights in Hungarian parliamentary elections.[27] Since 2010 the government has significantly intensified "the attempt to institutionalize a Hungarian nation which transcends state boundaries and includes not just the citizens of Hungary-proper, but all the ethnic Hungarian minorities living on the territory of the former Austro-Hungarian Monarchy."[28]

The student travel program lies at the intersection of this new "transnational" nation building project and educational policy. The *Határtalanul* program consists of three distinct grant competitions that schools can apply to annually. My study focuses on the largest and most inclusive program, which targets thirteen-year-old "seventh-grade" students in middle schools. In fact, the long-term aspiration of the *Határtalanul* program has been to have the entire cohort of Hungary's thirteen-year-old students take an organized class trip to a Hungarian heritage site in neighboring countries. This cohort is seen as key to implementing the program's general principle that each and every (homeland) Hungarian student should have the opportunity to take a class trip to visit ethnic kin communities in neighboring countries at least once during their public-school education.[29] No similar schemes or government subsidies exist for sponsoring students of these age groups to travel to other foreign countries.

The ultimate political goal of the program is to foster ethnic national consciousness across borders and educate young Hungarians that territorial borders of the state and those of the nation are not necessarily the same. It promotes the idea that ethnic Hungarians beyond the border should be viewed as part of the Hungarian nation, and their habitat as part of Hungary's past, and that "motherland" (*anyaország*) Hungarians owe a special responsibility to these diaspora communities that suffered from ethnic discrimination especially in the post–World War II era.

Határtalanul's main architect and first director, Örs Csete, saw a widespread lack of knowledge about transborder Hungarians as the urgent reason for establishing the program.[30] He argued that this ignorance was the product of forty years of forced silence under communism when the peace treaties that ended the two world wars—the 1920 Treaty of Trianon and the 1947 Paris Peace Treaty that reinstated the Trianon borders—were treated as taboo subjects. If these events were discussed at all—on the pages of history textbooks, for instance—they always had to be portrayed as just punishment for Hungary's fascist, irredentist, and oppressive activities. As a result, in Csete's view, generations of Hungarians today have known close to nothing about Hungarians in the "external homeland" (*külhoni magyarok*).

His intention was to raise awareness about the geographic fragmentation of ethnic Hungarian communities as a legacy of Hungary's twentieth-century history, especially because still roughly a quarter of all ethnic Hungarians are born and live outside of Hungary proper.[31] The first step toward a new idea of a nation that transcends this geographical fragmentation lies in the "removal of borders" (*határtalanítás*). This signifies, according to Csete, "the multiplicity of symbolic and concrete activities that completely disregard or overstep, so to speak, state borders and generate connections between people, organizations and institutions. These are the kinds of activities that work against spatial fragmentation and connect members of the nation spiritually without any, anyways totally unrealistic, (physical) change of borders."[32] The *Határtalanul* project was devised to put these ideas into practice by creating a "subject knowledge enhancement (*tudásbeviteli*) program that facilitates national unification, targeting young generations and providing them an opportunity to learn about these issues through lived experience."[33]

Another, more indirect aim of the program is to promote tourism to these areas inhabited by ethnic kin, especially to Transylvania in Romania. Ethnically based heritage tourism has deeper roots there and can be developed into a viable ethnic enclave industry. The Hungarian government has been offering significant grants and subsidies to ethnic Hungarian businesses in this field. The long-term hope for *Határtalanul* trips is that they will sow the seeds of interest among members of a new generation, who will later return to those same areas as regular tourists.[34]

Tourism to former Hungarian territories, first and foremost to Transylvania, began in the mid-1970s and was linked chiefly to the so-called Dance House movement, a folk revival movement that by the 1980s had grown into a significant countercultural social movement.[35] Transylvania became a prime destination for movement members who flocked to rural areas in search of authentic folk heritage (peasant songs, dance music, traditional performance techniques, living handicraft traditions, folk dresses) uncorrupted by communist modernization. From the 1980s onward, travel to these areas was also linked to political dissident groups in mainland Hungary that organized trips to deliver aid and donations to deprived communities as a show of solidarity to Hungarian minorities that suffered harsh discrimination under Ceausescu's dictatorship.[36] Charity-related activities remained an important motive for regular travel to Transylvania after 1989.[37] Similarly, in the early 2000s some civil society organizations, like the Rákóczi Union (Rákóczi Szövetség) started organizing student exchange trips that brought ethnic Hungarian high school students from neighboring countries to Hungary to celebrate, for instance, national holidays together with Hungarians. After the collapse of communism, religious tourism rapidly developed as a niche, as Transylvania is home to an iconic Catholic pilgrimage site in Şumuleu Ciuc (Csíksomlyó). There the Christian festival of Pentecost attracts between 50,000 and 100,000 attendees each year, making it one of the largest annual gatherings in all of Romania.[38]

It is in this larger context of expanding tourism that promoters of *Határtalanul* emphasized the potential multiplier effects for small businesses in the hospitality industry both within Hungary and in the "external homeland." These include travel agencies, bus companies specializing in travel to these Hungarian populated areas of neighboring countries, motel and B&B owners, tour guides, local Hungarian-owned restaurants, and other food venues. Moreover, Hungarian schools in neighboring countries, many of which have been constructed or renovated with the Hungarian government's financial support, lease their dormitories for lodging visiting school groups. The resulting earnings can be reinvested to maintain and operate the schools, thus increasing the long-term stability of these important Hungarian institutions.[39]

Class Trips as a Vehicle for Cross-Border Ethnic Unity

The *Határtalanul* mobility program is expertly designed and carefully managed by the government. The methodical framing and the elaborate application and reporting requirements seem to ensure the trips have the desired ideological impact without making the program overly prescriptive or rigid. Though only a small fraction of school applications is rejected, the application process is competitive and makes serious demands on schools that apply.

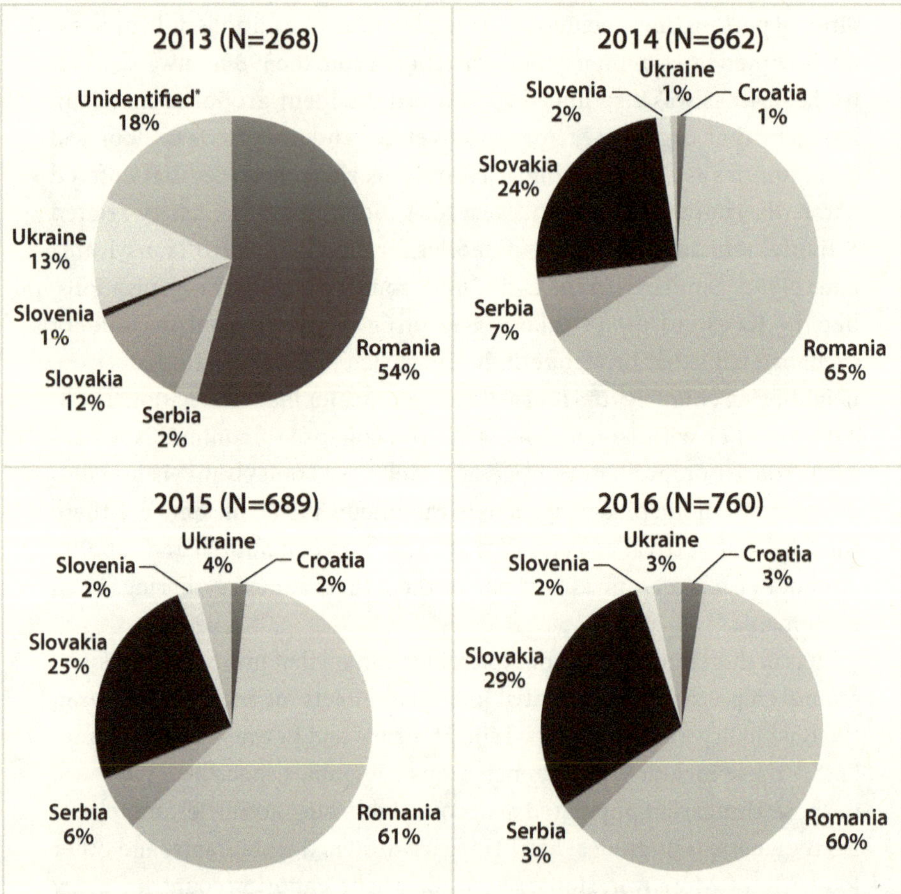

FIGURE 4.2. Class trips by destination, 2013–2016. The original summary data did not specify the destination country of the trips for 2013. That country was determined based on the short descriptions of each trip. For unidentified cases, the descriptions did not contain sufficient information to ascertain the destination country.

This is in line with the neoliberal disposition of the program: Schools should not take for granted that they will be funded and should work hard to prove they deserve the money, and they will be accountable for how they spend it.

Trips typically last from three to five days and are structured around a distinct theme, such as visits to the birthplaces, workplaces, or final resting places of important Hungarian literary figures across Transylvania. They follow in the footsteps of "great Hungarians," tour the memorial sites of the 1848–49 revolution, delve into folk art and folk music heritage, map the sites of mythic legends in Transylvania, or discover traditional mining towns in Slovakia. Applications must include a detailed daily schedule that specifies the group's morning, afternoon, and evening routine. They also need to indicate if the activities involve interaction with local Hungarian communities (e.g., joint activities with students from the same age group, participation in local holiday celebrations, or contributions to the local community's well-being). This aspect is highly incentivized to increase the "experiential value" of the trips by promoting active socialization between homeland and transborder Hungarians (figure 4.2).

The program imposes no specific thematic requirements on the trips, which stems from its more neoliberal attitude. Its creators put their faith in a corporate branding approach to foster participation rather than in simple top-down, administrative enforcement of meticulously predefined and closely censored political agendas. A corporate-style logo that pictures a stylized figure stepping over a border is prominently displayed on all program materials and at program-related events.[40] Its use by the funded schools is mandated, especially in media coverage about the class trips. Örs Csete underscores that the program intends to attract students and not deter them, which is why it would be counterproductive to make the trips mandatory. Therefore,

> the aim is to create a buzz among these young people that projects these class trips to the external homeland as a trendy thing, the school celebration of national unity as a youthful community event, and the House of Hungarians as a cool, cutting-edge place. As far as the class trips are concerned the "*Határtalanul*" label has already grown into a *new brand*. The class trips are self-generating and when successful, more and more students will want to travel, especially if the trips are going to be supplemented by other projects (grants, competitions, endorsement by celebrities) and be publicized using social media platforms popular among young people (Facebook, YouTube, etc.).[41]

In other words, schools and students should not be forced to participate. Instead, they should feel that if they do not engage with the program, they will miss out on something "fun, cool, and meaningful." The very idea of travel and class trips as means of spreading new visions of national belonging reflects this branding philosophy. Class trips promise to be particularly effective because students, almost by definition, return from them satisfied, pretty much regardless of the destination, since "the very fact that they can get away from home generates excitement."[42] This premise applies even though the school trips are conceived as study trips, rather than merely recreational ventures, emphasizing the experiential acquisition of knowledge.

That said, the application process, the expected outcomes, and reporting are highly regulated. Schools are required to organize preparatory classes prior to the trip and evaluation sessions after, submit detailed photographic documentation of the trip's key activities, submit samples of students' travel diaries, and prepare a two-minute summary video of their travel experiences. Schools also must arrange for media coverage of their trip in local newspapers or on radio and TV channels.

In addition to these core requirements, schools are encouraged—though not formally required—to take on some optional responsibilities. Most important, these involve integrating the class experience into celebrations of the aforementioned National Unity Day on June 4. Schools are also urged to organize information sessions in which they will promote the trip to their school's younger students to motivate them to apply to the program when they become eligible. All the core and optional activities as well as expenses must be painstakingly documented in the final report, which results in a sizeable dossier.

Government support of *Határtalanul* covers the full costs of travel and accommodation for grant recipients. This counts as generous support in an otherwise severely underfunded public education system. It makes a significant difference especially for smaller schools in rural and underdeveloped areas, which would otherwise be unable to finance comparable class trips. This is probably, in part, why the program is popular among public schools. Many schools apply recurrently, even though the administrative burden applications inflict on the candidate schools must also have some deterring effect. The substantial financial support and the elaborate requirements make schools eager to prove that the trip will be edifying by cramming the program with educational and ritual activities.

Class Trips on the Road: School Narratives of Traveling "Without Borders"

How do schools adapt the government's framework on the road? How do participating teachers and students narrate their trips? What do they think they have learned about Hungary and diaspora Hungarians? Here I will discern the central narratives that emerge from the school reports for the stratified random sample of 120 class trips for which I obtained the full dossiers. I identify three key narrative frames around which the trips' activities were consolidated, and which appear consistent over the years. The first outlines the practices through which the trips assume a narrow and exclusionary ethnic focus, highlighting how ritualistic affirmations of ethnic Hungarian identity constitute the core of the activities, even though the program does not expressly prescribe them. The second frame reveals how the trips foreground a "frozen," distant and mythical Hungarian past, carefully avoiding any critical confrontation with the twentieth century's violent history and firmly ignoring the present situation of transborder ethnic kin communities. The third frame demonstrates how the program allows for grassroots radical nationalism to seep into the classroom and public education. The final section explains how these frames shed light on the ways in which the class trips function as vehicles for far-right political indoctrination.

IN SEARCH OF ETHNIC KIN: RITUAL REAPPROPRIATIONS OF ETHNIC HUNGARIAN SITES

All the territories in which key destinations of the class trips are located have been historically multiethnic, multilingual, and multireligious, including those areas that still have or once had majority ethnic Hungarian populations.[43] Yet, the tours almost uniformly and exclusively focus on the Hungarian aspects and heritage of these destinations. They carefully ignore or edit out any details of the environment that would entail interaction with other ethnic groups and cultures.

For instance, nearly all settlements, from small villages to large cities in Transylvania, normally have names in three different languages: Romanian, Hungarian, and German, reflecting their ethnically mixed populations. Nonetheless, the schools use only the Hungarian names of the settlements and various landscapes in all their official materials and in interactions with the students as well.[44] This is true not just for Transylvania but also for the trips to other neighboring countries. A typical moment during the preparations for the trip is to consult the map of the area that the itinerary will cover.[45] As a rule, these maps are only in Hungarian, which is not always practical because at the destinations, such as in Slovakia, bilingual signs are often severely restricted or outright banned. Moreover, school documentation often does not even refer to these regions as being in a foreign country, but instead uses the old, pre–World War I Hungarian designations: Upper Lands (Felvidék) for Slovak and Southern Lands (Délvidék) for Serbian destinations. These terms carry strong historical and political connotations, as they identify these areas as parts of the Kingdom of Hungary. Their usage was mostly purged from public discourse after World War II. Although these categories lived on informally, they appeared only recently in official parlance or in public schools.

In general, the adjective "Transylvanian" is treated as a synonym of "Hungarian." When students are asked to enumerate famous Transylvanian writers, artists, politicians, or public intellectuals in preparatory exercises or as part of assignments before and on the trips, they are always expected to generate names of Hungarian personalities. A popular stop on the class trips to Transylvania is the Hajongard (Házsongárd, Hasengarten) cemetery in Cluj-Napoca (Kolozsvár). It is massive, covering some fourteen hectares, and considered one of the city's most picturesque sites. It was established in the late sixteenth century in response to a plague epidemic and was always a public cemetery, providing a final resting place to residents regardless of their ethnicity or religion. School visits to the cemetery often involve an assignment during which students are divided into groups and given names of famous Transylvanian writers, whose graves they are to find on their own and record their inscriptions or photograph them as proof.[46] The schools' lists always include only Hungarian writers, ignoring famous Romanian writers and other public figures buried in the same cemetery.

In addition to educational exercises, the trips are packed with ritual activities that all serve to symbolically reclaim pieces of Transylvania, Slovakia, and Serbia as Hungarian. These practices effectively leverage the performative and affective capacity of heritage tourism.[47] They connect ethnic identity with space, sensory experience, and affect. Even if the repetitive performances are often habitual and unreflexive,[48] they exert a strong emotional pull over the students. About 60 percent of the photos that are enclosed with the final school reports record such moments of the trip. Ritual activities often occur several times a day and range from laying wreaths decorated with the

Hungarian flag, to placing ribbons in the red-white-green tricolor of the Hungarian flag, to reciting poems by the Hungarian poet whose statute or grave they honor and singing the Hungarian national anthem and the Szekler anthem, which, along with the Szekler flag, have generated numerous ethnopolitical controversies in Romania.[49] The sites for these ritual exercises typically encompass plaques, homes, memorials, statues, and graves of Hungarian historical figures and events, though they sometimes include such curious *lieu de mémoire* as the favorite pear tree of the iconic nineteenth-century poet Sándor Petőfi, who died in the 1848–49 revolution.[50]

The physicality of the sites and the materiality of the markers framed by collective singing and declamation of poems are employed to turn Hungarian identity into a deeply emotional and almost mythical experience. As one teacher notes in their final report, after laying the wreath and singing the national anthem in the crypt of Francis II Rákóczi in Košice (Kassa), Slovakia, "we all felt that history, the Hungarian national past touched our souls."[51] Likewise, a student describes in his diary a visit to the thirteenth-century Romanesque church of Arača (Aracs) in Serbia: "When we were there, we sang the national anthem to the memory of our ancestors. I felt the power of the past in all my bones. There was a curious, unspeakable silence in the ether that I can still vividly recall. This memory will remain with me forever."[52] And on a trip to the graves of the martyrs of the 1848–49 revolution and War of Independence in Arad, Romania, a student remarked: "It was heart-wrenching to see the many Hungarian memorials that are visited by many people who come to lay wreaths. This way we could really experience the idea of belonging together as a nation. We could experience this beyond words."[53]

Besides reappropriating sites as Hungarian in ritual performances, a common motif runs through especially the preparatory phase of the program: the suggestion that students are not really going to a foreign country but will visit an extension of Hungary. In a radio interview on a local station in Szolnok, a midsize city near Budapest, the reporter chats with some students and their class teacher who are about to embark on a trip to Serbia, which they consistently refer to as the Southern Lands (*Délvidék*). The teacher explains that the goal of the tour is "to discover Hungary beyond the border" and "introduce students to the culture and situation of the Hungarian population that was torn away from us."[54] Her ultimate hope is that, with these class trips, students will eventually learn what it means "to travel from the home to the homeland" (*otthonról haza megyünk*). Incidentally, this phrase is also the business motto of one of the travel agencies, Csillagösvény, that specializes in offering package tours and providing grant-writing assistance to interested schools.[55]

The fuzzy line between home and abroad is captured by another teacher's statement underlining how important it is for "the first foreign trip that students take to lead them to the territories of historical Hungary."[56] In the project diary, the teacher also talks about how the excitement at going to Transylvania was mixed with the challenges of properly preparing students for the trip, some of whom had never crossed the Hungarian border before. The big question was, the teacher added, "whether we could successfully convey to them that we will not be traveling to Romania, but to Transylvania, and we will meet Hungarians who are just like us. It is often said that the storm of history had scattered us, but despite this the Hungarians of the Carpathian Basin belong to one and the same nation and this unity cannot be called into question by any other ethnic group (*népcsoport*)."[57]

Students were indeed trying to wrap their head around this idea. One of them noted in his diary: "We really learned an awful lot [on the trip], among other things, the fact that Hungary has a border with itself."[58] Another classmate made a similar point in highly emotional terms: "This trip took us to a seemingly unknown country, but we had to realize to what extent their life is also our life . . . now I no longer dare to call them 'Serbs' [referring to Hungarian minorities in Serbia] because they are also Hungarian, truly Hungarian in their faith and soul . . . in the future I will also strive to live as a true (*igaz*) Hungarian."[59] Some students believe this was in fact the best thing about the trip: "What I liked most about the trip is that we went abroad, but it still felt like as if we had been at home."[60]

Because the *Határtalanul* mobility program was ultimately established to foster a sense of national belonging between homeland and transborder Hungarians, the class trips are expected to include activities through which students engage with local ethnic kin communities. This mostly takes place in the form of visiting local Hungarian schools or orphanages and spending time with students of the same age group. The interactions involve semi-structured group conversations at the local school about how everyday school routines (e.g., subjects, grading, vacations) in a minority Hungarian school in Transylvania or Slovakia compare with those in Hungary. Schools also often bring small in-kind donations, most important, Hungarian-language books. At times, local Hungarian students join the visitors on a walking tour of the host city. But most often, joint programs consist of some mix of folk dancing, singing of folk songs, and playing a team sport, usually soccer. These interactions are highly ritualized and ceremonial and thus often quite awkward. Unstructured time for more informal exchanges between the travelers and local Hungarian teens is minimal. Visiting Hungarian students develop contradictory attitudes from these encounters, displaying a tendency to simultaneously romanticize and orientalize their experiences. They tend to perceive diaspora Hungarians as "better": more authentic, more proud, more bona fide Hungarians, yet they are often taken aback by signs of economic underdevelopment and poverty in neighboring countries.

The trips are in fact characterized by stark ethnic insularity. Contact with members of ethnic groups other than Hungarian is not encouraged and, due to the design of the trips, is almost completely eschewed. As a result, groups end up having only chance encounters with Romanians, Serbs, or Slovaks. These often turn out to be uneasy experiences that reinforce negative stereotypes about the ethnic majority and their tense relations with Hungarian minorities.[61] This is in part because these impromptu interactions mostly occur in prominent public places where Hungarian visitors perform ceremonies to symbolically reclaim elements of the cityscape, which non-Hungarian locals perceive as an affront. One such incident took place in Arad (Arad) in Transylvania at the memorial to the martyrs of the 1848 revolution, where one of the school groups was booed by Romanian spectators at the site, which quite disturbed students.[62] In another case, students laid a wreath in Albeşti (Fehéregyháza) at the bust statue of Hungary's most famous nineteenth-century poet, Sándor Petőfi, who also perished in the 1848 revolution, that was defaced by obscene Romanian graffiti (figure 4.3).[63]

IN SEARCH OF A DISTANT AND MYTHICAL HUNGARIAN PAST

The historical periods evoked by the destinations similarly reinforce the ethnic insularity and one-dimensional narrative of the trips. They combine the narrow focus on Hungarian ethnicity with an attention to events and sites that reference a distant past, eliciting uncritical and uncontroversial interpretations. The overwhelming majority of the trips target highly canonized sites linked to historical figures and events that span from the sixteenth to the nineteenth century, steering clear of the contentious history of the twentieth century beyond the breakup of the Austro-Hungarian Monarchy.[64] The historical heritage highlighted on these class trips does not simply transmit some "invented history."[65] Rather, the trips frequently focus on historical periods and events for which fact and fiction are hard to separate. Legends, miracles, and folk ballads are treated as an inherent part of

FIGURE 4.3. Student reciting a poem in front of Hungarian poet Sándor Petőfi's statue, which was covered in Romanian graffiti ("Hungary sucks"). ha-13-01-265.

historical memory, which lends a mythic quality and experience to historical consciousness and ethnic identity while anchoring them in space.[66] The class trips thus serve as a medium for reterritorializing the national (and especially ethnic) imagination by reconstructing mythic landscapes: They reconnect legends to concrete physical sites and places.

Sites that students typically visit include famous medieval castles of the Voivodes and Princes of Transylvania (e.g., Hunyadi, Bethlen, Thököly, Rákóczi) and of other prominent aristocratic families (e.g., the Károlyis); churches of various denominations (mostly built during the Middle Ages); battle sites of the 1848–49 revolution and war of independence; graveyards of fallen and executed revolutionaries and naturally deceased notable Hungarians; the homes and mansions of literary figures, politicians, and public intellectuals; and the so-called thousand-year border in Ghimeș (Gyimes), Romania.[67]

However, class trips are driven by an eager search not simply for a distant past but for a past enriched with myths, legends, ballads, and folk tales that unfold over breathtaking magical landscapes. Many of the destinations, especially in Transylvania, are indeed wellsprings of colorful and eventful tales. A teacher aptly articulates the pedagogical rationale behind focusing on legends: "Legends have educational value because they deal with resourcefulness, persistence, love, historical moments, courage, and the love of nature. In these regions, places, castles, saints have legends. Through legends we can get closer to the soul of people who live there, to their ways of thinking and their history."[68]

In the Anglophone world, Bram Stoker's Gothic horror novel *Dracula* and its countless adaptations are the most likely (and probably the only) association triggered by the mention of Transylvania. There is in fact thriving Dracula tourism at several sites that are linked to Dracula's real and fictional travels. These include the Bran Castle (Castelul Bran, Törcsvár), considered the home of Dracula; the city of Sighisoara (Segesvár), where the house in which Vlad the Impaler was born can be found; and the city of Brașov (Brassó, Kronstadt), where Vlad led raids against Saxon merchants.[69] In the 1990s there were ambitious plans to build a massive Dracula theme park, though the idea was eventually dropped for fear it would impart an unfavorable image of Romania to visitors. Even though the original Dracula novel had Hungarian connections, and Sighisoara (Segesvár) is a popular stop on the class trips, students do not visit the city to see Vlad's home but rather to remember one of the key battles of the 1848–49 revolution, a decisive defeat by the Russians.[70]

Hungarians are in strict pursuit of their own ethnic legends. There are class trips organized entirely around historical, religious, and folk legends that are associated with the visited regions. Students sometimes receive assignments that ask them to invent and write up a legend on their own.[71] Many of the scenic natural sites that serve as regular stops on the trips are steeped in myths and legends. For instance, the Killer Lake (Lacul Rosu, Gyilkos-tó) in the high mountains of the Eastern Carpathians in Hargitha County is a natural dam lake that was formed by a landslide due to an earthquake in 1838. But when Hungarian students make a visit there, they recount a folk ballad that offers a much more poetic version of the origins of the lake. According to the ballad, a beautiful young Hungarian woman, Eszter Fazekas, was snatched by a local bandit who took her into the mountains and tried to coerce her into marrying him. In her despair, Eszter shouted to the mountains for help. They responded with loud thunder and lightning and dumped rocks and debris on the area, killing both Eszter and the bandit, as well as a local shepherd with all his sheep. The collapsed slope blocked the canyon river and the lake was formed. The barren treetops of pine trees that used to grow on the slopes can still be seen sticking out of the lake. Students are told that when visitors look closely at the surface of the water on a sunny day, they might see Eszter's green eyes looking back at them.

CRACKING THE DOOR OPEN FOR RADICAL NATIONALISM

As noted earlier, the mobility program does not contain specific prescriptions regarding the thematic content of the trips. It provides no ready-made templates for furthering a new vision of the Hungarian nation that transcends state boundaries and incorporates diaspora communities. This contrasts sharply with how ideological programming in public schools worked under communism when ideological expectations were handed down as top-down directives and deviations from the one-size-fits-all model were rarely tolerated.

Yet, that the mobility program does not require uniform ways of promoting the idea of a "borderless" ethnic nation does not imply that it has no normative political aspirations. The *Határtalanul* program, for instance, also opens the door for radical nationalist tropes. It does so seemingly by oversight and indifference: It does not discourage schools from engaging in radical nationalist clichés and does not sanction such content in any way. Rather, it canalizes and institutionalizes ground-up popular sentiments that can often come from individual teachers or local tour guides who privately entertain radical nationalist beliefs.

It is not always easy to draw a clear line between "mainstream" and "radical" or "extreme" nationalism.[72] In Hungary, however, a particular set of symbols and themes is closely associated with a radical nationalist milieu.[73] In the context of these school trips, radical nationalist symbols relate primarily to interwar irredentist propaganda and cultural iconography that were absent from public schools before 2010. These symbols were taboo in official contexts until 2010, but they have been widely known and are increasingly widespread in popular culture. I identified and traced four key symbols in the dossiers of the class trips: the uncritical use of revisionist Trianon propaganda material from the interwar period, references to the work of the Transylvanian writer and Romanian war criminal Albert Wass, the use of songs and lyrics by so-called national rock bands, and the propagation of "Transylvanian" runic script among the students.[74]

Table 4.1 shows the frequencies (and percentage value in the representative annual samples) with which these radical symbols were incorporated into class trip curriculums. It reveals that each year about half the classes used at least one radical symbol during their trip.[75] The irredentist "Greater Hungary" image was the most commonly occurring example, followed by references to the life and work of the Transylvanian writer Albert Wass. While, as table 4.1 indicates, these radical symbols did not completely dominate the trips, the frequency and manner of their use must still be interpreted as alarming. Any evocation of these symbols was inconceivable in public school classroom environments before 2010, and they have no place at all in a formal educational context, unless they are critically examined. School-based activities related to these trips have played a crucial role in normalizing the presence of these symbols in public schools. I will discuss some examples of how these symbols were used on the trips and why they are radical nationalist in nature.

Radical nationalism is allowed to penetrate the class trips partly through the institutional link that was created between the program and the celebration of National Unity Day (Nemzeti Összetartozás Napja), to commemorate the Treaty of Trianon and promote the idea of an ethno-national community with transborder Hungarians.[76] Schools follow no uniform script for celebrating this event, but the *Határtalanul* program expects—even if it does not formally require—participating schools to incorporate their class trip experience into their celebration of the holiday.

The establishment of this holiday is not the main problem per se. The Treaty of Trianon indeed remains a radical turning point that had devastating consequences for Hungarian history, and it must be carefully examined, critically analyzed, publicly debated, and remembered. But rather than being an occasion for thorough evaluation and critical reflection, the new holiday has served to recycle a simplistic victim narrative from the interwar period. There is no politically untainted vocabulary (visual or verbal) to talk about the causes and consequences of this event, in large part because this topic could not be openly discussed under communism. The post-1989 period has

TABLE 4.1. Use of radical nationalist symbols on class trips*

	"Greater Hungary" image	Albert Wass	Runic script	"National rock"	Other	At least one radical symbol	N
2013	9 (30%)	5 (17%)	3 (10%)	2 (7%)	2 (10%)	14 (47%)	30
2014	8 (27%)	5 (17%)	2 (7%)	4 (13%)	5 (17%)	13 (43%)	30
2015	6 (20%)	2 (7%)	3 (10%)	2 (7%)	4 (13%)	12 (40%)	30

*Figures for 2016 are not included here because missing data is still being petitioned under a Freedom of Information Act Request.

been dominated by a loud backlash against this political silencing, which has revived bitter resentments over the partitioning of the country after World War I.

In most cases, class trips introduce radical nationalist motifs through materials used to explain how ethnic Hungarian communities emerged after the Treaty of Trianon that drastically redrew the country's borders. In preparatory classes, teachers frequently rely on various representations of "Greater Hungary": maps and images that depict Hungary with its pre-1920 borders. At times, students also literally perform "Greater Hungary" at holiday celebrations or as part of a trip activity with transborder students on their trip. They usually group together wearing red, white, and green T-shirts in the school gym or on the outdoor sports field to form a Greater Hungary shape with the Hungarian tricolor (figure 4.4).[77] A few dossiers include photos of flower beds in the shape of Greater Hungary planted in public squares of local municipalities.[78] This motif is a visual trope that was omnipresent in Hungary in the interwar years.

In the interwar period, the outline of "Greater Hungary" became the visual symbol that most effectively encapsulated the perceived atrocity of Trianon.[79] But, simultaneously, this image came to signify the aggressive irredentism of Hungarian politics between the world wars. This is why its use became taboo during communism and remains controversial today.[80] Moreover, "Greater Hungary" images shown as illustrations in class presentations are often the very images that were used by the interwar political propaganda machinery of the government and other organizations demanding the reinstatement of the old borders. This detail is never revealed to students, nor do the presentations ever explore the causes or varying views of the events. They narrowly focus on their consequences—the massive territorial, economic, and population losses, as well as the loss of natural resources, urban centers, and vital infrastructure—to emphasize the injustice that was inflicted on Hungary. In 2013, for instance, 30 percent of all the schools used "Greater Hungary" images this way while preparing students for the trip. In that year's sample, in only one school, from Budapest, did the teacher's presentation about Trianon adopt a somewhat more critical approach in the form of presenting competing explanations for the treaty's causes and complexities.[81]

The second most common item that infuses class trips with radical nationalism is the presence of the Transylvanian writer Albert Wass. Of the thirty schools in both 2013 and 2014, 17 percent included in their itinerary a visit to either his former home or his grave in Transylvania, learned about his work and legacy during the preparatory and the evaluation sessions, and

FIGURE 4.4. Students making the shape of today's Hungary within "Greater Hungary." hat-14-01-0510.

incorporated excerpts from his work into the program they performed at the school on National Unity Day.

Wass was condemned as a war criminal in Romania in 1946 and escaped to the West, settling eventually in Florida in 1951. He was sentenced to death for inciting a Hungarian military unit to massacre a Romanian orthodox presbyter, his family, their Hungarian maid, and a handful of local Romanians and Jewish merchants in 1940 when Hungary reclaimed parts of Transylvania. Wass denied the charges, and the United States refused three separate Romanian requests that he be extradited. But his death sentence was not revoked either in Romania or in Hungary after the end of communism. Despite repeated requests for a retrial, he was never rehabilitated and could not return to Europe. He ended his own life at the age of ninety in Florida in 1998. Although he was a leading figure in the cultural and literary life of émigré Hungarians in the United States, he was virtually unknown to Hungarian audiences until the collapse of communism because until then his books were not published in Hungary (and were banned in Romania). His popularity skyrocketed in the post-1989 era, and a cult-like following developed around him while his reception remained polarized and politically contentious.[82] Wass's relative prominence on the school trips is a tell-tale sign of how the trips uncritically introduce radical nationalism to schoolchildren.

But even if one grants him some benefit of the doubt regarding his conviction as a war criminal, his work will sadly speak for itself. His writings are peppered with irredentism, ethnocentrism, chauvinism, and anti-Semitism. For instance, his monumental historical novel *Sword and Scythe* (*Kard és kasza*) tells the story of successive generations of a Hungarian aristocratic family who lived in the Transylvanian plain from the eleventh to the twentieth century, drawing on Wass's own family history. The book ruminates over the responsibility of Hungarian landowner aristocrats who permitted more and more Romanian peasants to settle in Transylvania to work their land, until they began to outnumber ethnic Hungarians and irrevocably changed the region's ethnic composition. Another of his popular novels, *Give Me Back My Mountains!* (*Adjátok vissza a hegyeimet!*), written in 1949, was added to the National Core Curriculum in 2020, discussed in chapter 2, despite its unconcealed anti-Semitism, attesting to the growing normalization of radical nationalist content in public education. Class trips that embrace Wass do so with no reflection on his controversial involvement in World War II or the political ideology grounding his work.

Third, radical nationalist symbolism crops up in the type of music used as soundtracks to the two-minute video diaries of the trips that each school must submit as part of their final report. It is also sometimes performed during preparatory and information sessions, as well as the June 4 celebrations of National Unity Day. The music in question is from contemporary Hungarian rock bands that play a recent genre of political rock music labeled "national rock," which has strong roots in the skinhead music scene and can be loosely understood as the local equivalent of white power music.[83] The genre emerged around 2000 and has rapidly gained in popularity. It uses rock instrumentation, and its lyrics focus on national history and expressions of patriotism. They are often inspired by military and folk songs and embrace radical nationalist, irredentist, anti-Roma, anti-Semitic content. Music from well-known national rock bands, such as Ismerős Arcok (Familiar Faces), Szkítia (Scythia), and Kárpátia (Carpathia), accompanied the trips of several schools. The song "Without You" from Ismerős Arcok—where "you" refers to transborder ethnic Hungarians—served as a soundtrack to one school's video diary, with its recurring chorus, "No matter what happens while we live and die / we will always share the same blood."[84] Another school played Szkítia's piece entitled *Trianon* at their National Unity Day ceremony, with its unequivocally irredentist lament:

> No border can divide us,
> as we address God in the same language!
> Hungarians suffer from Trianon,
> Tell me why we let this happen, why?
>
> No border can divide us,
> as we address God in the same language!
> Trianon was used to tear apart
> ancient Hungarian blood relatives.

Many of these bands, especially Szkítia, perform in a folk-rock style, and students sometimes believe that these songs are actually folk music.[85] The excerpts from lyrics used on the trips unabashedly espouse "blood-and-soil" nationalism with racist overtones.

Szekler runes or Szekler script is another marker of radical nationalist influence lurking over the trips. The Szekler runic alphabet is said to be a rune-like script, similar in appearance to Nordic runes, that was used in ninth-century Transylvania. This script is a source of political controversy because it pits popular belief, according to which it proves the ancient origins of Hungarians as an ethnic group, against academic scholars who have largely questioned it as a legitimate object of linguistic and historical research; some have even dismissed it as a hoax dating from the Middle Ages. Runes enjoyed popularity in interwar right-wing circles and the Scouts movement, and as such they were suppressed during communism. The script's popularity was revived in the Hungarian diaspora in the United States and then in Hungary by amateur linguists and historians.

In popular culture, runic writing has seen a spectacular revival in the past two decades. Almost all radical nationalist websites are "bilingual"; runic calligraphy is a popular motif in garment design; children learn it in after-school programs; and many villages and small towns in Hungary now display the name of the settlement in runic script below the official Hungarian sign. Popular interest in runic script is also linked to the exploration of other, related mythic origin stories of Hungarians, including presumed links to Huns, Scythians, and Sumerians. Schoolchildren are especially drawn to runic writing because to them it feels like a cool secret code, a cipher. On the trips, runic script is used to make the educational aspects of the trips more fun. Study quizzes about the trip include exercises with runes, or students are instructed to search for examples of runic signs during the trip.[86]

What Can We Learn from the Trip Dossiers?

One question about the materials schools included in the trip dossiers is whether they exhibit any selection bias. The program's intentions are clearly communicated by the government, and schools and teachers who prepare the applications and reports are well aware of them. Hence, it is not terribly surprising that the final reports contain narratives that largely fall in line with government expectations. Yet, every year there were a few trips in the sample that did not just resound the ideological mantra of the program. Sometimes they focused on an ecological project, or their activities were dominated by playful programs with a long-time partner school in Serbia, as opposed to being studded with the usual visits to museums, churches, memorials, and cemeteries. These outlier cases attest that applications that did not perfectly fit the ideological mold were not automatically rejected. Rejection rates have in fact been low (below 5 percent), and most are rejected for failing to meet formal requirements, such as missing key official documents. As the section on radicalism suggests, there is also some variation in the extent to which the trips are doctrinaire and didactically political.

One could still argue, though, that samples from student diaries, for instance, were handpicked to demonstrate that the trips were successful in meeting the program's ultimate objective: increasing awareness about transborder Hungarians while embracing them as part of an ethnically homogeneous Hungarian nation. But the dossiers include a fair number of student diaries that merely enumerate trivial details with little evaluative commentary: the stops on the trip, the food they ate (e.g., "we had soup and meat with apricot for dinner," "we had a tasty breakfast"), when they went to bed and woke up. At times, students share anecdotes about silly situations (getting stuck in an elevator), pranks they played on each other at the hostel where they stayed (spraying whipped cream into the palms of sleeping classmates and cracking up when they woke up), or that they spent the evening doing karaoke and playing foosball or pool late into the night.[87]

Rather than a set of carefully curated student essays, then, the dossiers seem to reveal that schools and the teachers who have to compile the reports are overburdened by the extensive reporting requirements. The sheer amount of paperwork and certifications schools have to produce for the final report leave teachers little time and energy to dwell on the supporting materials. They seem to have tried to include a bundle of evidence from the trip, sometimes ad hoc, to document principally that the money they received was indeed spent on the activities they proposed in the original application. The enclosed visual materials illustrate this fittingly. Typically, seventy to one hundred photos from a trip are enclosed with each dossier on a CD. It is unclear who exactly took them, or whether they are from the same person or different people, from teachers or students or both. The selection always includes photos that are repetitive, not at all informative, or terribly clumsy: out of focus and poorly composed. It seems nobody thought about or had the time to painstakingly sort through the photos to generate a compelling visual diary. This again supports the assumption that not everything that normally makes it into a dossier is selected solely to meet the funder's ideological expectations.

Another important concern can be raised about the long-term impact of the program. Although empirically testing their effectiveness is beyond the scope of this research, studies of Birthright Israel tours—which share similarities with the *Határtalanul* program—have confirmed that such trips exert tangible impact on participants.[88] The Hungarian students' trips may have been filled to the brim with educational activities and moral imperatives toward transborder ethnic kin, but there is little direct evidence that these thirteen-year-old students really absorbed, or always genuinely identified with, the lessons they were spoon-fed. In fact, there is some evidence to the contrary. For instance, in a longer interview with a teacher and three students at a local radio station, the reporter was prodding the three girls to talk about what they learned about Transylvania on the trip. But they mostly just nervously giggled and struggled to recall any meaningful experiences from the official program. They only lit up when they could talk about the informal fun they had on their journey: staying up late, pulling each other's leg, or sharing the adventure of a foreign trip with their school friends. Pap similarly found in interviews he conducted with high school students after their trip that while their informal experiences were vivid, they perceived hefty study-related activities as more of a drag.[89]

Still, although students may not readily recall all the informational minutiae of the trips, they do seem to take away the general frames about Trianon as a crime against Hungary and the idea of an ethnic nation that reaches beyond national state borders. The examples from student diaries also signal students' strong emotional involvement, and they overwhelmingly report a positive impression of their trip, which they will remember as a memorable and pleasant school experience.

This chapter draws attention to how extracurricular activities in public schools like field trips and student travel serve as important means of political socialization and a practice through which the nation can be actively reimagined for new generations. The use of tourism, with its focus on the "leisure migration" of people,[90] is also a clever way to cloak political objectives vis-à-vis students. By using the Hungarian *Határtalanul* program as a case study, my research demonstrates how the government mobilizes heritage tourism to introduce new ideas into public schools about national belonging: a "borderless," ethnically homogenous nation that embraces ethnic diaspora communities and reclaims ethnic Hungarian heritage sites in neighboring countries as a reminder of Hungary's grandeur and ethnic superiority before the dissolution of the Austro-Hungarian Empire. The ethnic Hungarian diaspora is also exploited in the anti-immigrant discourse by the government and far-right civil society groups. They argue that the European Union gives priority to protecting the rights of non-EU immigrants while ignoring the rights of "autochthonous minorities," such as ethnic Hungarians in Romania, Slovakia, or Ukraine.

My analysis reconstructs the legislative, institutional, and interpretive framework that defines the program's objectives and parameters, underscoring its voluntaristic and neoliberal features. By juxtaposing this framework with the school's narratives, it demonstrates how the relatively lax control over the trips' content in tandem with the government's reliance on heritage tourism's informal, experiential, and affective power can offer grassroots radicalism an entry point into public education, enabling the normalization and institutionalization of radical nationalism. I identify three key narrative frames that schools invoke to facilitate this process: (1) a zealous search for Hungarian ethnic kin and material heritage in neighboring countries that creates ethnic insularity in a multiethnic environment while recycling a one-dimensional victim narrative about Hungary's territorial losses; (2) a focus on vernacular histories inscribed in mythic landscapes that reconnect legends to concrete physical sites and places beyond state borders; and (3) radical nationalist symbols that openly celebrate irredentism.

Tourism plays an "organic role in the making of peoples, in the manufacturing of places and the manipulation of pasts."[91] The Hungarian example thus highlights the general significance of how heritage tourism can introduce popular forms of nationalism into public education and thereby foster their institutionalization, how ethnic diaspora communities continue to shape the symbolic boundaries of the nation, and how new forms of "borderless" nationalism reinvent irredentism as a cultural and economic practice, especially in former empires that continue to resent their demise. The power of mythic pasts and landscapes that transcend territorial borders cannot be overstated in these tragic times when Russia and Ukraine are fighting a war over parts of a land that Russia claims have always belonged to it.

5

Reinventing Nomadic Heritage

ANTI-WESTERNISM AND MYTHIC ORIENTALISM

On a bright spring morning I was idly strolling in Brooklyn Bridge Park when I got a surprise call from my brother in Budapest. He asked me if I was still planning to write about the horseback archery revival movement in Hungary. When I replied yes, he chuckled and said that I should know that he did one of those commercial ancestry DNA tests and the results showed a tiny but detectable percentage of genetic material from Central Asia in our family's DNA. So, my brother continued amusedly, when I write about the modern-day horseback archers' nostalgic yearning for the ancient nomadic lifestyle of the vast Eurasian steppe, I should be aware that this story might hit closer to home than I would like it to.

Theories about the Asian roots of ethnic Hungarians have abounded since the Middle Ages, sparking fierce scientific and political debates especially since the Enlightenment while exerting a remarkably strong hold on the popular imagination. Hungarians indeed came from the East, from the Urals—the mountain range that divides Europe from Asia—and settled in the Carpathian Basin in the late ninth and early tenth centuries.[1] They also garnered a reputation, documented by Western chroniclers, as fearless nomadic warriors who practiced a kind of guerilla warfare, launching surprise invasions into Western Europe until deciding to reluctantly adopt rather than stubbornly resist Western ways of life. However, the details of Hungarians' ethnic and geographical origins remain fragmentary, highly contested, and always a fodder for political struggles.

Political and popular interest in Hungarians' kinship with various Asian ethnic groups has tended to surge especially in times of rising discontent with the West. Throughout its history, Hungary has grappled with the tension of trying to decide if it belongs to the East or the West. It has oscillated between these two cultural and geopolitical poles since its founding, to the extent that it has been described as a "ferry country," constantly shuttling back and forth between East and West.[2] The West was basically a shorthand for "Europe," the developed and prosperous geopolitical center that offered a desirable model to follow but also presented a threat to national culture. The East, in turn, was the ultimate place of origin, the "mythical, ancient homeland to which Hungarians could retreat when disillusioned with the West" that "embodied the attitude of dissent, opposition, and national independence."[3] While the civilizational tug of war between East and West has been particularly intense in Hungary, it is by no means a uniquely Hungarian trait and has significantly shaped national identity politics in Poland, Russia, and Turkey.[4]

Unsurprisingly, Hungary's illiberal turn after 2010, which was galvanized in no small part by increasingly loud criticism of the West's dogmatic liberalism, has provided fertile ground for the renaissance of eclectic ideas about Hungarians' deep historical, cultural, and genetic connections with the East. Popular pseudo-theories about genetic kinship were even used to explain and justify the introduction of new economic policy measures that would promote an "Eastern opening" toward countries like Russia, Turkey, China, or oil-rich Central Asian republics such as Kazakhstan.

The minister for national economic development, György Matolcsy, was, for instance, captured in a video by a liberal online news portal propagating such theories when fielding questions at an open forum with local residents in 2012.[5] He advocated expanding economic relations with Asian countries that, in his view, made perfect sense because of our genetic kinship. He emphasized how proud he was that Hungarians descended from Asia, which can also be proven by shared genetic markers, such as many Hungarian newborns displaying a small red spot on their bottom just like their Japanese counterparts.[6] The video went viral and became an instant meme. It turned out that the story was not completely bogus, though quite off the mark. Matolcsy was alluding to what is known as the "Mongolian spot," a bluish-gray congenital birthmark that was described in the 1880s by Erwin Bälz, a German anthropologist living in Japan. The birthmark is supposed to be prevalent in Asia and among Native Americans but relatively rare in Europe among infants of Caucasian descent. Its incidence in Hungary is similar to European figures but is slightly higher in parts of eastern Hungary that are home to the descendants of Cumans, a Turkic nomadic people from Central Asia.[7]

While Matolcsy's anecdote circulated primarily as a source of amusement, it was also emblematic of the widespread resurgence of interest in Hungarians' Asian roots, prompting a shift in national self-perception, a revisionist turn in the obsessive historiography of the ethnogenesis of the Hungarian people, and growing geopolitical and ideological attraction toward the East (Russia, China, and Turkey in particular). And it is no accident that I started this chapter with genetic examples. Namely, recent developments in genetic research have also been enlisted to supply "hard," natural scientific evidence for ethnic kinship with Asian people and for identifying Hungarians' migration trajectories into the Carpathian Basin, where present-day Hungary is located, through the rapid rise of archaeogenetic research in historical archeology.[8]

The emergence of horseback archery has played an important role in this process as a lifestyle movement that spans many variations as a modern sport, martial arts, cultural heritage protection activity, reenactment, and "lifestyle reconstruction" (*életmód rekonstrukció*) practice, as well as being a tool of "experimental archeology" (*kísérleti régészet*). It had a pronounced countercultural edge before 2010, to be embraced by the Fidesz government after the illiberal turn because of its broad popular appeal. The government has hoped to exploit the popularity of this lifestyle movement in its efforts to rewrite the larger cultural canon. Namely, the vernacular historical narratives that are disseminated through horseback archery promote a revisionist paradigm shift in historiography, popularize a mythical imperial past and Hungarian ethnic superiority, center traditional illiberal values (heteronormativity, masculinity, discipline, traditional gender roles, kinship-based, ethnically homogeneous communities), and, above all, provide historical depth and gravity to Hungary's opposition to Western European values and civilization.

Building on interviews with horseback archers from a variety of groups, ethnographic observations from multiple visits to horseback archery camps, trainings, competitions, horse shows, and large regular festivals like Kurultáj, as well as related books and media coverage on horseback archery, I argue that the revival of horseback archery provides important insight into understanding the appeal of mythic Orientalism as a source of anti-Westernism to the populist far right. This chapter examines how horseback archery is revived through consumer and lifestyle practices that function as a medium to reinvent, stage, materialize, and spread mythical history about Hungarian greatness, drawing on narratives about Hungarians' nomadic Asian origins and resistance to Western European influence. I begin by showing how horseback archery was introduced to the broader public through the culture war frame, focusing on one celebrity practitioner who has played a key role in its reinvention. But then I demonstrate that horseback archery is more than just the obsession of one high-profile player and is quite a differentiated cultural field. I delve into its variations from competitive sport to heritage-based lifestyle to amateur archeology preoccupied with revisionist historiography, laying bare their political implications. Throughout the chapter I also pinpoint intersections between horseback archery and other fields of cultural production explored in previous chapters to show how it is linked to larger "circuits of commerce."[9] The final section uncovers the deeper ideological roots of mythic Orientalism as a form of anti-Westernism, highlighting how it provides popular cultural backing to contemporary far-right politics.

Reviving Horseback Archery: Restoring Hungarian Greatness Through Anti-Western Narratives

CULTURE WARS OVER HUNGARIAN "GREATNESS": HORSEBACK ARCHERY VS. THE HOLOCAUST

Horseback archery was catapulted into public view in 2016 when an independent film, *The Horseback Archer* (*A lovasíjász*), a documentary portrait about Lajos Kassai, the man who is credited with reinventing horseback archery as an international sport, arrived in Hungarian cinemas. The film was produced and directed by a well-known actor and TV personality, Géza Kaszás, as a passion project. It follows Kassai's journey, from the 1980s when he was trained in communist Hungary as a mechanic for agricultural machinery and became obsessed with re-creating the bow and arrow that were used by Hungarian warriors around the ninth-century conquest of present-day Hungary, to his becoming an internationally known pundit of horseback archery as a modern-day competitive sport. Kassai's horseback archery system became accredited in 2013 as an academic program at the Hungarian University of Sports Science (Testnevelési Egyetem) and was awarded "*Hungarikum*" status, which is a seal of excellence reserved for

Hungarian products, inventions, practices, skills, and knowledge—that is, tangible and intangible cultural heritage of exceptional quality that represents the very best of Hungary's distinctive national culture and highest forms of achievement.[10]

The film was shot mostly in Kassai's "Valley" in southwestern Hungary, a large estate he gradually developed over the past thirty years where he keeps his horses, trains his followers, holds regular races, receives visitors for open days, organizes camps and tours for schoolchildren, and lives with his family and free-roaming animals (pigs, ducks, goose, cattle), species of carefully selected breeds that are claimed to be "indigenous" to Hungary. His Valley is a clear testimony that even though horseback archery can be a modern sport, true commitment to it entails a way of life; it's much more than just a recreational activity.

The director embarked on making the film because he was smitten by the spirit of the Valley: the "positive outlook on life, the momentum, and the pure energy" that permeated the place and Kassai's lifestyle.[11] Kaszás basically spent three years closely shadowing Kassai in the Valley, participating in trainings and related communal activities, and following him on several foreign trips to China and Canada to capture and convey the spirit that so captivated him in the first place. He was especially impressed by the commitment, passion, and determination with which Kassai has built his empire and successfully popularized his horseback archery racing system, not just in Hungary but abroad as well. Not to mention his praise for the way in which Kassai coupled the establishment of this modern sport with efforts to "recover the legacies and wisdom of ancient Hungarian ancestors" and reviving debates about the Central Asian origins of ethnic Hungarians.[12]

The film's reception was quite polarized and channeled into the culture war. This also signaled that in 2016, six years after Orbán's political takeover, cultural production—particularly in areas like filmmaking—was still perceived to be controlled by the previous liberal establishment. The film's director, Kaszás, profusely complained about this in the right-wing media. He emphasized that he never received any state support for making the movie, implying that the distribution of state grants for film production continued to be afflicted by a liberal bias.[13] But, most important, he resented the Hungarian Film Academy's decision to deny the film's entry into the official Hungarian Film Week, even though *The Horseback Archer* was the most-watched Hungarian movie of 2016, bringing over 100,000 viewers to cinemas and special screenings.[14] While the academy never gave him a reason for why the movie was rejected, he suspected that the squeamishness had to do with his sympathetic portrayal of controversial theories Kassai and other experts espoused in the film about Hungarians' ethnic and geographic origins, most crucially the suggested ethnic kinship with the mighty Huns.[15] Mainstream scholarship has always maintained the pseudo-scientific nature of these views, although their popularity among the broader public, particularly in right-wing circles, has remained unabated and been palpably surging since the early 2000s, as confirmed by the film's indisputable success.

Right-wing media further dialed up the culture war fervor around the film following the decision to exclude *The Horseback Archer* from the Hungarian Film Week's program. It began to pit the film against another highly celebrated Hungarian movie of the same year, the *Son of Saul*, an innovative new film about the Holocaust by a young Hungarian director, László Jeles Nemes, which swept prestigious international movie awards in 2015, winning the Grand Prix at the Cannes Film Festival, as well as the Golden Globe and the Academy Award for Best Foreign Language Film. Radical right-wing journalists expressed their indignation over the disparity with which the state treated the two movies. Sándor Pörzse, chief editor of the far-right weekly magazine *Baricade* (*barikád*) and a parliamentary representative of the far-right Jobbik Party, begrudged that a "a state-subsidized Holocaust-film receives enormous media and government support while the other film [*The Horseback Archer*], for which funding had to be literally scraped together, is basically surrounded by silence, even though it deals with our unique Hungarian heritage that is recognized as a Hungarikum."[16] He also suggested that the Holocaust film was able to produce high viewership numbers only because it was so widely distributed across cinemas in the country and schoolchildren were able to attend screenings for free, thanks to state subsidies. By contrast, *The Horseback Archer* "was not shown in cinemas in basically any of the large Hungarian cities in the countryside or in the largest cinema chains, despite that there is no story that is more essentially Hungarian."[17] In a similar vein, prominent far right politicians like Dóra Dúró from Jobbik also complained that the Hungarian National Film Fund had awarded no support to any historic film between 2010 and 2015 that aimed to strengthen Hungarian national identity. And now, that one such film was finally made independently, it should be required viewing for all high school students.[18]

The duel between the Holocaust film that confronts viewers with Hungary's dark past and the portrait of a horseback archer who wants to make Hungary great again by reviving popular myths about the glory of ancient Hungarian warfare provided a perfect culture-war pairing. It showed how politicians, cultural producers, and media outlets located politically right of the Fidesz government continued to pound away at the government's cultural policy, attacking everything that smacked of liberalism, cosmopolitanism, multiculturalism, or reckoning with historical responsibility, pushing Fidesz to radicalize its own cultural agenda and yield—often quite willingly—to these far-right pressures. It also deployed one of the central tropes of far-right reasoning introduced in chapter 2 on book publishing: the reference to double-standards about how liberal cultural content is unquestioned and automatically favored (e.g., by government subsidies) even if it's "un-Hungarian," while illiberal content is shunned and hampered despite its "national value" and popular resonance.

STAGING THE HORSEBACK ARCHERY EXPERIENCE

Incidentally, it was also in the same year in which *The Horseback Archer* came out that I visited the Kassai Valley. In November 2016 I attended one of the Valley's Open Days, held on the first Saturday of every month. The Valley is indeed quite scenic, a pleasant, hilly area with a small lake and stream, sprawling over approximately 15 hectares in the vicinity of a nature reserve, but also only a stone's throw from the capital city of the region, Kaposvár. In his memoir and countless interviews, Kassai described the spiritual experience through which he found this site.[19] It was his horse that galloped into the valley with him one day on their regular strolls. The valley ended in a cul-de-sac, forcing the horse to stop. As he was standing there in the bottom of the valley, a strange tranquility came over him, coupled with a mounting feeling that he had found his place in the world.[20] He tracked down the owners, a state-owned agricultural cooperative at the time, first leasing the area from them before purchasing it and setting up his archery base there in 1988.

The Valley's Open Days are carefully choreographed. I arrived just as the activities were getting under way. After paying the entrance fee, picking up some flyers, and quickly reviewing the house rules, which prohibit photography[21] and call for caution around larger animals like the buffalos, I hurried toward the "horse pit," a large, sunken field at the foot of the hills where a flock of geese was grazing, which doubles as the racetrack Kassai designed for horseback archery competitions. This is where the main show introducing the Kassai Valley to visitors takes place. The program began by a staged ritual in which a newborn baby of a young couple dressed in black and white traditional clothing was inducted into the local community by a priest after the couple and the baby were symbolically greeted by members of the community, who turned out to be the performers in the rest of the show. The ritual was a prelude to a horse show, performed to an eclectic mix of folk(ish) background music, in which we saw a series of drills that required serious acrobatic skills from the performers, including jumping on and off the moving horses and mimicking the flexing of a bow while riding.

I was surprised to see that women and girls made up nearly half of the performers, who were otherwise Kassai's students and members of the sports club, which is idiosyncratically called a khanate in the Kassai system. Historically, a khanate referred to a kinship-based tribal organizational unit associated with nomadic Turkic, Mongol, and Tatar societies that functioned as a polity, like feudal chiefdoms in Europe. The dynamic sequence in the show was followed by a more tranquil scene in which women were lying on the back of standing horses while men were circling around them with Nepali singing bowls. Kassai started using the bowls to relax and mentally prepare the horses and their riders for archery routines and races that require extraordinary concentration and coordination. Classic horseback archery was performed only in the last third of the roughly ninety-minute show. Here, however, only men shot arrows in various formations. In preparing to shoot from the horses, the climax of the show, they practiced by shooting onto the wall of the sunken field while performing folk dance steps—again, an element that Kassai incorporated into the training because of the affinity he noticed between the rhythm the archers need to internalize when shooting from the back of a horse and the typical rhythm of Hungarian folk dances. The most spectacular and complex sequence was performed by Kassai himself toward the end, which involved not just shooting arrows from the horse but juggling with a range of other weapons, including a spear, an axe, and a sword. In the finale, in a dramatic closing scene, a girl sat on a horse holding an enormous Hungarian flag in both hands and walked (on horseback) around the perimeter of the field while passing through the other performers.

Visitors stood and sat around the sunken field, rewarding the performers with enthusiastic applause. I estimated the size of the audience at around two hundred people, which exceeded my expectations. It consisted of mostly families, including lots of kids, many of them girls, with parents dominantly in their thirties and forties, and some foreign tourists. Most viewers looked middle class, judging by their attire and comportment. I suspected most of them came from the countryside, which was confirmed later during a Q&A session with Kassai.

FIGURE 5.1. Sabretaches sold at the *Kurultáj* festival. Photo by author.

People were dressed in sporty, casual street clothing, but they often sported small accessories that identified them beyond doubt as drawn to right-wing subcultures preoccupied with Hungary's prehistory.[22] For instance, there was a man with a classic sabretache (*övtarsoly*), a pouch for everyday belongings typically part of men's attire in the Conquest period worn on their weapon belt (figure 5.1),[23] or a woman dressed in a nondescript gray outfit but donning a large decorative hairpin with a Turul motif (figure 5.2), the Turul bird being a mythological bird of prey featuring prominently in Hungarian origin stories and the clan symbol of Hungary's first ruling dynasty, the ninth- and tenth-century Árpád house. Decorative disks bearing the Turul motif worn at the end of hair braids were ornaments that distinguished Hungarian noble women in this period.

These symbolic historical artifacts were revived as modern fashion accessories in the 1980s when interest in Hungarian prehistory, such as the mysteries of the geographical and ethnic origins of the Hungarian people and their language, Hungarians' migration patterns from the East, and the period of the Conquest, became a manifestation of counter-establishment popular culture.[24] These items are not replicas but evolved as a genre of folk craft that is inspired by the material culture of the Conquest era. They are reintroduced

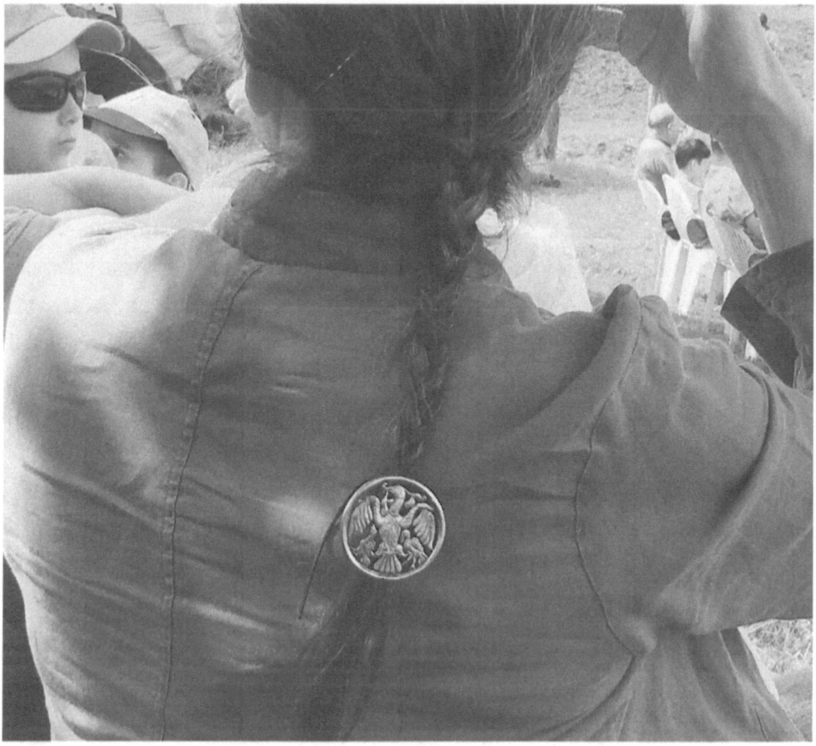

FIGURE 5.2. Woman wearing a Turul hairpin at a horseback archery show in Pomáz. Photo by author.

to be part of contemporary everyday wear while simultaneously emanating a cultural and political statement. They can be found as staples at the arts and crafts fairs I wrote about in chapter 3 and will be discussed later in this chapter as well.[25]

At the end of the show, Kassai announced to the audience that those interested in a more informal Q&A with him were welcome in the covered riding hall after a short break. He suggested we first explore the estate, sampling the food available for purchase and for consumption on site at the main building, walking around the estate, and meeting the animals (racka sheep with their unusual spiral-shaped horn, buffalos, rabbits, hens and cocks, and the horses, of course). Most visitors stayed to try the various dishes (sausages, goulash, mutton stew) and tasted the cheeses, smoked meat, and preserves from local organic producers. There was also a small store in a building near the entrance, erected in the style of Hungarian organic architecture, selling books mostly published by Püski, the publisher featured in chapter 2, including Kassai's memoirs and literature on Hungarian prehistory.[26] Other archery equipment, such as Kassai's signature bows, was also among the merchandise, as well as impressive, delicately detailed, full leather armor for a horseback archer.

I walked over to the riding hall to the Q&A with Kassai, catching a glimpse of the 170-year-old original Kazakh yurt that serves as the setting for unconventional history lessons Kassai regularly delivers to visiting groups of public school students about the Hungarian Conquest and nomadic lifestyle. The riding hall is decorated with large graphic portraits of Hun, Avar, and Hungarian warriors from the Conquest period hanging from the ceiling. I instantly recognize the style and can tell that they are drawings by Zalán Kertai, who describes himself as a painter specializing in heritage protection themes with an emphasis on "Hungary's thousand-year-old military history and martial arts, and the visual imagery of contemporary Hungarian military heritage protectors."[27] But to most people, his drawings are familiar as graphics on T-shirts from the *Rege* brand that is very popular in this subculture (figure 5.3).[28]

At the Q&A participants were particularly interested in Kassai's portrait film. They would have liked to be able to purchase it on DVD and organize screenings, possibly inviting Kassai, too. The film clearly boosted the visibility of horseback archery, especially Kassai's version of it, generating tangible demand for the sport. There were also many questions about his horseback archery system. We learned that he basically built a franchise system, which he had marketed within and beyond Hungary. He specified the size and dimensions of the racetrack, the basic organizational units (e.g., tribes, khanates), the ranks members can attain and the requirements for membership, the logistics of competitions, the scoring system, and the reporting of results. He approves and licenses each racetrack and trains referees. In Kassai's view, the franchise system facilitates access to the sport because it enables members to use their own horses and organize competitions where they live.

A flyer I picked up at the entrance pictured horseback archery bases across the country mapped on to a Greater Hungary image, showing that altogether there were three khanates (larger clubs) and eight tribes in Hungary—including one khanate and three tribes in Slovakia. In addition, there was one tribe each in Austria, the United States, and Canada. Kassai's khanate also has an international chapter with members from China, Bulgaria, Romania, Norway, and Czechia. To raise the international profile of his system, Kassai established the World Federation of Equestrian Archery in 2020 with the intention of eventually getting horseback archery to qualify

FIGURE 5.3. T-shirts from Rege brand with Zalán Kertai's graphics of Conquest-era warriors wrapped in a runic alphabet sleeve, sold at the *Kurultáj* festival. Photo by author.

as an Olympic sport. The Kassai Valley, nevertheless, remains the center of worldwide horseback archery, where world championships and a recurring annual meeting are held for all member organizations.

Kassai took clear pleasure in bragging about his international fame and engagements. He claimed to have offered training in over sixteen different countries, such as Saudi Arabia, Qatar, the United Arab Emirates, South Africa, and the United States, where his training camp attracted people from all over the country, including Native Americans from the Pine Ridge reservation in South Dakota who were hoping he could help them reclaim their horseback archery heritage.[29] He also shared anecdotes about prestigious horse shows he was invited to all over the world, by Queen Elizabeth II, for instance, as well as about working as a trainer and consultant for Hollywood A-listers like Matt Damon for a role in the 2016 monster film, *The Great Wall*, in which he played a European mercenary warrior on a quest in imperial China.

But it turns out that participation in the horse shows has also been important for Kassai's business. He explained that he had started in local village festivals but now travels far and wide across the world to perform horseback archery routines in famous horse shows. The honorary fees he receives for his performances make a significant financial contribution to his enterprise. Revenues from the shows, as well as the experiential history lessons offered to schoolchildren and the local and international training camps largely cover the costs of maintaining the Valley. He acknowledged that he had considerable income from his signature products—arrows, bows, quivers, horse saddles—which horseback archers who decide to follow the Kassai system pretty much have to purchase, but that he reinvested this income in research and development and in keeping the Valley accessible to less well-off users, too.[30]

Kassai repeatedly emphasized that his chief mission was not about making money out of horseback archery. Rather, he contended that even his approach to the business side of horseback archery grew out of his identity as a martial artist, driven by a calling to follow the path of ancient warrior ancestors. Horseback archery in his view is a martial arts school that is a vehicle for personal growth and self-development. It is "an institution that embodies historical continuity with the ancient past. It is simultaneously a mental, cultural and physical activity."[31] This is also, in his view, what clearly distinguishes it from how archery is practiced in the West simply as a sport, prioritizing physical performance. Hungarian horseback archery is more in line with Eastern traditions, where sport is seen as offering a way toward psychological growth and self-awareness. In addition, it aims to significantly strengthen community and raise national self-awareness. This is why, for instance, as part of the admissions requirements into a Kassai club, candidates have to recite a Hungarian poem and perform a Hungarian song. "This is not required to become a horseback archer," he says, "but to become part of the community." And "as this is a martial arts school, community must be made up overwhelmingly of warriors."[32]

The importance of community not only was stressed during the Q&A at the Open Day but was formalized as an objective of the Kassai system in the application materials for *Hungarikum* designation. According to this statement, community building is a fundamental goal of horseback archery and is actively promoted through camps, open days, races, horse shows, living history lessons, or training camps.[33] The focus on community building also serves to bridge the three foundational aspects of horseback archery—cultural heritage preservation, martial arts, and sport—organizing them into an entire way of life. To this effect, visual markers such as clothing are essential binding elements, too. Members are expected to wear a kaftan of the color that corresponds to their rank, carry their weapons in adequate quivers, and dress their horses properly as well. The tribal and khanate chiefs always sport a Bocskai at official events, which is a stripped-down version of the formal Hungarian dress from prewar Hungary that I discussed in detail in chapter 3. This example again shows how these different subcultural networks intersect to make up a larger "circuit of commerce."[34]

However, when Kassai discussed during the Q&A how today people experienced a painful absence of and pressing need for authentic communities and how his horseback archery program was hoping to fill this void, he painted a deeply conservative vision of what he understood to be a "community." His notion centered on the maintenance of a hierarchical order with clear roles for everyone, a centrality of discipline, and the organization of activities that reinforce traditional, heteronormative gender roles. He contended that, most important, members needed to be able to follow orders and respect hierarchy. Apparently, a martial arts–inspired vision of a cultural community leaves its members little room for freedom.

WHAT MAKES HORSEBACK ARCHERY POLITICAL?

But what does Kassai's vision about reviving horseback archery have to do with far-right populist politics? He, in fact, always distances himself from any involvement in party politics when asked publicly. At the same time, he has been whole-heartedly endorsed by far-right politics and media as a cultural icon—a role he seems to have cherished and played along with.[35] He has also reciprocated this attention by accepting invitations to talk shows, lectures, panel discussions, festivals and other public events organized by well-known far-right figures. He has similarly used his growing celebrity status to make provocative gestures towards left-wing and liberal media. He often portrayed himself as a rare social conservative who was willing to talk to the other side. He demonstratively gave a long interview on the most influential leftist-liberal YouTube channel, Partizán whose founder, chief editor and his interviewer, Márton Gulyás is an openly gay, left-wing activist.[36] Under the pretense of being open to a reasoned discussion of vastly opposing political and cultural viewpoints, he seems to use these platforms to disseminate his profoundly conservative worldview, including his homophobic views on gender issues or the bogus theories about Hungarians' ethnic links to ancient Huns.

But the more profound political power of Kassai's world comes from his ability to present modern-day horseback archery as a means to re-create and relive Hungary's historical greatness. Kassai's historical greatness narrative is rooted in a mythical orientalism, in ethnic Hungarians' Eastern origins and the superiority of the warfare practiced by nomadic tribes over their more developed Western opponents. These themes feed neatly into contemporary anti-Western sentiments fomented by Orbán's far-right politics such as the constant likening of the European Union to a colonizing force and a threat to Hungary's sovereignty. Horseback archery thus shows that nostalgia and mythical history serve as key resources for populist politics and that culture and lifestyles practices help provide popular resonance to this political project.

The time of the ninth- to tenth-century Conquest is such a fertile ground for nostalgia for the far right because its living memory is replete with catchy stories about how Hungarians, a recently arrived nomadic migrant group, did not only successfully resist Western European attacks and pressure to adopt Western Christianity but prevailed over Western European armies thanks to Hungarians' more sophisticated warfare skills that relied on masterful horseback archery tactics. Every Hungarian is familiar with the Latin slogan "A saggitis Hungarorum libera nos Domine!" (Save us from the Hungarians' arrows Our Lord!, or *A magyarok nyilaitól ments meg Uram minket!*), which was allegedly included in the prayers of Western Europeans at the height of Hungarian military expeditions to the West in this period, indicating the might of Hungarian armies.[37] This popular historical legend was also highlighted in Kassai's official bid for recognizing horseback archery as a *Hungarikum*. He stressed that "our ancestors led military campaigns from the Byzantine Empire to Bremen," and "contemporary chroniclers all agreed that Hungarians were unsurpassable when it came to battle spirit, discipline, and horseback archery."[38] According to Kassai, modern-day horseback archery helps to make this history part of living memory again and restore Hungarian pride, which is seen to have been deliberately repressed under communism and post-1989 liberal regimes.

But Kassai's reinvention of horseback archery as a modern sport does not simply recover and carry on the legacy of Conquest-era Hungarian warriors in the form of nostalgia; it also offers a present-day feeling of greatness. The way he set up the sport to be international enables him—and other practitioners—to make inflated claims about the performance of Hungarian horseback archers as being the best in the world. While it is true that Kassai's horseback archery system has followers beyond Hungary, he seems to constantly overstate the extent and significance of this international presence. In interviews he often contends that he is building a "world empire," a "worldwide organization," whose physical center is his Valley, while also emphasizing that spreading the sport is a vessel for spreading Hungarian culture and "making Hungarian culture visible all over the world."[39] There is, however, little hard evidence for the wide international reach of the Kassai system when one explores the competition reports or the website of the World Federation of Equestrian Archery. Yet, Hungarians repeatedly describe themselves as being "world leaders" in this field, with Kassai collecting the most trophies overall, attributing their excellence in key part to the deep historical roots that horseback archery has in Hungary. Again, this might technically be true based on actual competition results, but it is also somewhat of a misrepresentation given that the overwhelming majority of the practitioners are Hungarians, and they incidentally make up the rules of the game.

Nevertheless, the rhetoric that the sport successes of modern-day horseback archery confirm and allow to reclaim Hungary's historical greatness has proved to be powerful and has lent itself to political exploitation—hence Kassai's celebrity status bolstered by the far right. Kassai has also always promoted these far-reaching interpretations in his public statements by emphasizing the national character of the sport and how it captures the essence of the Hungarian spirit. Namely, "Hungarians follow nothing and no one in a servile fashion and are only willing to stand behind a leader who transcends mediocrity and exhibits charisma and exceptional ability. But then they follow with their hearts and minds."[40] Based on this quote, it's not hard to see why Viktor Orbán would be sympathetic to Kassai's depiction of Hungarian national character.

This attitude is also keenly internalized by members of the sports clubs adhering to the Kassai system, as evidenced, for instance, by interviews I conducted with one of the Kassai tribes. The chieftain proudly explained to me that at the 2014 world championship, for instance, there were nine Hungarian competitors, and they took the first nine places in the competition out of approximately sixty contenders. Similarly, in 2019 there were six Hungarian competitors, and they finished in the first six places, demonstrating that Hungarians completely rule the game.[41] In his view, this hegemony also has to do with our long traditions in horseback archery and with Kassai's efforts to revive these traditions. In turning it into an international sport, his goal was to do so by marketing it explicitly as a "Hungarian sport" to foreigners as well. Interest in this version of horseback archery would thus simultaneously express interest in and reverence for Hungarian culture and for Hungarians' superior horseback archery skills. When I asked the chieftain if some people could interpret this kind of pride invested in horseback archery as overly nationalistic, he and his wife, a fine artist who is also an active member of the Kassai tribe, immediately protested that they were not nationalistic and that their pride in Hungarians' mastery of horseback archery had nothing to do with nationalism. They were only proud of Hungarian achievements without looking down on others. This is a common trope on the right against accusations of nationalism, insisting that it is okay to be proud of being "better" than anybody else because in their view this does not necessarily imply that others are inferior.

Horseback Archery: From Modern Competitive Sport to Lifestyle Trend to Experimental Archeology

While Kassai certainly looms large over the revival of horseback archery in Hungary, this is by no means a one-man show. Not all contemporary horseback archers follow the Kassai system, and there is quite some diversity across different strands. There are groups that are more focused on the modern sport aspect of the revival and less on the cultural heritage dimension, groups that are preoccupied with the historical authenticity of every detail, and groups in between these two poles that embrace its lifestyle elements. This variety suggests that horseback archery has evolved into a differentiated field of cultural production serving diverse consumer interests while always tied to a larger cultural mission. Yet, it also highlights similarities in the ways in which horseback archery is commercialized primarily through festivals, local and international horse and reenactment shows, competitions, nomadic lifestyle summer camps for children, or alternative, experiential history lessons for primary and secondary school students.

HORSEBACK ARCHERY AS MODERN SPORT AND REVIVAL OF HUNGARIAN HORSE-RIDING CULTURE

The headquarters of the most sport-centered horseback archery association are found just outside Pomáz, a small town near Budapest, northwest of the capital on the suburban commuter train line. They are located on an impressive plateau at the foot of a mountain range and at the border of the Duna-Ipoly National Park. While this place is not as sweeping and imposing as the Kassai Valley, it also has been linked to a larger cultural and political mission. The training, competitions, shows, and festivals take place on the grounds of the "Hungarian Castle" (*Magyar Vár*), and this is where the stables are located. The site is part of 25 hectares of land owned by Sándor Herpai's family business, who donated it for the Hungarian Castle foundation, a civil society organization Herpai set up with a Hungarian émigré, János Horkovics-Kováts, returning from (West) Germany, where he worked for decades as a gynecologist before developing a passionate interest in Hungarian prehistory.[42] The main objective of the foundation is to preserve, protect, and promote Hungarian national culture and national self-awareness. To this effect, they "support every idea, effort, and activity that aims to broadly disseminate and enrich the history and culture of the Hungarian people while also boosting tourism to Pomáz and the Pilis mountains." They feel their work is indispensable because Hungarian self-esteem has been deliberately quelled by coercive political forces, including communism and European integration. They are concerned that "because of a fear of rising Hungarian national awareness, Hungarian values and culture have been highlighted and presented in an unnaturally subdued manner. A tangible consequence of this has been the spread of low-quality, expressly harmful 'cultural' content, mostly coming from the Western world. In this context, Hungarian society also fails to be sufficiently familiar with its own cultural traditions."[43]

The founders' initial vision entailed the construction of a historical theme park that would have sported replicas of typical medieval castles from each of the sixty-three counties (*vármegye*) that made up the Hungarian Kingdom before the Treaty of Trianon in 1920. Their plans were inspired by similar international examples, such as the Warwick Castle in Britain or Neuschwanstein Castle in Germany. These ambitions, however, never panned out, and only a much more modest "castle" and a few additional service buildings were erected on the land. But the foundation has pursued its cultural mission by organizing and hosting a broad range of programs since 2004, including folk dance gatherings, patriotic-themed summer camps for school children, May Day picnics with horse shows, and horseback archery competitions.[44]

The horseback archery academy that operates here is one of the largest in the country.[45] It is run by the Némethy family, who were originally Kassai students but parted ways with him, developed their own system, and eventually became his competitor. Although they claim to prioritize horseback archery as an athletic activity, the head of the family still repeatedly referred to the deep cultural and historical roots of horseback archery in an interview

I conducted with him, as well as his family's close ties to prewar Hungarian equestrian traditions that were shattered by communism.[46] He married a German woman and lived in West Germany in the 1980s, selling IT systems and computer software to Hungarian companies. They wanted to raise their two sons bilingual and bicultural, and this is how they ended up sending them to a nomadic-themed summer camp near Pomáz, where they lived in yurts and were introduced to horseback archery. As he put it, "This is where they [his sons] were transformed from uptight, pedantic Germans into nomadic, dirt-tolerant Hungarians." After the family resettled in Hungary, they trained under Kassai but increasingly questioned his methods and got into personal and professional fights with him. They wanted to start a Kassai tribe, but Kassai didn't approve, which became the final push for them to leave and start creating their own brand of horseback archery. In many ways, they seemed to have copied straight from Kassai's playbook—slightly changing the size of the racetrack and the competition rules, using different bows and arrows, holding competitions on Korean-style racetracks too—but they claim their system is much more open, modern, and professional and treats horseback archery chiefly as a contemporary sport. They also entertain international aspirations and have been recruiting foreigners to their system, predominantly from France and Germany.

Yet, as the head of the family described, what distinguished the spirit of horseback archery in Hungary was the understanding that it is a mix between a sport, culture, and tradition, in contrast to Swedes or French, for whom this is just a sport, or Koreans and other Asians, for whom horseback archery primarily has represented culture and heritage for hundreds of years without a break in continuity. For Hungarians, the old traditions had to be reconstructed from scratch because communism completely wiped out Hungary's longstanding horse-riding culture (*lovaskultúra*). It forced horse breeding farmers into communist state cooperatives, annulled the conservative, aristocratic, and gentry (*úri, dzsentri*) middle class that used to keep horses and participate in equestrian sports, not to mention the military cavalry officers who also disappeared after World War II. That Hungarians are a proud "horse-riding nation" (*lovas nemzet*) has been a popular trope in defining Hungarian national character, one that was again eroded under communist rule. This is also why post-1989 right-wing governments, especially since 2010, have vowed to restore horse-riding culture to its former glory and have viewed horseback archery as significantly contributing to this effort. Other initiatives include the opening and generous public financing of a National Equestrian Theater (Nemzeti Lovas Színház), where plays are performed by actors on horses, or the annually held, high-profile historical horse race, the "National Gallop" (Nemzeti Vágta), which was established in 2008 to commemorate the legacy of Hungarian hussars.[47]

These examples show that even though the Némethy Academy in Pomáz claims to be the most sports-driven horseback archery club, its work and identity are still very much anchored in right-wing populist political, cultural, and historical beliefs and social networks. The site that they operate from, the Hungarian Castle, is dedicated to a political and cultural mission to raise Hungarian national consciousness. The Némethy Academy has had its base there since 2009, largely as a courtesy of the owners, paying heavily discounted rent, because they see their activities as a close fit with their larger ideological agenda. Members of the horseback archery club regularly participate in the cultural programs of the Hungarian Castle, such as the horse shows at the May festivities or the annual reenactment ceremony to commemorate the 907 Battle of Bratislava, in which Hungarian forces annihilated the German (i.e., East Francian and Bavarian) army, thanks to the effective tactical deployment of horseback archers.[48] The Némethy Academy and its activities make up an integral part of the Hungarian Castle's agenda, as I witnessed during my half a dozen visits to various events over the past four years, including May festivities, regular trainings, and horseback archery competitions (figure 5.4).

NOMADIC HORSE-CULTURE AS A LIFESTYLE CONCEPT

It is true, though, that the Némethy Academy is more open than Kassai to other horseback archery groups that are less interested in it as a competitive sport and pursue it more as a holistic lifestyle practice complemented by other cultural heritage protection–themed horse-riding pursuits (e.g., reenactments, historical horse shows, historical long-distance riding tours). One such group is the Steppe Fox Nomadic Cultural Heritage Association (Pusztai Róka Nomád Hagyományörző Egyesület), which is based just outside Karcag, a town in Central Hungary in the Northern Great Plain region, with a small contingent of members who live in Pomáz. The group was set up by a farmer who specializes in livestock farming. He leases land from the Hortobágy National Park in the *Puszta*, a UNESCO World Heritage site, a protected cultural landscape that encompasses a vast area of plains and wetlands in Eastern Hungary devoted to traditional forms of land use and husbandry, including the grazing of domestic animals, and the preservation of the pastoral society that has defined this area for two

FIGURE 5.4. Training at the Némethy Academy in Pomáz. Photo by author.

millennia. After 1989 the farmer's family moved to a *tanya*, a remote and isolated farm typical to this area that is maintained through self-sufficient farming. They raise traditional Hungarian animal breeds here, such as the Hungarian Gray beef cattle (*szürkemarha*), the Hortobágy Racka, and herding dogs like the Mudi, while also keeping horses. Traditional, self-sufficient farming on a *tanya* was an intentional lifestyle choice for them. It represents an ecologically sustainable and nature-centered holistic way of life that is simultaneously rooted in expressly antimodern, anticapitalist, and antiglobalist sentiments.

The Steppe Fox Association was founded to organize those who live and work in the surrounding area into an even tighter community. For them, horseback archery is something that is organically connected to their everyday life and not some recreational activity they take up for a few hours after their 9-to-5 office jobs and over the weekend. The story behind the name of the organization reveals another reason for the keen interest and commitment to nomadic cultures and their way of life, which includes horseback archery. The steppe fox is native to the steppes, semideserts, and deserts of Central Asia, reaching into Mongolia and northern China, and is also called the corsac fox, derived from the original Turkic name, *karsak*, which is the same word as the name of the city Karcag, where the group is originally from. The overlap is no random coincidence but has to do with the history of the region, where large populations of Cumans, a Turkic nomadic people from Central Asia, settled in the thirteenth century, seeking refuge in Hungary from the Mongolian invasion of the Kievan Rus' in today's Ukraine. Many residents still consider themselves descendants of Cumans, and many place-names and geographical designations of parts of the *Puszta* uphold their memory. As the name choice demonstrates, the Steppe Fox Association puts a strong emphasis on horseback archery and other traditional horse-riding activities as ways to carry on this Cuman legacy.

The association's main activities revolve around performing in historical horse shows (fifteen to twenty per year) at various festivals, not just in Hungary but in the pre-Trianon ethnic Hungarian territories in neighboring countries as well as in Kazakhstan or Germany. This is also how I had first seen them a few years ago at the May festivities at the Hungarian Castle grounds in Pomáz. They participate in horseback archery competitions and popularize traditional "ethnosports" like the Eurasian horse game *köböre*, known as *buzkashi* in Persian, that was brought to Hungary and preserved by the Cumans.[49] A BBC journalist described this game as "rugby on horseback with a dead goat as a ball."[50] They also hold an annual "Nomadic horse-culture as lifestyle" (*Lovasnomád életmód tábor*) summer camp for children at their *tanya* to teach them nomadic lifestyle skills. The children live in authentic yurts and learn to ride and tend to horses, as well as the basics of horseback archery. The association's members have attended the World Nomad Games in Kyrgyzstan, Turkey, and Kazakhstan, and Kazahkstan's Great Steppe Race, which is an endurance horse race over a 500-km-long course that covers treacherous terrain and is similar to the Mongol Derby, which re-creates the 1000-km-long postal route established by Genghis Khan in 1224.

Even Steppe Fox members who were not originally from this region and had no Cuman ancestry were captivated by these mythical narratives of nomadic cultural heritage and the lifestyle lessons they offer for today. One member I interviewed described how he got involved with the group shortly after he graduated from college with a B.Sc. degree in geography. He was researching traditional forms of husbandry in floodplains, and he met one of the Steppe Fox's founders through his fieldwork. After college he decided to take an internship on their farm and worked for room and board with a friend, herding sheep and the Hungarian Gray cattle. They had no background with horses and didn't know how to ride but were offered the opportunity to learn at the farm. He was not interested at first, but it turned out that getting around on horses was quite practical in this line of work, so he eventually learned to ride. This was just a year after the Steppe Fox was formed in 2004, so they also started telling him about horseback archery, which he wasn't interested in at all. And then one day they asked him to help out at a horse show, and there, when he saw the warriors parading on horses in impressive historical attire and shining armor, he was overtaken by a feeling that "it would be great to be riding with them."[51]

He added that "in the mid-2000s there was a real boom in heritage preservation, not just when it comes to horseback archery, but all of a sudden, it became trendy to wear a sabretache (*tarsoly*), sport items with the Greater-Hungary image, or attend various Hungarian prehistory lectures; there was definitely a surge of interest in these issues." As we talked about the Steppe Fox's founding and how he joined, he shared another anecdote that established the group's ties to Conquest history, another crucial narrative anchor in this world. He told me that even though the Steppe Fox was formally launched in 2004, members always joke that the group's history can be traced back to the Conquest because one of the founding members played the role of the young Árpád—the prince who led Hungarians in their conquest of the Carpathian Basin at the turn of the ninth and tenth centuries and was the founder of the first royal dynasty that ruled Hungary until the thirteenth century—in the 1996 feature film that was made about the Conquest to mark its 1,100-year anniversary.[52]

My interviewee has remained an active member even though he moved back to Pomáz and bought a farm for himself, where he continues to be engaged in traditional, self-sufficient farming, keeping mostly cattle and horses and producing and selling milk and cheese. Although he participates in horse shows and horseback archery competitions, his personal goals and motivations coincide with the stated mission of the group: While he respects the professionality of the horseback archer sportsmen and the attention to historical authenticity prized by the experimental archeologist wing of horseback archery, he adopts a more laidback attitude and focuses on the lifestyle elements that connect organically with a nature-centered traditional lifestyle. When I asked him if there is any politics embedded in this attitude, he responded that he usually tries to stay away from direct political action, "but I think that people who are involved in cultural heritage protection and in these circles [horseback archery] are chiefly, if we have to draw a boundary, if we just split things in half, all on one side. I don't really know any horseback archer who would be very lefty . . . people who are active in heritage protection tend to be overwhelmingly conservative."

REWRITING THE HUNGARIAN PAST THROUGH EXPERIMENTAL ARCHAEOLOGY

The third strand of horseback archery besides the sports and the lifestyle-centered varieties is chiefly preoccupied with the historical authenticity of the practice and its tools. It has fueled the rise of "experimental archeology," which has played a significant role in shifting the official canon on Hungarian prehistory, demonstrating the power of amateur historians in rewriting academic historiography. Experimental archeology denotes efforts by archeologists, historians, specially trained artisans, or even self-taught enthusiasts to re-create archeological artefacts to generate and test archeological hypotheses. It can involve reconstructing artifacts with historically accurate technologies, re-creating the techniques and methods by which these objects were made, or modeling and testing the ways in which they must have been used. Living history or historical reenactment are distinct from experimental archeology and can be considered its recreational counterparts.

There are various archeological parks and sites devoted to experimental archeology. Butser Ancient Farm in the UK is one of the earliest examples where theories of construction, use, and materials were tested, including a Stone Age farm, a Roman villa, and an Iron Age village. The Danish Lejre Land of Legends open-air museum features reconstructed buildings from the Viking era, among others, and runs experiments in prehistoric living and technologies. In Eastern Europe such archeological sites, like Biskupin in Poland or Kernavė in Lithuania, have often served as vehicles for raising national consciousness, symbolizing the exceptional prehistoric achievements of Slavonic ancestors in Biskupin or upholding national distinctiveness in the face of Soviet assimilation pressures in Kernavė.

Horseback archery in Hungary has proved to be a rich terrain for experimental archeology for several reasons. On the one hand, by revisiting theories about Hungarians' kinship with Huns and Scythians that have been heavily contested and sidelined by academic historiography, it addresses obsessions at the heart of Hungarian national identity: the geographical origin and ethnogenesis of the Hungarian people. On the other hand, it relates to a historical period that left few tangible traces behind. The nomadic lifestyle of migrating Hungarian groups can only be reconstructed from sporadic and fragmented material artifacts, and, more recently, the genetic analysis of human (and animal) remains. The incomplete and patchy history has endowed this period with an air of mystery, generating a particular fascination for popular culture, as writers, artists, or amateur enthusiasts have tried to fill in the evidential gaps and imagine the way of life of Conquest-era Hungarians.

Generations of Hungarians have, for instance, been deeply influenced by the drawings of Gyula László, an archeologist-historian-fine artist who published several volumes depicting Conquest-era everyday life.[53] Incidentally, he also developed a controversial and never substantiated theory about the Conquest, the so-called double-conquest (*kettős honfoglalás*) thesis, contending that the Conquest took place in two waves, with the first wave arriving in Hungary already in the seventh century, i.e., almost three centuries earlier than suggested by established scholarship.

Such dubious theories are indeed quite common in Central and Eastern Europe. They are often used to make territorial claims based on indigeneity and are mobilized in chauvinistic and nationalistic political projects. One of the best-known such theories is Romania's Daco-Roman continuity thesis, which claims that today's Romanians are descendants of old Roman conquerors. It is used to prove that Romanians are an "indigenous" ethnic group and have more territorial rights than other ethnicities (e.g., Slavs, Hungarians) who migrated later to the area. But similar contests over the ancient roots of ethnic groups to legitimate competing territorial demands are at center stage in other parts of the world as well, in the Middle East in particular. Palestinians' insistence, for instance, that modern-day Palestinians are direct descendants of the Canaanites who inhabited the region before Israelites, and are therefore entitled to the land, has been politically mobilized in the Israeli-Palestinian conflict.[54]

In the post–World War II era, the more communist historical scholarship marginalized the study of Hungarian prehistory as a way to suppress questionable ethnic origin stories and their chauvinistic implications, the more these alternative theories were embraced by extra-academic amateur historians and prehistory enthusiasts who often shared right-wing, anticommunist sentiments. Hungarian prehistory thereby also became a thematic linchpin of countercultural activities before the end of communism and an important intellectual preoccupation of the Hungarian ethnic diaspora abroad (chiefly in the United States). It is also important to note that books promoting these alternative histories were often published by the right-wing publishers scrutinized in chapter 2. Following its return to Hungary from the United States, the Püski press, for instance, made the revisionist treatment of Hungarian prehistory one of its publishing priorities.

The revival of horseback archery was intimately linked with a renewed interest in Hungarian prehistory. A seminal treatise published after the fall of communism, entitled *Horseback Archery and Prehistory,* came about as a collaboration between an archeologist and a self-taught prehistory buff.[55] The first author, an archeologist reviewed the scientific literature on "Eurasia's arrow-flexing horseback-riding people" in the first part of the book, stressing that Hungarian horseback archery culture can be traced back to the Scythian-Hun era in Siberia and Central Asia. The second author, an amateur prehistory fan and a software engineer by training, put the existing scientific theories to test by re-creating various horseback archery tools and techniques (e.g., shooting backwards from a horse). This second part of the book was presented as the first systematic application of the experimental archeological approach to horseback archery. The author was also quick to make dramatic statements about the significance of horseback archery for Hungarians' overall survival as a nation:

> Without horseback archery, there would be no Hungarians, neither the country, nor the language. And to not realize the significance of the activity without which we would have been dissolved in the sea of various peoples is more than irresponsible. Neighboring ethnic groups had two generations to find the antidote [to horseback archery warfare] but were unable to do so, and then we gave up this art of warfare voluntarily because the political needs [of the country] had changed. Even 100 years later the crusade armies only dared cross Hungary without making a stop . . . because a bad move could have led to the annihilation of the united forces of Western Europe.[56]

And in taking stock of the lessons experimental archeology has to offer to horseback archery, he noted that "in testing feasibility we discovered subtle details that will convince posterity of the intellectual superiority of these people who lived off animal husbandry rather than just dwelling on the overpowering physical violence used by them."[57] This argument that the technological and tactical sophistication of Conquest-era horseback archers not only outshined Western military technology at the time but also parallels or even surpasses modern warfare techniques is frequently reiterated in horseback archery circles and is taken as a token of Hungarian ethnic superiority.

The book's second author and Hungarian prehistory enthusiast, György Papp, maintained a horseback archery school in a small village in Western Hungary near the Austrian border devoted to his experimental archeological mission. Others have followed suit, forming an important niche in the field of horseback archery. One of these schools I visited is called the Resonant Arrow Historical Archery School (Zengő Nyíl Történelmi Íjász Iskola) and is based in a small suburban village northeast of Budapest. I met the founder Attila and his chief aide, the twenty-one-year-old Nelli, on a sunny summer day at their school. They showed me around the stables, and we sat down for the interview under an imposing walnut tree at a massive wooden table that displayed various historical bows and arrows. Attila explained to me that the school's name denoted a type of special arrow used by nomadic horse people in Eurasia that softly whistled when it was shot. According to some archival sources, they used this design to create special sound effects, and when large numbers of archers simultaneously shot their arrow, this sound amplified the overall effect of the attack on the enemy. Attila thought this would be an attention-grabbing name when he set up the school in 1999. The horseback archery part of the business is supported from his main source of income, which comes from tending horses that are owned by people who "like to ride but live in the city and have no room to keep horses or time for caring for them." For a monthly rental fee, he takes care of their horses. This practice is quite widespread among horseback archery schools and provides financial stability to the smaller schools in particular.

Attila first followed and competed in the Kassai system, and just like Kassai and other horseback archery schools, he also reached out to younger generations by offering a summer yurt camp program. But over time he became increasingly interested in emerging historical and archeological research on the history of horseback archery. In 2015 he was invited to a festival called Hunnenfest in Asparn near Vienna, Austria, where he and his fellow horsemen had to perform how horseback archers fought in a battle. This was when he realized that he was more interested in accurately reconstructing the Hungarian horseback archery tradition than in competing in Kassai-style races.

As a result, he decided to shift the focus of his activities in this direction. This involved, for instance, incorporating a history component on the tests administered to horseback archery students or developing a theme to perform at horse shows that follows the historical progression of horseback archery techniques through the examples of Scythians, Huns, Avars (Eurasian nomads), Hungarians, and Ottoman-Turks. It also entails a commitment to working with special horses, not the ones typically used in horse-riding schools and dressage clubs. These so-called *Hucul* horses have special cultural significance because they are thought to be the closest to breeds that Hungarians' nomadic ancestors used.[58] They are smaller, stockier, and calmer than the Western breeds that replaced them, which makes them more suitable for horseback archery. The rediscovery and renewed popularization of this heritage horse breed is often discussed in horseback archery circles in the context of anti-Western sentiments, as it is praised to be "the only Hungarian horse whose breeding has no trace of Western culture."[59] The Hucul breed was even declared a Hungarian national treasure by a parliamentary decree in 2004.[60]

Most important, however, is that historical and archeological research now makes up a fundamental part of Attila's engagement with horseback archery. He has collaborated with academic researchers on various experimental archeology projects;[61] published an article on the use of steppe-type composite bows and arrows made of horn and sinew in the *Quarterly of Military History* (*Hadtörténeti Közlemények*), a peer-reviewed scholarly journal of the Hungarian Institute and Museum of Military History;[62] coauthored another article that appeared in *Hungarian Archeology*;[63] and was headed with Nelli to the Genghis Khan Museum in Mongolia for a research trip in the fall of 2023. Incidentally, he is also the author of a young adult novel, *Altináj*, that follows the adventures of a boy and his beloved horse, part of a nomadic tribe in Hungarian prehistoric times in the Don-Donets region of today's Ukraine.[64] The book builds on archeological research from the period and hopes to awaken interest in Hungary's nomadic past in younger generations. It has not only been embraced enthusiastically by far-right media platforms for its portrayal of Hungarians' illustrious nomadic horse culture but was also recommended to middle school students as an elective reading by the National Core Curriculum.

Prehistory enthusiasts like Attila have had an increasing impact on shifting the official historiography of Hungary's nomadic and Conquest era past, making it more accommodating to theories (e.g., kinship with Huns and Scythians, ethnic origin stories linked to various Central Asian locations) that have been held to be controversial and unwarranted by evidence in academic circles but had broad support in right-wing popular culture.[65] The influence of amateur historians has been facilitated by the government's top-down reorganization of the research infrastructure of the Hungarian Academy of Sciences—including the establishment of a special Hungarian Prehistory Research Group in 2012—and the opening and lavish funding of the Institute of Hungarian Research in 2019 as a flagship institution of the parallel academic institutional system established by the Fidesz government after 2010. As discussed in previous chapters, these efforts serve to institutionalize a new right-wing cultural canon in the historiography of foundational moments of Hungarian history, such as the Conquest era.

The Ideological Roots of Anti-Westernism

Festivals that incorporate various horse shows and reenactments are central to horseback archery groups in Hungary as a source of both income and public visibility, as my interviewees reiterated. One must-go festival mentioned by representatives of every strand of horseback archery was Kurultáj, the largest cultural heritage festival not just in Hungary but in all of Europe, which occupies a unique place in the world of horseback archers and other cultural heritage protectors.[66] Kurultáj is a "tribal assembly" of Hun-Turkic nomadic cultures that takes place in the eastern Hungarian *Puszta*, a steppe landscape with some of the largest sand dunes in Europe. It is a high-profile, three-day international event that has been organized every two years since 2008. Horseback archery competitions and reenactment battles take center stage, while the event also hosts a large market fair and an archeological exhibition (figures 5.5 and 5.6).[67] The overall significance of horseback archery for the event is made evident by its logo, which shows a backward-shooting horseback archer riding on a horse and miraculous deer simultaneously. The festival includes a designated area for yurts for participants who want to camp at the site, and an open-air food court with vendors selling traditional Hungarian, Turkish, and Central Asian dishes. It also offers folk music concerts, lectures by academic and amateur historians on Hungarian prehistory, ethnogenetic and archeological research, esoteric interpretations of Hungarian national mythology, folklore and language theories, as well as shamanistic ceremonies, a nomadic wedding ritual, and various activities for children.[68] The number of visitors has grown steadily over the years, from around 45,000 in 2008 to 210,000 by 2016 and over 250,000 by 2024, and are staggeringly high numbers for Hungary, which has around ten million inhabitants.[69]

The festival's objective goes beyond mere entertainment and performance: It uses the festival format to disseminate knowledge claims about ancient nomadic cultures.[70] It tries to seamlessly blend the more lighthearted commercial aspects with serious "scientific" lectures and exhibitions that aim to rewrite the Hungarian past—an aspiration shared with experimental archeology. For a few days during the festival, participants can "'buy,' 'take on,' 'listen to,' or 'taste' the Hungarian 'heritage' and re-experience the glorious past that might have never existed in reality, but have been re-created by the power of creative imagination."[71]

FIGURE 5.5. Entrance to the main festival stage at *Kurultáj*, with image showing Attila the Hun, his name also spelled out in runic script. Photo by author.

I participated in this event three times between 2018 and 2024 and can attest that attendance signals serious commitment to the festival's cause and requires plenty of stamina from visitors. The days in August during which the festival is held are usually among the hottest of the summer, which make the *Puszta* an unforgivingly harsh environment with the scorching sun and the endless sand dunes bereft of shade-providing trees, certainly

FIGURE 5.6. Display from on-site archeological exhibition at *Kurultáj* showing a facial reconstruction based on archeological finds and a painted portrait of what the man could have looked like in real life. Photo by author.

giving visitors a sense of the hardships that their nomadic ancestors had to endure. Moreover, the performers and reenactors wear Conquest-era period clothing, sporting heavy leather boots, richly embroidered long kaftans, and fur or felted hats (figure 5.7). My visits to this event were surely among the most physically straining field trips I have had to undertake. Attending Burning Man in Nevada would probably feel closest to the Kurultáj experience. The consistently high visitor numbers in the face of these challenging conditions demonstrate that there is real interest in and demand for the festival's themes.

Most notably, however, the festival has been endowed with special political significance from its onset in 2008, underscoring that it has always

FIGURE 5.7. Reenactors at *Kurultáj* preparing for their show, wearing heavy leather, felt, and fur clothing. Photo by author.

been more than just an arcane cultural heritage show. At the beginning, it was endorsed and financially supported by Jobbik, the most far-right political party in Hungary at the time, for its subversive and countercultural approach to Hungary's past, ethnic origin myths, and antagonistic relationship to Europe. After Fidesz's landslide election victory in 2010, Viktor Orbán also recognized the festival's popular appeal and the broader political usefulness of the national identity narratives that prehistory enthusiasts celebrated with the event.[72] As a result, the government gradually extended its tutelage over Kurultáj, pushing out Jobbik as the festival's political underwriter.

The growing mainstreaming of the event was spurred on by the rapidly increasing financial support that it has received from the government. In the first few years, the organizers managed to raise only about 11–12 million HUF through state grants awarded to civil society organizations. Until 2018 the Turkish government was also one of the sponsors of the festival, providing about 20 percent of the 73 million HUF total support.[73] In 2018, however, the Hungarian government (the Ministry of Human Resources) became the main underwriter of the event, providing 300 million HUF and raising the amount of support to 700 million HUF by 2024. The substantial subsidies, for instance, enable the organizers to keep the festival free of charge to the public. Similarly, in 2010 the deputy speaker of Parliament, Sándor Lezsák, became the main patron of the event, and since 2018 the speaker of the National Assembly and founding member of Fidesz, László Kövér, has opened the festivities. The government thus officially endorses the event together with the often dubious cultural content it propagates.[74]

Yet, Kurultáj is also meaningful because the festival presents a crucial link between popular culture, consumerism, and more ambitious ideological projects. The political mainstreaming of the event, thanks to the government's growing interest in it, is one clear illustration of this link. But Kurultáj carries the legacies of a more elaborate political ideology, called Turanism, that has shaped the political right in Hungary since the nineteenth century.

Turanism emerged as a pan-ethnic movement articulating a cultural and political framework that aimed to unite various ethnic groups that shared their inner and central Asian origins and therefore close cultural, ethnic, and linguistic bonds.[75] The term "Turan" was coined by Persians to denote the nomadic tribes of the Central Asian steppe north of Iran.[76] Until the Enlightenment, the steppe kinship of Hungarians with Huns was largely taken for granted and the theory of a Scythian-Hun-Turkic-Hungarian continuity was widely accepted. But then, and progressively in the second half of the nineteenth century, Hungarian and German scholars started questioning these interpretations as ungrounded and unscientific.

Based on new developments in linguistic research, they proposed an alternative theory, according to which Hungarians were not Turkic but Finno-Ugrian people. This sparked a heated scientific and political debate, referred to as the "Ugrian-Turkish War," which ended with the triumph of scholars advocating the Finno-Ugrian connection.[77] The initial academic debate became highly politicized and gradually gave way to views that defenders of the Finno-Ugrian theory were acting in the interest of Habsburg rule and Austrian dominance, trying to undermine Hungary's rightful claims to a glorious past and diminishing its ethnic and cultural significance.

The competing Ural-Altaic thesis that maintained Hungary's Turkic and Central Asian ethnic and linguistic kinship did not disappear after this battle but became a countercultural position that was still supported by various Hungarian academic and political circles and especially by the Hungarian public at large. It also became increasingly embraced by Hungarian nationalist circles as a counter-ideology against Western-oriented depictions of Hungarian historiography.[78] The pan-Turkic ideology of Turanism was popular in Turkey, too, but for Hungarians it became a counterpoint to other powerful pan-nationalistic movements (e.g., Pan-Slavic, Pan-Germanic) of the late nineteenth century that Hungarians felt threatened and isolated by.[79]

Turanism's popularity in Hungary was similarly related to the Orientalist Zeitgeist that swept across Europe around the fin de siècle. But by contrast to Western Orientalism, Hungary's interest in the Orient was in many ways unique because it revolved around the emotionally intense search for the very origins of the Hungarian people: their "ancestral home" and ethnic kin.[80] It spurred a big wave of explorations to Central Asia and the Middle East, reviving the efforts of Hungarian explorers who had been searching for the nation's ethnic and geographic origins at least since the first such recorded journeys to the Caspian Sea and the Ural Mountains in the thirteenth century.[81] This eventually stimulated the founding of the Turanian Society (Turáni Társaság) in 1910 by Hungarian travelers, academics, and political elites "to scientifically explore, maintain contacts with, as well as popularize 'the East' through public lectures, language courses, expeditions, and the issuing of the journal *Turán*."[82] Orientalism also inspired a search for a distinctly "Hungarian national style," which was true to Hungarians' Eastern roots, making a significant impact in cultural fields such as fine arts, literature, and particularly in textile arts and architecture.[83] These enduring cultural vestiges remain important because they create contemporary resonance for "Eastern ideas and spirits."

The sharp rightward political shift of Turanism unfolded in the interwar period. The Treaty of Trianon, with its massive territorial and population losses, not only devastated Hungary after World War I but sowed the seeds of deep resentment with the West, blaming it for the unjust settlement. Turanism provided an outlet to canalize and radicalize these anti-Western sentiments. Yet, Turanists were smitten by Italian fascism too, admired Mussolini, and reached out to Turkish sympathizers as well.[84] Turanism became rapidly racialized, asserting that Turanian people could be identified through specific racial attributes, thus fully espousing racism and anti-Semitism. By the 1930s Turanism had grown into the political and cultural discourse of the radical right in Hungary.[85] Because of its close associations with fascism, racism, and anticommunism, after World War II Turanism was completely marginalized by the communist regime.[86] The Finno-Ugric version was cemented under communism as the canonized ethnic origin story, and questioning it remained taboo and relegated to countercultural circles.[87] Turanism was not all destroyed, though, it was just dormant and largely sustained by the Hungarian diaspora in the West until 1989.[88]

Turanism's revival did start sluggishly after the fall of communism, which is not surprising in view of the widespread euphoria in Hungarian society over the once-in-a-lifetime opportunity to "return to Europe," that is, to the West. It began to accelerate, however, around the time of Hungary's accession to the European Union in 2004 and went into full swing after the 2008 financial crisis, as discontent with Europe as a civilizational aspiration, the European Union as a governing institution and source of economic prosperity, liberal democracy, globalization, and neoliberal market capitalism swelled.[89] It was the new far-right party, Jobbik, which emerged as a political party in 2003, that reintroduced the "Turanian idea" into public political discourse and adapted it to define primarily its foreign policy.[90]

As Turanism calls for the unification of the Ural-Altaic people, "including the Turks of Turkey, the Turkic people of Central Asia, Tatars, Hungarians, the aboriginal tribes of Siberia, and even the distant Mongols, Manchus, Koreans, and Japanese," its revival primarily signaled Jobbik's rejection of Hungary's Western orientation and place in the Euro-Atlantic alliance, calling for an alternative by turning to the East, to ancient ethnic kin for new allies.[91] While this geopolitical vision might, at first, seem delusional for the twenty-first century, it resonated with supporters because it revoked a powerful historical imaginary of Hungarian greatness. Jobbik's updated version of Turanism also practically expressed itself in an Anti-American, anti-Israel, anti-European, but pro-Turkish, pro-Palestinian (pro-Islam), and pro-Russian foreign policy stance.[92]

The Jobbik-backed Kurultáj became the cultural focal point of the Turan revival, providing a broader popular cultural base to its far-right political platform. Kurultáj's main organizer, András Zsolt Bíró, an anthropologist and president of the Hungarian-Turanian Foundation, has been at the forefront of using archaeogenetic research to prove that Hungarians are related to people in Central Asia. He has participated in several expeditions to Central Asia and on a trip to Kazakhstan in 2006 collected genetic evidence to support his hypothesis that members of the Madjar tribe in northwestern Kazakhstan are indeed related to Hungarians.[93] His work—despite the many questionable aspects of archaeogenetics—is now upheld as incontrovertible evidence for Hungarians' Turkic roots, in yet another major blow to the Finno-Ugric theory. With Kurultáj's growing visibility, Bíró has also become one of the public celebrities of the nomadist revival, although not quite matching the stature of the horseback archer, Lajos Kassai.[94]

The activities of the Hungarian-Turanian Foundation similarly highlight and actively foster the transnational aspect of this anti-Western cultural-political movement.[95] Nomadic horse people are described as all "belonging to the same family" and "making up a civilization just like Christianity."[96]

Turkic nations are always invited to Kurultáj, and high-ranking representatives regularly attend the event to celebrate the shared nomadic heritage and the cultural bonds with the peoples of Central Asia. Turkish prime minister Recep Tayyip Erdoğan's son, Bilal Erdoğan, attended the conference in 2022, while representatives of the Turkish Agency for Cooperation and Coordination as well as the Emre Yusuf Turkish Cultural Institute regularly attend the event. And as a gesture of reciprocity, Hungary is invited to similar events in Central Asian states, such as the World Nomad Games, receives institutional support for its archeological expeditions, and was accepted as an observer member of the Organization of Turkic States in 2018, being the only EU country in the organization.

But it would be a mistake to think that the sole purpose of Kurultáj's nomadic pageantry is nostalgia. Present-day nomadic warriors do not just reminisce about the past but produce new knowledge by reconstructing how things "really" were. They do this with the intention of rectifying existing historic canons to reshape Hungarian identity in the image of the recovered glorious past. "The costumes, music, collective performance and food all function to build reality, to share a common past, to see the continuity with it and to point to a better future."[97]

This aspect of the nomadist revival—that the better future lies with the East rather than the West—captured Fidesz's attention because it resonated with its geopolitical vision of an "Eastern opening." In Viktor Orbán's view, an "Eastern opening" toward countries like Russia, China, Turkey, and Central Asian countries (e.g., Kazakhstan, Azerbaijan) would allow Hungary to recover its agency in economic and foreign policy matters while defying the expectations of the European Union. As Orbán put it at a conference shortly after his return to power in 2010: "Figuratively, or simplistically speaking, we are sailing under western flag, but an eastern wind blows in the world economy."[98]

In the following years, in a highly theatrical exchange of blows, Hungary refused IMF help and pressured the organization to leave the country in 2013 as a show of sovereignty but also as a rejection of the West. Meanwhile, Hungary has partnered, for instance, with Russia on such major energy projects as the building of a new atomic reactor and with China on infrastructural and manufacturing investments, including a Budapest-Belgrade high-speed train line and several EV battery–manufacturing plants. The "Easter opening" is, however, not only an economic discourse but—as one can see through its links to Turanism—a cultural and ethnic-racial discourse as well.[99] These broader civilizational overtones make it akin to Russian Eurasianism and

Turkish neo-Ottomanism, which offer ideological and intellectual scaffolding to anti-Western attitudes in these countries.[100]

Viktor Orbán was widely criticized for acting like a "rogue president" shortly after he assumed Hungary's six-month European Union presidency in July 2024. He drew the ire of EU leaders for launching an unauthorized "peace mission" with surprise visits to Ukraine, Russia, and China, claiming to work toward brokering a peace deal between Russia and Ukraine. Many in the EU considered his talks with Vladimir Putin in Moscow, the first such visit by an EU leader since 2022, and Xi Jinping in Beijing just the tip of the iceberg in what turned out to be a rocky presidency that Orbán tried to use to undermine the European Union.

This chapter, however, suggests that Orbán in many ways follows a long tradition that compels Hungarians to be a thorn in the side of Western Europeans. Tracing the revival of horseback archery underscores the deep historical origins, popular cultural embeddedness, and political affordances of this attitude that has fueled recurring waves of anti-Western sentiments in Hungary. Ever since Hungarians' nomadic ancestors migrated to Europe and decided to settle there, they have been torn between assimilating to Western (European) ways of life and resisting those very same ways in favor of adherence to their Eastern (Asian) roots.

The chapter shows how the popular revival of horseback archery—originally a warfare closely associated with Central Asian nomadic cultures—as a modern-day sport, cultural heritage activity, and lifestyle practice highlights the role of mythic orientalism as a key source of anti-Westernism in Hungary and its use as a political resource by contemporary far-right populism. It demonstrates that consumption and lifestyle practices provide an excellent tool to revive and spread mythical history because they make it attractive, tangible, accessible, and easy to circulate. These are incidentally the characteristics that amp up their political appeal, too.

Horseback archery can be commercialized in a variety of ways—as a competitive sport, recreational activity, cultural heritage protection, historical reenactment, nature-centered lifestyle, "lifestyle reconstruction," or hobby archeology. One does not necessarily have to become a member of a sports club and invest in expensive gear but can consume horseback archery as a spectator, making engagement with it accessible at variable price points to consumers from different class backgrounds. It can be staged for experiential consumption, as we saw in the case of the Kassai Valley or the Hungarian Castles' performance events, various local and national festivals such as

Kurultáj, incorporating horse shows and heritage themes, or nomadic summer camps and alternative history lessons targeting children and teenagers.

The various sites of consumption, festivals in particular, function as important nodes in broader "circuits of commerce,"[101] connecting horseback archery to similarly minded cultural producers in other fields that were discussed in previous chapters, such as fashion or book publishing—examples of which are included throughout the chapter. Multiple forms of commercialization amplify horseback archery's visibility way beyond just the close circle of active practitioners.

Horseback archery's focus on specific historical themes and periods—the Conquest era of the ninth to tenth centuries, the search for the ancestral homeland and ethnic kin in Central Asia, nomadic lifestyles and migration trajectories—is consequential both for how it is commercialized by cultural producers and appropriated by politics. As mentioned earlier, these historical themes lend themselves to heavy mythologization simply because of the sheer scarcity of hard evidence that would enable a comprehensive scientific reconstruction of these historical periods. Therefore, just like in the case of the heritage tours examined in chapter 4, the boundaries between myth and history are constantly blurred to fill the evidential hiatus and produce narratives of historical greatness. Contemporary consumer culture lends a powerful mechanism for bridging the gaps, allowing cultural producers to create a historical imaginary that captures the popular imagination. Politically, the deeply ingrained popular cultural narratives that are steeped in mythic Orientalism and attribute Hungarian greatness to anti-Western attitudes create a strong popular base for supporting the government's anti-EU stance and its opening toward Eastern autocratic states, such as Russia, Turkey, and China.

It is important to underline that the political mainstreaming of mythical histories promulgated by horseback archery is not a linear, top-down process. To the contrary, the process is similar to what I noted in chapter 4 with respect to the "Without Borders" heritage tourism program. The government embraces bottom-up popular cultural narratives because it hopes to capitalize on their antiestablishment and countercultural legacies and their effectiveness in mobilizing nostalgia to shift the cultural canon that was established by the communists and maintained by post-1989 liberal governments. The Hungarian government, for instance, enables the production and dissemination of revisionist histories about Hungarian ethnogenesis by providing financial support for events like Kurultáj, by establishing parallel research institutions such as the Institute of Hungarian Research, and by offering cultural visibility to horseback archery and nomadic heritage at official events and celebrations.

This is also why the nostalgia that animates horseback archery generates more than just sentimental longing for national greatness and geopolitical prowess. It becomes a driving force behind historical revisionism that denounces academic historiography and the existing historical canon. The government's backing of these grassroots efforts to rewrite the past helps to institutionalize a new national canon that can then be passed down to future generations through public education and commemorative rituals.

Hungary's most important national holiday, August 20, offers a case in point. This day is dedicated to commemorating the founding of the Hungarian state and the state's founder, Hungary's first Christian king, St. Stephen. Celebrations conclude at the end of the day by a spectacular fireworks show along the Danube on both shores, accompanied by a narrated light-painting show projected over Parliament and the Chain Bridge. In 2024 the thirty-minute show began with a silhouette of a horseback archer appearing over the Parliament Building produced by 1,300 drones, going on to recount "Hungary's watershed historical events and myths." The MC announced to the audience that "the narrator is an old shepherd who will tell us the legends and myths that we told our children at home so that they can also be proud of being Hungarian and being able to live in this Hungarian culture that has deep roots and can give us large wings." He said that the legends were indeed true in the sense that they can give us strength in our contemporary struggles "for self-determination, autonomy, sovereignty, independent Hungarian decisions in the European Union, Transylvania, the Upper Lands [i.e., Slovakia], Trans-Carpathian [i.e., Ukraine], and the Southern Lands [i.e., Serbia]." Following the MC's introduction, three-fourths of the show dealt with the mythical history of Hungarians' Eastern nomadic origins; their kinship with the Huns; the enormous power, conquests, and death of Attila the Hun; and the "return" of Hungarians to the Carpathian Basin to "reconquer" it. Only the last few minutes were fleetingly devoted to St. Stephen, even though the holiday is celebrated in his honor, making clear the relative symbolic weight the government attributed to the power of mythic Orientalism over Western values.

6

Conclusion

As I was working on this conclusion in the spring of 2025 in Budapest, art movie theaters started screening a new documentary, *Riefenstahl*, about Leni Riefenstahl, the German filmmaker best known for creating the defining visual imagery of Nazi Germany through the propaganda films she shot for Hitler, including *Triumph of the Will* (1935) and *Olympia* (1938), about the 1936 Berlin Summer Olympics. One screening was attended by the film's producer, Sandra Maischberger, a renowned German political TV talk-show host, who probably did one of the last live interviews with Riefenstahl at her hundredth birthday in 2002—she died at 101.

Maischberger was disappointed with this historic interview; she felt she couldn't coax anything genuine out of Riefenstahl, and this was in part why she became interested in further researching her life and producing the documentary after Riefenstahl's estate was made public in 2016. Under Andres Veiel's direction, the film explores the many controversies around Riefenstahl's relationship with Hitler and the Nazi political leadership—alluding to the contemporary relevance of such Faustian bargains—building on a trove of new materials from her private estate but also from ample archival footage from West German TV talk shows from the 1970s, as she was apparently a frequent guest on the talk show circuit in this period. While the film is not a conventional biographical documentary, viewers still get a glimpse into Riefenstahl's career trajectory.

Interestingly, although Riefenstahl is primarily known as one of the most skillful propaganda film makers of all times, it turns out that she started her film career in a humbler genre. The so-called mountain film (*Bergfilm*) was a popular cultural genre in Germany in the 1920s, focusing on stories of mountaineering adventures in the Alps, depicting humans' heroic struggle against nature, always returning from the peak having experienced profound character transformation. The first mountain film featured the ascent of Mont Blanc by an American climber, Frank Ormiston-Smith, in 1903, but the genre was codified in Germany and is considered an "autochthonous" national popular cultural genre like the American western.[1]

Riefenstahl's breakthrough came in 1932 with *The Blue Light* (*Das Blaue Licht*), the first film she produced, directed, and starred in, which was very unusual for a woman at the time.[2] The film has a mystical, fairy tale setting in a mountain village. Riefenstahl plays the protagonist—a village outcast, considered a witch by the villagers because she can climb the cliffs effortlessly while young men die in droves trying to reach a grotto that hides beautiful crystals periodically illuminated by the full moon. It was supposedly this film that caught Hitler's eye. He was impressed not only by Riefenstahl's rock-climbing skills but also by her portrayal of nature and the human body. A meeting was arranged between Hitler and Riefenstahl in 1932, which eventually led to her propaganda film commissions.

This is yet another example of how the state's political propaganda machine mines nationalistic popular culture, and how it proactively scouts cultural producers to create content that resonates with everyday people. Riefenstahl's artistic talent sadly served one of the most violent and oppressive regimes of modern history. Her story, nevertheless, remains a timely reminder of the dangerous potential and enormous political power of cultural production.

This book's main goal is also to call attention to the workings of cultural production in the rise of populism by identifying fundamental mechanisms that underlie populist politics. It shows how restoring the nation as the ultimate source of collective identification is a central objective of far-right populism, and how cultural production plays a pivotal role in reimagining the nation as an exclusionary, ethnically homogeneous, and anti-immigrant collective, in sharp contrast to liberal visions of global multiculturalism. Far-right populism assigns special political significance to cultural production and views culture wars as a political tool to disrupt a liberal cultural canon and replace it with a right-wing cultural hegemony to deepen its political rule. The previous chapters have demonstrated that this cultural shift is advanced not merely in a top-down manner by right-wing cultural and political elites but through grassroots popular cultural production. Far-right popular culture derives its vitality from countercultural, antiestablishment attitudes and practices and produces mythical narratives—akin in many ways to "deep stories"—that are also commodified and circulated through multiple consumer markets.[3] Radical nationalist "circuits of commerce" emerge in and connect different fields, from fashion to tourism, facilitating the expansion of far-right cultural production and consumption. When far-right populists gain political power to form governments, as in the case of Hungary, they strategically embrace elements of popular cultural production that help cement their political legitimacy.

Donald Trump's win of the US presidential elections in 2024 is the latest major political development that dramatically contributed to the worldwide expansion of far-right populist politics. He launched his presidency with a barrage of executive orders that offered a preview of his second term's political priorities in shock therapy–style. He followed the advice of his former chief strategist, Steve Bannon, about taking a "flood the zone" approach to his political and media opponents by overwhelming them, and the broader public, with a bewildering range of initiatives. Close parallels between his and Viktor Orbán's inaugural actions have been widely noted in the media in relation to anti-immigration measures, attacks on civic organizations, legacy media, an independent judiciary, and LGBTQ+ rights, as well as an apparent general contempt for the rule of law.[4]

Executive orders that address culture war issues occupy a prominent place in the Trump administration's stack, including banning DEI policies from federal government and requiring employees to report any colleagues who attempt to promote DEI efforts "in disguise"; crashing transgender rights and recognizing "only two genders, male and female"; "eradicating anti-Christian-bias"; and renaming the Gulf of Mexico the "Gulf of America," with the aim of "Restoring Names that Honor American Greatness." Besides the executive orders and budget cuts for the arts, humanities, and public media, Trump also installed himself as chairman of the board at the Kennedy Center for the Performing Arts to control the programming at one of the most eminent national cultural institutions in the United States. He purged the Center's board and filled it with new appointees, including a new director, who are loyal to him. And in perhaps the boldest move yet, he renamed the center after himself.

Some of the immediate consequences for books, for instance, involved suspending for a "compliance review" Julianne Moore's children's book, *Freckleface Strawberry*, in schools serving the children of US military personnel and civilian defense employees, and removing Kathleen Turner's book about Ruth Bader Ginsburg from library shelves.[5] The Defense

Department announced the compliance review of library books to ensure that its schools' instructional materials were aligned with Trumps' new executive orders—specifically "Ending Radical Indoctrination in K-12 Schooling" (#14190) and "Defending Women from Gender Ideology Extremism and Restoring Biological Truth to the Federal Government" (#14168)—that aim to address "gender ideology and discriminatory ideology topics." PEN America's 2023–24 Book Ban Report, *Cover to Cover*, reveals that there has been a rise in the number of bans of picture books and graphic novels that are often early literacy tools and are now targeted for featuring non-mainstream characters (LGBTQ+, people of color) and broadly understood presentations of nudity.[6] This confirms that appealing to child protection has become a general far-right political tactic, pioneered chiefly in Viktor Orbán's Hungary, as described in chapter 2, to curb freedom of speech.

Trump's culture war measures are indeed closely reminiscent of changes that unfolded in Hungary after the populist turn in 2010. The one significant difference, however, is that in the United States they are now happening much faster. In Hungary, culture war issues were always central to Fidesz's political agenda, but their conversion into policies and legislation was a more gradual process; the pace was stepped up significantly only after 2018, after Fidesz's third sweeping election win. The acceleration of the far-right crackdown on liberal culture and its institutions illustrates how populist regimes learn from each other by engaging in mimetic isomorphism.[7] Many of Trump's executive orders are clearly illegal, even unconstitutional, and are being tested in courts to reveal whether democratic checks and balances can restrain his presidential overreach. Yet, even if several executive orders are blocked by judges, the unequivocal political messaging, especially about cultural values and identity politics, will continue to pack a punch.

In this book I have argued that developments we currently witness, for instance, with the evolving second Trump presidency in the United States, that throw a spotlight on the cultural aspects of far-right populism are not epiphenomenal. Culture as "a web of significance,"[8] consisting of symbols and myths organized into narratives that guide meaning-making in everyday life, has been understood and enlisted as a crucial political instrument by the far right. Culture wars have been decisive in building overall loyalty to far-right populist politics, helping to overshadow economic policies that often actually hurt the average voter. Toppling the liberal cultural hegemony has been a key political goal of far-right populists. This is why a closer look at cultural production affiliated with the political right provides a lens into how culture is exploited as a political resource. It illuminates especially how the nation is restored as the foremost political collective and reimagined as an exclusionary community that draws hard boundaries along ethnic, racial, and gender lines, starkly reversing decades of expanding inclusiveness.

Hungary's relentless rightward trajectory is replete with idiosyncratic elements, but it also offers plenty of general lessons that apply well beyond its borders. In the following discussion, I outline three key mechanisms that emerge from the four case studies discussed in the previous chapters and carry broader relevance. I also highlight examples from other countries suggesting that these mechanisms can serve as analytical starting points for more in-depth comparisons in future research. Such comprehensive comparisons, however, lie beyond the immediate objectives of this book. The three mechanisms my book identifies operate at different scales of generalization. At their most general, they elucidate how cultural production and cultural producers enable the rise of far-right populism by crusading to subvert taken-for-granted liberal cultural canons.

First, I show that, contrary to widespread assumptions according to which authoritarian regimes unilaterally dictate cultural measures from the top,[9] far-right populist governments endorse right-wing grassroots and popular culture, which they elevate into the national cultural canon upon their rise to power. This move serves a dual purpose: it helps to dislodge the perceived and real liberal cultural hegemony while also endowing the government with broad popular support. Hence, the government actions we see in the United States through Trump's seemingly top-down executive orders are not happening in a social vacuum. They have not been cooked up by a reclusive party vanguard but respond to sentiments that have been brewing in society for a long time. The book bans, which have been largely initiated first by pressure groups and local grassroots organizations like Moms for Liberty and have targeted books with LGBTQ+ and racial justice themes, foreshadowed Trump's executive orders on "ending radical indoctrination in public schools" and "gender ideology extremism." The grassroots organizations have also grown into well-funded and organized groups that are now lobbying for state legislation to expand book bans and criminalize librarians, bringing this type of censorship to a new level. Some of these state laws—in Idaho, for instance—demand that "harmful" books be segregated in their own space, which is a big challenge for small public libraries. This mirrors regulations that were passed in Hungary after the *A Fairytale for Everyone* book controversy explored in chapter 2, which require the removal of LGBTQ+-themed books from the children's book section and an extra layer of wrapping in cling film in bookstores.

This mechanism is at play in each of the cultural fields I examined in Hungary. Several authors and books that were zealously promoted by small far-right book publishers, even though they were severely tainted by their past associations with fascism, are "rehabilitated" and canonized by the government through incorporation into the National Core Curriculum for public schools. Folk-inspired fashion is increasingly touted by the new political elite and receives official recognition through high-profile exhibitions and induction into national arts collections (not just ethnographic collections), thereby lifting it into both high culture and the national cultural canon. Officially shunned but popular radical nationalist and irredentist symbols (e.g., Greater Hungary image, runic script) make their way into public schools through the experiential educational framework of the government's heritage tourism campaign. Revisionist and scientifically unsubstantiated ideas about Hungarian ethnogenesis promoted by amateur archeologists and horseback archery enthusiasts are validated by government support and public recognition in the "duplicate," "government-friendly" research institutes set up after 2010. The crackdown on liberal institutions like universities, research institutes, performing arts venues, and West-oriented NGOs in tandem with the establishment of progovernment parallel institutions provide the institutional infrastructure that facilitates the acknowledgment of and state support for right-wing cultural producers' work.

The popular cultural elements of the right are also frequently associated with countercultural currents and movements—not just in Hungary—that have viewed themselves as marginalized by liberal cultural dominance. In the United States, for instance, these would include antiscience activism such as antivaxxers and fringe doctors, or various media platforms and content creators of conspiracy theories. For example, Jack Posobiec, senior editor of the far-right publication *Human Events* and a right-wing activist podcaster, came onto the scene first spreading the Pizzagate conspiracy theory. In the United States, media markets (e.g., the podcast industry) are also more differentiated and extensive and less directly regulated by the national government than in Europe. These media platforms often adopt names to spotlight their countercultural spirit: An important right-wing media outlet in Canada is called "Rebel Media," and Steve Bannon's podcast is named "War Room." Right-wing alternative media are now invited to join the White House Press pool, which they claim they have been marginalized from by liberal legacy media. Far-right governments hope to appropriate some of the rebel chic and antiestablishment cachet of these popular movements to flaunt the disruptive and revolutionary fervor of their politics that purports to usher in a radically new political era.

The second general mechanism that this book pinpoints draws attention to how identity narratives that reimagine the nation circulate in multiple different forms and through multiple different channels. That is, "deep stories"[10] are deep not just because they are told over and over again but because they are embodied and reinforced through different carriers and conduits. Qualitative social science has explored deep stories primarily with the help of interviews, discourse analysis, and ethnographic observations, generally paying less attention to nonverbal forms through which they can be manifested and diffused. My case studies of different cultural fields show that the same narrative can simultaneously surface in multiple forms and shapes.

The Trianon trauma, for instance, which is a narrative essential to the far-right populist reimagining of Hungarian national identity, emerges in revisionist history books printed by far-right publishers, dominates the visual imagery of cross-border heritage tourism for public school students, and shapes the aesthetic repertoire of folk revivalist fashion. Mythical stories about the Central Asian origins of ethnic Hungarians have inspired fiction and "scientific" literature picked up by far-right publishers, contemporary remakes of pre–Conquest era archeological finds, orientalizing attire for horseback archery shows, the nomadic lifestyle concept, as well as jewelry and fashion items. Simultaneously, narratives about communism's responsibility for suppressing patriotic and national sentiments, and for censoring authors (e.g., Albert Wass, Cecile Tormay, József Nyirő), topics (Trianon, revisionist Hungarian origin and pre-Conquest histories, cross-border ethnic Hungarian diasporas), and symbols like the Greater Hungary image or folk fashion motifs permeate each field of cultural production.

The fact that the same narrative crops up and materializes in multiple forms in various fields helps to amplify and deepen these very narratives. And their incarnation in commodity form makes consumer markets a particularly important and potent conduit for the circulation of these narratives. Markets endow cultural producers with agency to disseminate political messages outside the conventional realm of political discourse while providing an infrastructure for effectively spreading these messages. Right-wing cultural producers have in fact relied on markets to pursue a cultural-cum-political mission, viewing the economic rationale of their businesses as subordinate to this higher calling. This attitude also fosters the emergence of politically defined and motivated "circuits of commerce"[11] not just in one field, as we saw in the case of folk-revivalist fashion, but in different fields of cultural production that connect and intersect.

Books by the charismatic founder of the horseback archery movement, Lajos Kassai, for instance, are published by the Püski family press, as are many of the new revisionist histories of the pre-Conquest era that have animated horseback archers. Similarly, the fashion producer Katalin Hampel, who revived the Hungarian dress with its aristocratic flair, published a volume containing her life history interview with the right-wing religious press Kairosz. The joint owners of the Igéző fashion brand pointed to Lajos Kassai as one of their cultural role models. Middle-school students encounter traditional Transylvanian folk fashion on their heritage tours, learning about the folk dress patterns that are revived by several of the fashion brands discussed in chapter 3. Several fashion brands sell their ware at heritage festivals like Kurultáj, which are key meeting points for horseback archers. These connections across fields facilitate the scaling up of these politically committed circuits of commerce, intensifying and expanding their prevalence.

The specific substantive theme of the narratives will, of course, vary greatly across countries, but the general mechanism I have described remains similar. The Conquest-era mythology that reanimates the fierce Hungarian settler spirit in today's horseback archers may at first seem peculiar. But at a closer look, its cultural meaning is not so radically different from the myth of the American West that upholds the frontier spirit as a cornerstone of American exceptionalism. More precisely, right-wing historical identity narratives in Hungary, for instance, revolve around Trianon—that is, fomenting resentment over "unjust" treatment by foreign powers and romanticizing ethnic and cultural supremacy over neighboring countries—around denying responsibility for the Holocaust, and around mythical ethnic origin stories. By comparison, in the United States. they center on white Christian supremacy (traced all the way back to the Doctrine of Discovery, 1493), which is also closely linked to downplaying, and even denying, the legacies of slavery and enduring structural racism, while glorifying the Confederacy and resistance to the Reconstruction in the post–Civil War era. These narratives then elicit attacks against critical narratives, such as the 1619 project by Nikole Hannah-Jones in *The New York Times* or stories of historical injustices against Black people. Donald Trump's ordering of a comprehensive review of all Smithsonian museums to "seek to remove improper ideology"—that is, to correct for an overly "woke" curatorial approach and an "overemphasis" on slavery—exemplifies this backlash.[12]

Such forms of historical revisionism are a staple of far-right politics not just in Hungary or the United States but also in Israel, Turkey, or Poland, where, for instance, a law was passed in 2018 that made it a civil offense to imply any Polish responsibility in the Holocaust.[13] Historical revisionist efforts do not simply intend to "erase history"[14] but actively rewrite it to serve contemporary political agendas, feeding off a powerful mix of popular nostalgia and resentment. Moreover, they are not confined to insular academic and political debates but assume multiple popular incarnations in different cultural fields, as illustrated for Hungary in chapters 4 and 5 of this book.

The first two mechanisms I have described so far both highlight how grassroots right-wing culture gets disseminated, scaled up, validated, and bolstered by the state. The third mechanism is at a lower level of generalization and underscores the importance of far-right populism's geopolitical dimension. It shows that the populist reimagining of the nation often involves significant geopolitical repositioning. As liberalism is closely linked with Western (i.e., North American and Western European) civilizational norms, cultural values, and political governance structures (e.g., electoral democracy), the rejection of liberalism also entails a move away from Western standards and models of a good society. This is how anti-Westernism becomes a defining element of far-right populism in countries that have historically had an ambivalent relationship with the West. This includes countries like Russia or Turkey but even countries in the Global South, such as India, that additionally associate the West with colonial rule.[15] In smaller countries like Hungary, anti-Westernism is fueled by an interstitial geopolitical position between East and West and a recurring experience of betrayal by the West at critical historical turning points (e.g., the end of World War I and II, 1956) when the West "abandoned" mostly Central and Eastern European states in the interest of restoring the global balance of power. The present unfolding of Ukraine's fate in the wake of the 2022 Russian aggression might just be the latest example of this historical pattern.

Cultural producers in these countries activate and recycle identity narratives that give historical depth and cultural resonance to contemporary anti-Westernism—manifested, for instance, in anti-EU attitudes—thus providing symbolic backing to far-right governments' geopolitical reorientation efforts. Chapter 5, on the revival of horseback archery and amateur archeology, offers the broadest range of such narratives for Hungary and its links to the government's "Eastern Opening" project. But chapter 2 also emphasizes how right-wing publishers relentlessly attack pro-Western cultural figures and label them unpatriotic (and sometimes even "deranged," as evidenced in the debates about the required reading list of the National Core Curriculum).

In Russia and Turkey, the same practice of tying pro-Western sentiments to a lack of patriotism is widespread, and both countries have long histories of anti-Western thought and cultural movements manifested in Eurasianism, Turanism, or Neo-Ottomanism.[16] And in the Global South, postcolonial nationalism becomes increasingly tied to anti-Western illiberalism.[17] Geopolitical repositioning also always sharpens political and cultural awareness of territorial borders and movements across them, which is illustrated, for instance, by how heritage tourism becomes a way to promote symbolic irredentism in Hungary. A renewed sensitivity to borders combined with imperial nostalgia can even escalate into outright territorial revisionism, as confirmed by Russia's and Turkey's aggressive foreign policy and military interventions.[18] Now, however, with the United States electing a far-right populist government, it remains to be seen how this turn of events will be reconciled with the strong anti-Western narratives in existing far-right regimes.

New Right political theories, discussed in the introductory chapter, pointed to intellectuals as the main champions of a new illiberal cultural hegemony.[19] But this book demonstrates that cultural producers more broadly play a central role in these political ecologies. They create cultural objects—often in commodity form—that adapt, reproduce, package, and circulate identity narratives. They act as the "cultural warriors" or "organic intellectuals" of the right to question the hegemonic liberal cultural frames and provide alternatives.[20] In today's politics, in which truth and facts no longer seem to matter and controlling the narrative is everything, cultural producers as experts at constructing narratives might have a particularly important competitive political edge.

The sociological study of cultural production has focused on how tastes are stratified by social class, following the direction set out by Pierre Bourdieu's seminal work and more recently extended to include closer attention to how class stratification interacts with race and gender.[21] But the Hungarian case illuminates that cultural tastes are also stratified by political worldviews, something that is becoming increasingly apparent in today's politically polarized environment. Cultural tastes are split between liberal and illiberal, progressive and traditionalist, pro-Western and anti-Western, or along urbanist and populist lines in Hungary. The stirring up of culture wars aims to expose the classification struggle over terms and forms of representation and turn it into an open Gramscian struggle for cultural hegemony. This book thus also hopes to motivate further research on the political stratification of tastes to help us understand why we find ourselves in such a starkly polarized and deeply antagonistic world.

Epilogue

On April 12, 2026, as this book was going to the press, Viktor Orbán and his party, Fidesz, suffered a devastating loss in the Hungarian national elections. At a record-high, 80 percent voter turnout, a new party, Tisza achieved a spectacular two-thirds victory. Orbán conceded with remarkable swiftness and the Danube embankment, with the Hungarian Parliament as dramatic backdrop, became the scene of euphoric street celebrations, especially by young people.

Ironically, Péter Magyar and his Tisza party triumphed in the elections with a populist message that rallied the Hungarian people against the Orbán regime's corrupt elite, tirelessly exposing the staggering corruption of Fidesz politicians, state officials, and the shady business oligarchs they helped to enrich—much like Orbán did in 2010 against the socialist government. But those who expect a frictionless return to Western-style liberalism will likely be disappointed. The new Parliament will be the first since postcommunist Hungary's inaugural democratic elections in 1990 that will include no party with a liberal or leftist program. Each of the three parties that will take up seats in the Parliament—the center-right Tisza, the remnants of the far-right Fidesz, and the extreme-right Our Homeland Movement—falls right of center on the political spectrum.

Péter Magyar is no poster boy of liberalism and social progressivism. When the Fidesz government banned the Budapest Pride March in the summer of 2025, he remained silent. His opposition to immigration is as rock solid as Orbán's. His political integrity is tainted by his long years of embeddedness in the Fidesz elite's inner circle as member of the Fidesz delegation in Brussels and the husband of a former justice minister. His campaign relied heavily on national symbols, at times smacking of ethnonational overtones. He delivered political speeches on the March 15 national holiday in a Bocskai jacket—something Orbán never wore—and marched around the ethnic Hungarian areas of Transylvania, Romania in a richly folk-embroidered vest, the political symbolism of which was examined in chapter 3.

It is with respect to Hungary's geopolitical orientation that he has promised the biggest break from the Orbán era, turning Hungary's East-West pendulum—discussed in chapter 5—back to the West, ending constant feuding with the European Union. But just how far the pendulum will swing back to the West remains to be seen.

And the tentacles of the Orbán regime reach deep into the economic, social, and cultural infrastructure of Hungarian society. A parliamentary supermajority can help to effectively dismantle these old structures but not without potential pitfalls. There is strong demand from voters for political purges in every domain and readiness on Tisza's part to meet these expectations. Such purges will, however, reinforce a polarized culture-war mindset, eventually generating resentment and a backlash—sentiments that were fueling many of the far-right cultural warriors in the Orbán era.

While Orbán's far-right populist regime is clearly over, populism remains alive and well across the globe from the United States, France, Germany, and Italy to India and Argentina, as the world uneasily awaits the 2026 midterm elections in the United States.

Methodological Appendix

My foray into radical nationalist cultural production began when I was studying "uncivil" society in Hungary in the early 2000s. I was mapping the rise of right-wing civil society organizations that significantly contributed to the spread of far-right populism in Hungary.[1] The webpages of many of these organizations were informative because they helped to situate these groups in a larger social network of like-minded organizations and actors, as almost all of them included a section on their webpage with internet links to "our friends." Among these links, I noticed many websites that were selling consumer items, including specialized books, maps, music, clothing and accessories, home décor, and other miscellaneous right-wing paraphernalia displaying radical nationalist symbols (e.g., Greater Hungary, runic script, irredentist slogans such as a popular T-shirt with the text "I'm older than Slovakia") that were rarely seen before in the public sphere and could not be openly used in mainstream political discourse due to their highly tabooed status.

By following these links, it became clear that there was a sizable and diverse culture industry that catered to a growing right-wing, radical nationalist populist subculture. I became interested in how cultural producers helped materialize radical nationalist ideas and increase their visibility by using the commodity form and markets to broadly circulate them, enabling sympathizers to expressly represent themselves as members of these loosely knit subcultural communities. It also felt that blurring the boundaries between political, economic, and cultural messages was an essential feature of both right-wing civil society groups and related culture industry players.

For a while I toyed with the idea of focusing on just one area of cultural production, preferably fashion or music, as these were the most frequently researched fields in longstanding scholarship on extremist youth cultures.[2] But I wanted to show that even though radical nationalist consumer culture in the era of far-right populism shared similarities with earlier consumer subcultures, it was not simply a variant of extremist youth subcultures, and it was integral to how populist politics mobilized cultural resources to reimagine the postliberal—i.e., the ultimately illiberal—nation and generate new cultural identities. This is why I decided to select several different, but at the same time representative, sites of cultural production, which could demonstrate that although they were not perfectly overlapping "circuits of commerce," they intersected in multiple ways, which facilitated the scaling up of their reach and impact.[3] Opting for four case studies that appeared particularly consequential based on my preliminary research—fashion, book publishing, heritage tourism, and horseback archery—certainly extended the empirical and conceptual scope of my research but also made the project more time-consuming and challenging from a methodological point of view.

The Challenges of Internalist Research into Far-Right Politics

Given that I had to tackle four quite different empirical domains, an ethnographic approach that would have been the most befitting method of choice for an "internalist" perspective that centers on insiders' understandings—on the "native's point of view"—was not really a feasible option. It has also generally been true that despite the rapid growth of far-right (extremist and radical) political activity in recent decades, ethnographic research that builds on intense and long-term engagement, participant observation of routine activities and events, face-to-face conversations, and interviews with members of these groups and movements has remained scarce.[4] The study of far-right movements has been dominated by an "externalist" approach that focuses on the "economic, social, attitudinal, or cultural environments that nurture organized racism and right-wing extremism rather than the dynamics of the far right itself."[5]

Difficulty of access is most often cited as the reason for the dearth of internalist research into far-right politics. The fact, however, that simultaneously there is a relatively copious amount of ethnographic research on dangerous organizations and milieus such as street gangs, drug users, or crime-ridden neighborhoods suggests additional reasons for the lacuna.[6] Lack of access does not only follow from potential threats of violence from such groups and other serious safety risks,[7] but from a more profound lack of interest in and moral ambivalence over closely engaging with the internal life of far-right political organizations.

Anthropologists and sociologists who most frequently embark on internalist research have had a strong preference for studying political movements and activism that pursue left-wing and progressive objectives that academics tend to more readily identify with. The personal rejection of right-wing politics almost requires disengagement from these actors who are portrayed as pernicious and even abhorrent, and researchers are accused of increasing the visibility of these groups by studying and publishing about them.[8] In fact, I, myself, have been criticized and questioned about my ethical stance along these lines when I, for instance, presented material from chapter 4 on heritage tourism at invited academic talks in Europe.

Engagement with far-right milieus is seen as justified mostly when it is undertaken from an activist perspective, which introduces another set of problems into the research process. Researchers driven by political activism chiefly aim to expose the harmfulness of the far-right groups they study and possibly undermine them, which can seriously limit research potential and yield awkward results.[9] Activist research agendas, while well-intentioned, run the risk of reducing far-right actors to one-dimensional stereotypes and oversimplifying their intentions, motivations, and experiences. This is a dilemma that researchers have frequently dealt with by either completely concealing their intentions from their subjects or eschewing direct interactions with insiders.[10] While I am not naïve about the possibilities of objective social science, I tried to devise research strategies for my project to avoid these traps.

As mentioned earlier, encompassing four areas of cultural production made the use of conventional ethnography—"deep hanging out" in the Geertzian sense[11]—impossible, so my fieldwork had to build on a careful mix of qualitative methods and data sources. Interviews with cultural producers were combined with ethnographic visits to events (festivals, fairs, exhibitions, guided tours, store visits, book talks, and panel discussions) and analysis of diverse media sources (print and social media) central to the respective fields of cultural production. The selection of interviewees and the nature of specific events and media are detailed in the individual chapters. To make the interviews more informative, I always tried to conduct them in an ethnographic context. I asked interviewees to pick the location for the interview and explain during the interview why it was meaningful to them. In most cases I conducted interviews in the ateliers, studios, stores, or workplaces of fashion producers and book publishers, in the outdoor camps of horseback archers, occasionally in the subject's private homes, or at major events, primarily festivals and fairs, that they regularly participated in.

Fieldwork was conducted in the summer months between 2017 and 2023. This somewhat protracted time schedule allowed me to repeatedly participate in major events that take place regularly every year, such as the Kurultáj festival for horseback archers or the major arts and crafts fair, the Festival of Folk Arts (Mesterségek Ünnepe), that is part of the annual August 20 national holiday celebrations. The repeat visits to these events helped to make my findings more robust. Overall, I conducted forty-eight interviews and made over three dozen visits to various events; many of the ethnographic visits involved extensive travel within Hungary, including some quite remote locations. Interviews were transcribed and analyzed in Atlas.ti and then triangulated with data from ethnographic observations and media sources, following inductive grounded theory principles.[12]

Walking a Fine Line: Interviewing People Whose Views Clash with Our Own

My self-presentation to prospective interviewees required careful consideration and reflection on how my social and cultural background would be most likely to influence the interviews and what responses it would elicit from my subjects, considering the challenges of internalist research on far-right political actors. I was always transparent about my professional identity, institutional affiliation, and research intent, but not always completely forthcoming about finer details (e.g., my political convictions) unless I was explicitly asked to talk about them, which never really happened.

Being a native Hungarian speaker from a US university created a fundamental ambiguity about who I was, which I tried to cultivate because it made participants think that I did not have an immediate stake in what was going on in Hungary, allowing them to talk more freely. My background as a Hungarian living in the United States with interests in Hungarian culture and events possibly made some of them think that I was part of the Hungarian immigrant diaspora in the United States, which is an important constituency of far-right Hungarian politics and a significant consumer base for Hungarian nationalist cultural products, as I explain in chapters 2 and 3. My general impression was that interviewees agreed to participate in my research because, based on their assumptions about my background and interest in their work, they were convinced that politically and culturally we were "on the same side" and that I wanted to study them because I agreed with their cultural agendas. They seemed to take this assumption for granted and did not probe me further or do background checks on my affiliation and research activity. So, in some way I benefited from a social homophily assumption suggesting that we are primarily interested in studying people who are similar to us. And it is true for Hungary, too, that liberal scholars do not seriously engage in systematic "internalist" empirical research about far-right groups.[13] The reaction from interviewees was also not a product of significant response bias because 90 percent of those I approached for an interview agreed to participate. The rest usually did not respond at all to my initial query, or the interview fell through because of scheduling difficulties.

There was only one occasion when I felt that I was "found out" and some doubt was cast over my identity, politics, and research purpose. I traveled to a picturesque but remote village in western Hungary to interview a horseback archer, a member of the Kassai School (chapter 5). The interview took place in the archer's family home which was located on a sizable estate that housed the horses and hosted their training. Their grounds have also served for years as a site of an annual summer workshop for foreign artists who are interested in thematizing horses in their work. The artists normally live in a nomadic yurt erected on the grounds, and their activities also involve an introduction to horseback archery.

This interview occurred in the middle of a summer heatwave. Because of the remoteness of the location I had to wait hours after my interview to catch a bus, so I asked the host if I could stay a little longer inside their home since there was no shelter from the scorching heat in the only roadside bus stop in the village. He generously let me stay. While waiting in the living room, his wife—a fine artist and also an active horseback archer—arrived home, and we struck up an informal conversation about my research. When she learned that I was affiliated with the New School, she mentioned that a while ago she spent a few months as a university exchange student in New York and that she thought the New School was a "very liberal, leftist institution," so she figured I probably think that horseback archery is quite nationalistic. Luckily, she left no time for me to respond but jumped right into an explanation for why it was not true that horseback archers were nationalistic. She asserted, for instance, that they only celebrated Hungarians' superior achievements, without simultaneously looking down on representatives of other nations.

This episode made it clear that my interviews would have played out quite differently if the interviewees had had more contextual knowledge about where I was coming from and what my published work was about. This was an exception, however, and no other interviewee was familiar with the New School, which is not a well-known institution in Hungary, particularly in conservative and right-wing circles. The interviewees generally either did not have the time or were not interested in looking up who I was, likely because of the tacit assumptions outlined here.

In my initial introduction to potential subjects and in the interview itself, I defined national cultural heritage as the focal point of the conversation. Besides using the trajectory of the interviewees' businesses as a general frame for the interview, I asked questions about their relationship to national cultural heritage, how they defined it, what made cultural heritage "national," and how this was reflected in their work as cultural producers. Did they intend to preserve, protect, or reinvent cultural heritage? Why did this matter to them, and why did they think it mattered to their customers? How did they find their customers, and who were they? Did they see their work as a business venture or as a cultural and/or political mission? How was their quest made easy or difficult under different political regimes and governments? By centering the interview on meanings and uses of national cultural heritage, I felt that I could more effectively elicit my subjects' views and narratives about changing conceptions of national belonging and the political implications thereof without tendentiously overpoliticizing the conversation, thus pressuring interviewees to talk about "their politics."

My concern with research that tends to confront interview subjects directly and assertively with questions about nationalism and right-wing political sympathies is that it usually yields unsurprising and noninsightful results. Interviewees—especially those who are not members of explicitly political organizations—can easily feel provoked. They also usually treat those questions as narrowly related to political party affiliations and electoral politics. Seeing how far-right populism aims to use culture as the Trojan horse of politics to combat and overcome liberalism, moving beyond a narrow understanding of the political as merely electoral and party politics seemed essential for my research.

Nevertheless, just like in the process of approaching subjects for an interview, I had to prepare for reacting to certain political and cultural statements that I strongly disagreed with during the interviews. In handling these situations, I was trying to preserve my ethical integrity without slipping into an activist mode and starting to argue with the subjects. Even though it was hard at times to restrain myself, I wanted to avoid turning the interview into a debate in which I tried to point out to the subjects how wrong they were. My main objective was to discern the subjects' worldviews and motivations even if they vastly diverged from my own.

The interviewees rarely made openly racist, xenophobic, or homophobic statements—which doesn't necessarily preclude that they espoused such views—but they did say things at times that I found politically and culturally unpalatable. In such cases, I did not egg them on or fake that I agreed with them, but I also did not express my disagreement. When possible, I tried to insert follow-up questions to dig deeper, but without revealing what I personally thought about the issues at hand. These situations felt a bit like a major holiday dinner with a large extended family when we try to have a conversation with a relative whom we only see at such events and who holds diametrically opposing views without blowing up the festivities. To reiterate, I decided to bottle up my own political convictions as much as possible and maintain ambiguity about my cultural (Hungarian-American) identity because I felt this was the best methodological strategy to elicit frank and uninhibited responses from interviewees, and not because I felt awkward about disagreeing with them on fundamental matters.

My use of mixed qualitative methods could not parallel the immersive depth of a full-blown ethnography, but it still has some advantages over an ethnographic approach. Ethnographies of far-right politics, for instance, tend to overemphasize the "groupness" of far-right supporters. Ethnographers usually embed themselves with activist groups and organizations, and this is largely why their findings suggest that adherents of far-right populist views are members of such clearly bounded groups. Until recently, far right ethnographies also centered on extremist groups (e.g., Ku Klux Klan, neo-Nazi groups, skinheads) as a largely fringe phenomenon, and this is partly why these studies sometimes exoticize their subjects and their environments in a way that is akin to academic ethnographies of hard-to-access, marginalized groups.[14]

By contrast, my approach shows that far-right populism constitutes a much more diffuse universe. The focus on cultural producers from different fields does not only extend the empirical scope of populist political activities but shows how various fields intersect and make up a loosely connected network. Similarly, it highlights a broader range of possible forms of engagement with populism than just affiliation with far-right organizations and movements. Consumer communities are "imagined communities" that do not require organizational membership or sustained face-to-face interaction. They also allow for various modalities and intensities of involvement. One can be, for instance, a committed member of a horseback archery sports club, participating in trainings and competitions while others might also adopt the nomadic lifestyle concept they propagate, but others can be more distant fans who attend horse shows and festivals merely as spectators. Cultural producers themselves are also not necessarily hardcore political activists, although even at the very minimum they are important enablers of populist propaganda through the narratives they disseminate with their products. My approach in general is also less likely to exoticize research subjects. In fact, the most disquieting aspect of my research was to realize how "normal" and "next door-neighbor-like" most of my subjects were—aside from the Whiskey Robber.[15]

Navigating the Labyrinthine Politics of FOIA Requests

Chapter 4, on heritage tourism, builds on a data source that deviates somewhat from the other chapters. Originally, I planned to follow the same strategy as for the other case studies and interview business owners who specialized in heritage tours to former Hungarian areas of neighboring countries. But then I learned about the *Határtalanul* program, in which the state brings heritage tourism to middle-school students and which promised to be an excellent case study within a case study, particularly as it became evident during my research that public schools constitute an important battleground for populist politics. Capturing the hearts and minds of new generations is a clear priority for the Orbán regime.

Since the program was sponsored by taxpayers, I theoretically had a right to access data compiled about the trips by the relevant public agency. I formally contacted the state official in charge at the Ministry for Human Resources, which was overseeing the program at the time. I did not have high hopes that the official would respond, but I thought it was worth a try. To my surprise, I received a timely response and was referred to the person running the program. I met this person at the ministry and received a surprisingly warm welcome. I was allowed to look into the data right away on this first visit, to be able to narrow down what exactly I needed.

It was when I told the program director that I needed copies of the data base that contained summary information about all the trips and was also going to need the full dossiers for specific trips after I selected a random representative sample from the overall pool that the troubles began. At this point, it turned out that I had to make a formal Freedom of Information Act (FOIA) request to the ministry to obtain the data. It is important to note here that by 2017, when I was making this inquiry, FOIA requests in Hungary had become highly politicized. This instrument was not widely used before Fidesz's return to power, but after 2010 it became a major tool for investigative journalists and various activists to expose and combat corruption, as well as the government's general lack of transparency and accountability.

Yet, government institutions were quick to adjust to these challenges and swiftly invented a series of little technical and legal tricks to delay and derail

FOIA inquiries. For instance, from 2015 onward, institutions started charging petitioners hefty fees for the "extra labor" demanded from government employees to prepare materials for FOIA requests (e.g., locating, retrieving, and photocopying relevant documents). Sometimes these charges were so flagrantly high that this prevented petitioners from getting the data. Questioning unreasonable charges, rejections, and slow response times required filing a legal complaint, which could only be settled in a lengthy court procedure. And then Covid and the Russian invasion of Ukraine brought about further restrictions because they enabled the government to declare, and repeatedly reinstate, a state of emergency.

After I filed my FOIA request for the summary database on the total of 2,374 school trips, I had to wait only a few weeks to get the data file through official channels. But instead of sending me the original Excel file that I worked with on my visit to the ministry, they converted this master file into a pdf document. One or two columns did not even properly convert, which made them useless for my purposes. I chalked this off to being one of the tricks they used to sabotage FOIA requests, although I cannot completely rule out that it was just incompetence. I contacted the program director, who agreed that this was a problem, and that given that my request was formally approved, they would be willing to send me the right file directly, even though this violated official procedures somewhat—namely, after an FOIA request is filed, all communication and document exchange should occur through the legal department.

After reviewing the summary file and selecting a random sample of 120 class trips (see chapter 4 for data and selection strategy), I submitted another FOIA request for the full dossiers of the selected trips. I received no response for months. I tried to contact the program director and learned that the person was now working for a different program on cross-border ethnic Hungarians but was still in the same department so would check on the status of my request. A couple of days later, I got a call asking if I could come into the ministry the following day—the person would get the requested dossiers delivered by then, given that my earlier FOIA request was actually approved for these materials. The following day I was shepherded into the office of an employee at the Ministry of Human Resources who was on sick leave, and my dossiers were piled up on a cart in the room. The dossiers had plentiful contents in mixed media, including printed program questionnaires, handwritten student essays and drawings, CDs with videos and photographs from the trip, countless invoices, and newspaper clippings (see chapter 4), so it took quite a while to work through them.

One day while I was working at the ministry, my "mentor"—the former program director—stormed into the office and told me to pack up immediately and leave the building. I was told I would get a call about when I could return. I was dumbfounded by all the secrecy and drama, as I believed I was operating within the bounds of existing rules. The reason I had to flee was a raid by a personnel inspector. Apparently, government ministries conduct random personnel checks in their buildings. An official can show up unannounced to inspect whether everyone who is supposed to be working in the building is in fact there, and, simultaneously, that there are no unauthorized people (who are not staff members) on the premises. I returned the next day and continued my work uninterrupted until I went through all the dossiers, but after the raid my file-copying activities acquired a bit of a communist era samizdat vibe.

The difference the support of a ministry insider makes, however, became soberingly clear a few years later when I tried to obtain some missing data. The reporting process for the trips can be very drawn out. Often there is a long back-and-forth between the ministry and the school over missing materials—invoices, proofs of delayed media appearances, post-trip follow-up activities, and so forth—so in some cases it might take almost two years to approve the report and close the dossier. This is why when I conducted my "undercover" operation in 2018, there were still some selected 2016 dossiers missing. I tried to petition these files in 2020, only to encounter insurmountable obstacles.

As Covid descended, the Hungarian Parliament approved state-of-emergency measures that had important implications for FOIA requests. FOIA materials can be acquired as copies prepared and delivered by the respective government agency, or petitioners have the right to access requested documents in person on site. In my case, the latter option was crucial because of the eclectic nature of the dossier contents, many of which could not be easily copied. The state-of-emergency declaration eliminated the in-person option, which was justified as a Covid safety measure. Interestingly, when the state of emergency was renewed in the wake of the Russian aggression in Ukraine, it remained unexplained why the ban on in-person document viewing remained in effect, but it did. I no longer had an insider contact because my "mentor" no longer worked in this policy area, and meanwhile oversight of the program was transferred to a state-owned non-profit foundation. I could not get beyond the legal department this time. My last FOIA request yielded some copies of documents that clearly amounted to a small fraction of the materials in the dossiers. My complaints about the incompleteness of the received files remained unanswered. I even consulted a lawyer specializing in FOIA cases but was discouraged by how long the court process might take.

Overall, I am still not sure why the original program director went to such lengths to help me. There was no informal connection between us that would have explained such transgressions on their part, and they also did not strike me as a political dissident who was hoping to undermine the Orbán regime from within. The program director struck me as a professional career bureaucrat who specialized in working on cross-border ethnic Hungarian diaspora projects and did not give much thought to the political implications of the work. But I would clearly not have been able to write chapter 4, analyzing an important piece of how populist propaganda operates in public schools, without this person's help, even though as a Hungarian citizen I was legally entitled to access these materials.

Weighing Questions of Anonymity

There are competing views in qualitative social research about how best to protect research subjects and what level of anonymity to grant them. There are those who consider guaranteeing full anonymity to all informants as a bare minimum, firmly distancing themselves from ethically tainted and exploitative research that marred some past ethnographic research in anthropology and sociology. Others, although remaining a minority, argue that protecting subjects from harm is possible even when using their real names.[16] A trend I see among my PhD advisees is to go for full anonymity because this is the fastest way to attain Institutional Review Board (IRB) approval for their dissertation research without seriously considering the pros and cons of such an approach. IRB regulations also differ across countries, so the standards for comparative research are more complicated and variable.

In the case of my research, fully anonymizing my subjects would have been virtually impossible. In the field of cultural production in a small country like Hungary, key players usually all know each other, or of each other, and the populist, radical nationalist niche is highly distinctive and interconnected. It would be hard to describe the work of the fashion producers or book publishers I interviewed if I wanted to make them fully unrecognizable. For instance, I would not have been able to use any images in the chapter on fashion because the brand would have been immediately recognizable. Similarly, mentioning a specific book gives away the name of the publisher.

Or talking about the incorporation of controversial books into the National Core Curriculum without mentioning specific works that can easily be linked to publishers would be impractical. And these are all small businesses, so once the name of the fashion brand or the publisher is known, the owners are easily traceable. This is how I located my interviewees in the first place.

But, most important, I opted for using the real names of my subjects—except in cases where I was explicitly requested not to do this—because most of them also have had a public persona. They have often talked publicly about issues I interviewed them about, openly airing views that they shared with me. They also have not engaged in illegal or unconstitutional activities that could be linked to them through my research. Of course, when I felt that somebody could be compromised in their private or professional lives, I made sure to maintain their anonymity. This is why I don't reveal any details about the person who helped me to get access to the *Határtalanul* files for the heritage tourism case study. I also did not use the real names of "ordinary" actors who have no public persona, like some members of horseback archery clubs quoted in chapter 5.

Finally, as a historical sociologist I was always a bit puzzled by excessive anonymization because I have considered my research to eventually become the historical imprint of an era. I use the real names of the actors, brands, publishers, and businesses to truthfully—as much as this is possible—document the actors, events, practices, and processes that are key to understanding the cultural dynamics of far-right populism in early twenty-first-century Hungary and beyond.

NOTES

Chapter 1. Introduction

1. There is an award-winning book by Julian Rubinstein (2004) that narrates his story to an English-speaking audience. The film rights to the book were originally acquired by Johnny Depp, though he ended up not producing the film after all. There is also an audio cabaret version of the book featuring actors and literary figures such as Eric Bogosian, Gary Shteyngart, and Demetri Martin.

2. The Hungarian movie version was released in November 2017. It was written and directed by Antal Nimród, known for his Hungarian art-house classic *Kontroll*, about subway ticket controllers, and for the big-budget Hollywood movies *Predators* and *Vacancy*.

3. Rubinstein 2004.

4. See an extended discussion in the methodological appendix.

5. For the United States, see, for instance, Hochschild 2024.

6. Szombati 2018.

7. Hochschild 2016. Hochschild continues this journey to eastern Kentucky, an area of rural Appalachia, in her book *Stolen Pride* (2024) to probe how a once-centrist district came to embrace Donald Trump's politics and why white, blue-collar workers are trapped in a "pride paradox" that feeds cultural and political resentment.

8. See also Blee 2003, 2007.

9. See, for instance, Arato and Cohen 2022; Mudde 2019; Mudde and Kaltwasser 2017; Müller 2016; Norris and Ingelhart 2019; Rydgren 2006; Urbinati 2019. Even research that recognizes cultural polarization between social liberals and social conservatives as a driving force behind populism usually limits its attention to how these value differences translate into electoral support for populist parties (Norris and Ingelhart 2019).

10. Beaman 2016.

11. Trump 2024.

12. Berezin 2021.

13. Rosenthal 2020: 2.

14. Rosenthal 2020.

15. Wodak 2015.

16. Studies have noted, for instance, the parallels between Trump's and Orbán's electoral trajectories, making a comeback after a lost election more determined than ever to hold onto power; the mobilization of right-wing civil society; or the deconstruction of parliamentary democracy through legal means (Mudde 2022; Scheppele 2013).

17. Berezin 2021; Bonikowski and DiMaggio 2016.

18. Ignatieff 1993.

19. Fukuyama 1992.

20. Berezin 2021: 241.

21. Benedict Anderson (2006 [1983]: 141) also noted this tendency: "In an age when it is so common for progressive, cosmopolitan intellectuals (particularly in Europe?) to insist on the

near-pathological character of nationalism, its roots in fear and hatred of the Other, and its affinities with racism, it is useful to remind ourselves that nations inspire love, and often profoundly self-sacrificing love. The cultural products of nationalism—poetry, prose fiction, music, plastic arts—show this love very clearly in thousands of different forms and styles."

22. Bonikowski 2016: 429–30.

23. See, for instance, Billig 1995; Brubaker et al. 2006; Edensor 2002; Fox and Miller-Idriss 2008; Löfgren 1989.

24. Anderson 2006 [1983]: 6.

25. Anderson 2006 [1983]: 42–43.

26. Anderson 2006 [1983]: 34.

27. Banks 2024; Bourdieu 1984; Peterson and Anand 2004.

28. See, for instance, Levitt 2015; Rivera 2008.

29. See, for instance, Adams 2010.

30. Peterson and Anand 2004.

31. For recent examples of this approach, see Childress 2017.

32. For a similar analytical framework, see Lamont and Molnár 2001.

33. Lamont and Molnár 2002; Molnár 2017.

34. Molnár 2021.

35. Helleiner 2002; Helleiner and Pickel 2005; List 1885.

36. Goff 2005. Similar cases are also discussed by DeSoucey (2010) for foie gras in France and by Bowen and Gaytán (2012) for tequila in Mexico.

37. Portes and Manning 2005; Waldinger 1993.

38. Comaroff and Comaroff 2009.

39. See, for instance, Aronczyk 2013, 2019; Bandelj and Wherry 2011; Castello and Mihelj 2018; Kaneva 2011; Kania-Lundholm 2014; Koch 2020; Rivera 2008.

40. The state can, however, contribute to enabling and sustaining these niche markets after far-right parties attain political power, as I will demonstrate for Hungary in the following chapters.

41. Comaroff and Comaroff 2009.

42. Zelizer 2010.

43. See, for instance, Bennett 2011; Hebdige 1979; McKay and Goddard 2009.

44. Clarke et al. 2011.

45. Gaugele 2019; Miller-Idriss 2018; Pilkington et al. 2010; Ventsel 2022.

46. Pasieka 2024; Schwenck 2023.

47. See also Molnár 2017.

48. Zelizer 2010.

49. Bourdieu 1985.

50. Culture wars originated from the German *Kulturkampf* that began in the 1870s between the Catholic Church in Germany and the Prussian state, broadly concerning the separation of church and state. Later, culture wars have come to denote political and public debates that were animated by deep cultural fissures in society. In the United States, culture wars have primarily referred to consecutive waves of conflict between religious social conservatives and secular social progressives. In Hungary, even the culture section of a signature far-right weekly paper, *barikád*, that ran from 2009 to 2017 was titled *kultúr(h)arc* (culture war), underscoring the prevalence of a culture war mindset in contemporary politics.

51. Morrison 1988: 132.

52. Williams 2022.

53. Hunter 1991; Stanton 2021; Zimmerman 2022 [2002].

54. Hunter in Stanton 2021.

55. The Florida-based liberal arts college New College offers one of the most striking examples for these attacks, thanks to the ideological takeover of the school through the appointment of new trustees by the state's governor, Ron DeSantis (Young 2023).

56. de Benoist 2017.

57. Bures 2020; Bar-On 2021.

58. Burawoy 2019: 65; Gramsci 1971.

59. This interestingly contrasts with Bourdieu's theory about cultural domination, which is more widely applied in cultural sociology. Bourdieu argues that the cultural realm conceals the class stratification that underlies it. So, while for Gramsci culture is also the subject and object of class struggle, for Bourdieu it "dissipates class struggle" and is defined by a classification struggle over terms and forms of representation (Burawoy 2019: 66).

60. Bures 2020: 34.

61. Bar-On 2021.

62. Spektorowski 2003.

63. Bures 2023.

64. Bures 2023:18.

65. Moltke 2022.

66. Moltke 2022: 156. "Great replacement" was popularized by Renaud Camus in his 2011 book, *Le Grand Remplacement*, stating that ethnic French and white European populations are being replaced by nonwhite people, dominantly from Muslim countries, through mass migration and long-term demographic changes. This conspiracy theory has found growing support in Europe among anti-immigrant and white nationalist movements.

67. Gorski and Perry 2022; Moltke 2022.

68. Camus 2019.

69. In his teenage years, Békés was also a member of a Skinhead group Savaria Skins in his hometown in Szombathely.

70. Schmidt inherited (with her two children) her husband's real estate firm when he, a sociologist turned real estate mogul, died suddenly of a heart attack at age fifty-three in 2006. Mária Schmidt was listed twenty-first among the top one hundred richest Hungarians in 2024. As a historian, Schmidt has promoted a controversial, revisionist history of the Holocaust.

71. Békés published a sequel in 2025 under the title *National Maximum*, mainly just reiterating the message of the first book.

72. Békés 2023.

73. This is the same event at which his speech about the illiberal state was delivered in 2014.

74. Cited in Békés 2023: 2.

75. Békés 2020: 10.

76. Békés 2020: 88.

77. Békés 2020: 79.

78. Békés 2020: 105. What is understood by "culture" in the theories of the New Right remains diffuse, and the Hungarian interpretation illustrates this effectively. Békés offers definitions of culture, but they vary greatly throughout the book. At times, it refers to the culture industry (mainly different types of media) and cultural and educational institutions, and at other times, it denotes material culture, political culture, ideas, narratives, customs, symbols, behavior, traditions and heritage, collective myths and memory, discursive and cognitive dispositions, and even cultural capital (drawing directly on Bourdieu). Although generally vague and sprawling, these notions still cohere around a Durkheimean view of culture as critical to collective consciousness, to strengthening and emotionally deepening collective identities—first and foremost national identity in this case.

79. Békés 2023.

80. Orbán's crackdown on Hungarian universities has had a particular appeal to the Trump administration. J. D. Vance referenced it in several of his campaign speeches and media interviews as the model to follow in the United States as well. Similarly, Ron DeSantis's attacks on the public university system in Florida (e.g., his assault on New College of Florida, interventions into curricula targeting gender studies and sociology, political appointments of trustees) have been inspired by Orbán's tactics in Hungary (Stanley 2024: 125–27).

81. Békés 2020: 133–35.

82. Publishers like Antaios Verlag, research institutes like the Institut für Staatspolitik, and journals including *Sezession*, *Cicero*, *Junge Freiheit*, and *Criticón* (Göppfarth 2020; Moltke 2022; Moltke and Komfort-Hein 2024).

83. Békés 2020: 139.

84. Békés 2020: 389–90.

85. Hochschild 2016, 2024; see also Gorski and Perry 2021: 3–5, on white Christian nationalism.

86. It triumphed as Cambridge University Press's Word of the Year in 2017 (Rosenthal 2020).

87. See, for instance, Mudde 2004; Müller 2016; Norris and Ingelhart 2019.

88. Mudde 2004.

89. Mudde 2004: 543.

90. Mudde 2004.

91. Henley 2024.

92. Mudde 2019.

93. Henley 2024.

94. See, for instance, Finchelstein 2022, 2024; Snyder 2017; Stanley 2018, 2024; Ziblatt and Levitsky 2018.

95. Stanley 2024: xiii.

96. Stanley 2024.

97. Hochschild 2016, 2024.

98. Rosenthal 2020; Stanley 2024.

99. Hollander 2019; Sedgwick 2019.

100. Hollander 2019.

101. Rosenthal 2020: 110.

102. Laruelle 2022.

103. Sajó, Uitz, and Holmes 2021.

104. Zakaria 1997.

105. Laruelle 2022: 306.

106. Krekó and Enyedi 2018.

107. Paksa 2012. For preference for the term radical right in general, see also Sedgwick (2019), and for Scandinavia, see Teitelbaum (2017).

108. The extreme right rejects essential elements of democracy, such as majority rule and popular sovereignty, whereas the radical right accepts these basics while questioning the liberal aspects of democracy, including rule of law, minority rule, and separation of powers (Mudde 2019).

109. PEN 2025.

110. Békés 2023; de Benoist 2017.

111. Albert Wass, a best-selling Transylvanian novelist, was condemned as a war criminal by a Romanian Tribunal in 1946, and Cécile Tormay was a well-known anti-Semite, admirer of Mussolini, and right-wing activist, while also being a feminist, in the interwar period.

112. Kubik 1994.

113. See, for instance, Miller-Idriss 2018.

114. The Treaty of Trianon, signed on June 4, 1920, was the formal peace agreement that ended World War I for Hungary. It reduced Hungary's territory to one-third of its pre–World War I size and halved its population. Nearly one-third of all ethnic Hungarians were stranded beyond the new borders of Hungary in neighboring countries. Revisionist claims in the interwar period were largely responsible for Hungary entering World War II as a German ally. The post-1920 borders and status of diaspora Hungarians have continued to cause political tension with neighboring countries and serve as a source of deep resentment for many Hungarians.

115. Taylor 2021.

116. The data included summary information about 2,374 class trips and 120 detailed school reports (travel itineraries and explanations, student travel diaries, photographs, video recordings documenting the trip, local media coverage of the trips).

Chapter 2. Books as Weapons of Culture Wars

1. Szakács and Bayer 2019: 10–11.

2. Szakács and Bayer 2019: 11.

3. Szakács and Bayer 2019: 11.

4. Békés 2020, 2025.

5. See, for instance, Kovács and Trencsényi 2020.

6. See, for instance, Goncalves et al. 2024; Göppfarth 2020; Moltke 2022; Moltke and Komfort-Hein 2024.

7. Békés 2020, 2025.

8. Canon is what Pierre Bourdieu (1984) would call "legitimate culture," a framework that defines "common culture," a series of historical facts and cultural products (texts, images, sounds, material culture, etc.) canonized by cultural producers and institutions. Canons "are tenacious, they do change over time, mostly in slow motion. A canon functions as a standard in education and other fields, and determines what it is necessary to teach, to learn, and to know. A cultural canon is also used as a political instrument in the construction of a national cultural identity (Corse 1997)" (Bevers 2005: 390).

9. In 2020 Libri controlled two-thirds of the book market, Líra about a quarter, and small publishers the rest.

10. Interview with Leona Szy, originally at https://archiv.polgarokhaza.hu/index.php?mode=interju&cikk_id=175.

11. Bakos 2011; Kőrösiné 2016.

12. Morcsányi was the director of Magvető Press, the main publisher of contemporary Hungarian fiction, between 1995 and 2015, and his work was highly regarded in the industry.

13. Textbook publishing is somewhat of an exception and will be discussed later in the chapter.

14. Textbooks and academic books (especially hard sciences, engineering, and business administration) are the only areas that attract foreign publishers to the Hungarian book market.

15. It is difficult to translate the *Napkelet* title into English because the archaic Hungarian term indicates that the sun rises in the East, implying that light, enlightenment, culture, and refinement come from the East.

16. This idea about the binary division of Hungarian culture recalls sociological theories developed by the influential sociologist (and communist politician) Ferenc Erdei (1987). He argued that Hungarian society had a dual social structure (*kettős társadalom*). The conservative middle class, rooted in the remnants of the feudal aristocracy, was dominantly affiliated with the state and public offices, while the new bourgeoise middle class embraced capitalism and market institutions. Another version of this theory maps these parallel structures around a populist-urbanist split, where populists rally around traditional values, rural lifestyles, and autochthonous development

while urbanists regard themselves as pro-Western, cosmopolitan, urban, and supporters of capitalist modernization. For an example of how these binaries shaped the postwar architectural profession, see Molnár (2005, 2013).

17. The rise of Mediaworks is closely linked to Fidesz's systematic takeover of independent media through business oligarchs loyal to the government. The company was catapulted into the limelight in 2016 when it acquired in a hostile takeover and immediately shut down Hungary's most influential leftist-liberal newspaper, *Népszabadság*, originally owned by the socialist party, MSZP. By 2019, 80 percent of media in Hungary was owned by government allies (https://freedomhouse.org/report/freedom-and-media/2019/media-freedom-downward-spiral).

18. Békés 2020.

19. Hochschild 2016.

20. I had the misfortune of personally experiencing what it means to be subject to Lovas's attention. He published a short piece in the government-affiliated *Hungarian Times* (*Magyar Idők*) based on an article that was printed in the German daily, *Frankfurter Allgemeine Zeitung*, which partly discussed a public lecture I gave about my research at the American Academy in Berlin in 2017. His piece triggered some vicious hate mail I had never had to face before.

21. In some cases (e.g., Gergely Prőhle, former director of the Petőfi Museum for Literature) it can be proven that Szakács's attacks played a role in the eventual removal of the office holder.

22. https://mki.gov.hu/en/intezet-en/kuldetes-en.

23. Szakács's former friend and colleague Gábor Horváth-Lugossy became the first director of the Institute of Hungarian Research in 2019.

24. Borvendég 2020.

25. Bayer was a founding member of Fidesz and a close confidant of Prime Minister Viktor Orbán. He has built a reputation in large part on the notoriety that surrounds his media presence as a columnist for right-wing newspapers and a political analyst in regular TV appearances. He enjoys near mythical reverence in right-wing circles for "speaking truth to power" and deep disdain in the left for his brazen and unfiltered racism and anti-Semitism. In 2016 he received one of Hungary's highest honors, the Knight's Cross of the Hungarian Order of Merit, causing a public outcry and prompting many prominent public figures to return their previous awards in protest. While these public displays of criticism were bruising for the government—around a hundred former recipients returned their state awards—they didn't budge and retract his award, granting thereby an official seal of approval for the brand of hate speech Bayer's work represents.

26. Szakács and Bayer 2019: 66–67.

27. Bayer notes that besides the museum, there are eleven municipalities in Norway where streets or public squares are named after Hamsun and nine statutes, memorials, or memorial plaques, while he also has three statues in Oslo (though not in public spaces). The Norwegian Central Bank issued a silver coin in his honor, and a memorial center dedicated to him was opened in the Arctic (Szakács and Bayer 2019:78).

28. Szakács and Bayer 2019: 78.

29. Hóman was an acclaimed scholar in the 1920s, appointed as director of the National Széchenyi Library and later as director of the Hungarian National Museum, who became minister of religion and education in 1932, occupying this position until 1938, and then again from 1939 to 1942. He remained in office after the German occupation of Hungary in March 1944 and the coup d'état of the pro-Nazi Arrow Cross Party in October 1944, sponsoring legislation that called for the expulsion of Hungarian Jews. See figure 3.2 for an image of him.

30. Szakács and Bayer 2019: 43.

31. Szakács and Bayer 2019: 82.

32. Szakács and Bayer 2019: 68.

33. See chapter 1, note 118, for more on Trianon.

34. Olay 2023.

35. Dugin 2014.

36. With a portfolio of over 250 book titles, Arktos is considered "the most significant player in the field," according to its website. It was founded in India in 2009 by a Swedish businessman and former active neo-Nazi, Daniel Friberg, and an American editor, John B Morgan. The press relocated to Sweden in 2014 and to Hungary in 2015. Friberg is strongly influenced by the *Nouvelle Droite* (French New Right) and finds it important to make the works of authors like Alan de Benoist or Guillaume Faye available in English translation. Arktos publishes the key works of the European New Right and translates far-right European literature into English.

37. On the significance of Eurasianism for the far right, see Laruelle (2012).

38. The press was founded in 1939 as "Hungarian Life Publisher," changing its name to the last name of the family that always owned it during their exile in the United States.

39. Only a few (Gyula Illyés, Ference Erdei) joined the communist establishment.

40. The Hungarian equivalents of these terms (*Honfoglalás előtti idők* and *őstörténet*) refer respectively to the historical era that preceded the end of the ninth century, when Hungarians began to settle in the Carpathian Basin, and to ethnic prehistory.

41. Hubbes 2013: 225.

42. Paál 2005.

43. Hubbes 2013.

44. Máté 2004–2007.

45. Molnár 2017.

46. See, for instance, Goncalves et al. 2024.

47. György 2012.

48. National Core Curricula were passed in 1995, 2003, 2007, and 2012. The 2020 version is the heavily reworked version of the 2012 document (NAT 2020).

49. Joób 2020a.

50. Joób 2020b.

51. index.hu 2020.

52. Szily 2020.

53. https://magyartanarok.wordpress.com/2020/02/01/a-magyartanarok-egyesulete-allasfoglalasa-a-nemzeti-alaptanterv-2020-januar-31-en-nyilvanossagra-hozott-szovegerol/.

54. Joób 2020a.

55. Interestingly, his own books are published by presses like Püski, confirming his connections to the far-right milieu.

56. Hír TV 2020. Takaró uses only the Hungarian names of these multiethnic cities located in Romania and Slovakia, respectively.

57. Horváth 2020.

58. Kárpáti 2020.

59. Korompay 2020.

60. narancs.hu 2020a.

61. Bayer 2020.

62. Ott 2021.

63. Ott 2021.

64. Pataki 2021.

65. Pesl 2021.

66. As one commentator put it: "She went abroad to puke on our country" (Tóth 2021).

67. Mezey 2021.

68. Petrovics 2021.

69. Tóth, Facebook post, February 22, 2021.

70. "You will not even become a footnote in Hungarian literature" (Tóth 2021).

71. Tóth 2021b.

72. Pataki 2021.

73. Magyar Nemzet 2021.

74. mandiner.hu 2021.

75. Tóth 2021b.

76. Dúró was Jobbik's spokeswoman from 2007–2014 and the deputy leader of its parliamentary faction from 2014–16.

77. She stated that "The Our Homeland Movement does not tolerate that children are exposed to homosexual propaganda by sneaking this abnormal lifestyle even into children's books, which is a lie given that homosexual princes are not part of Hungarian culture. At our press conference today I'm destroying the propaganda book of homosexuality, which is an attack against children's healthy development and against Hungarian culture" (narancs.hu 2020b).

78. While such pressure groups in the U.S. challenged an average of 46 titles per year between 2001 and 2020, in 2024 they challenged 4,190 titles in 12 months (Poole 2025).

79. Same-sex couples, for instance, were excluded from the institution of marriage and family in the new constitution enacted in 2012. In 2020 the legal recognition of transgender people ended.

80. The journalist who made this argument in an opinion piece in *Magyar Nemzet* went as far as suggesting that the Nazi analogy doesn't work because the fact that the book was shredded and not burnt makes a huge difference. "Burning comes with suffocating smoke and ashes. By contrast, shredding causes no harm to the environment, only gets rid of filth, the paper can be recycled, potentially even into another book" (Franka 2020).

81. Dúró 2020.

82. Németh 2021.

83. Szilvay 2021.

84. Gajdics 2020.

85. Kékesi 2020.

86. Hetzmann 2020.

87. Hernádi 2020.

88. Szőke 2020.

89. Ironically, the attacker also complained that she received threats after her book-grinding appearance. There were several events organized in solidarity with her, for instance, by no other than the cultural warrior, Árpád Szakács himself.

90. Elek and Nagy 2020.

91. narancs.hu 2020c. They were consequently ordered to remove it.

92. Hetzmann 2020.

93. In reaction, the Hungarian government organized a referendum in 2022 with steering questions soliciting support for the Child Protection Act. The referendum was invalid, but those who voted overwhelmingly backed the government.

94. MCC is also part of the "parallel institutional infrastructure" that Fidesz has been building to create a network of government-friendly civil society and cultural organizations, like several other examples discussed earlier. Founded in 1996, it initially offered interdisciplinary training and scholarships to talented students (from high school to postgraduate levels) in the social sciences and humanities to complement their formal schooling. Over time it has extended its profile to publishing books and journals, offering mobility programs, organizing conferences and panel discussions, running outreach programs for diaspora Hungarians in neighboring countries, and setting up satellite campuses in Western European countries—that is, gradually evolving into the main cadre-recruiting and training organization of the Orbán regime. It is legally a nonprofit organization funded by government subsidies. In 2021 MCC received a major boost in funding,

as it was given control over 10 percent (each) of the shares of two of Hungary's largest companies, MOL, the Hungarian Oil and Gas Company, and the Richter Gedeon Pharmaceutical Company. Its overall assets amounted to 500 billion HUF in 2021.

95. These books also cannot be placed in the shopwindow and cannot be sold within 200 yards of a school or a church.

96. Meghji 2021.

97. Kristóf et al. 2021.

98. Labrisz worked with three different printing companies, some of which asked not to be listed in the book because of fears of retaliation and freezing their access to government subsidies for other jobs.

Chapter 3. Reviving Folk Traditions to Refashion the Nation

1. Fülemile 2023.

2. Kubik 1994.

3. Beaman 2015.

4. Piela 2021.

5. Lamont and Molnár 2002.

6. Novikov 2017.

7. See, for instance, Gaugele 2019; Miller-Idriss 2014, 2018; Ventsel 2014.

8. Miller-Idriss 2018.

9. Turner 2012.

10. Sewell 1992.

11. See, for instance, Feischmidt 2020; Molnár 2023.These reconceptualizations of the nation also led to state policies such as the 2011 Dual Citizenship Law, which grants extraterritorial citizenship to members of Hungarian ethnic minorities in neighboring countries that were part of Hungary before 1920, including nonresident voting rights in Hungarian national elections.

12. Taylor 2021.

13. See, for instance, Aronczyk 2013, 2019; Castelló and Mihelјs 2018.

14. Molnár 2017. Many classic works on nationalism emphasized the link between economic modernization and the rise of nationalism in the nineteenth century (e.g., Gellner 1983), but the present discussion explores the role of contemporary economic practices as markers of nationhood.

15. See, for instance, Aronczyk 2013, 2019; Kaneva 2011; Kania-Lundholm 2014; and Rivera 2008; Bandelj and Wherry 2011; and Melchior 2011 specifically for fashion.

16. See Billig 1995; Brubaker 2004; Edensor 2002; Fox 2006; Fox and Miller-Idriss 2008.

17. Comaroff and Comaroff 2009.

18. Bartlett 2019.

19. See, for instance, Bartlett 2019; Maxwell 2014, 2021; Tomc 2021.

20. Kimura, Peterson, and Lin 2022.

21. Gu and Lu 2021; Ling and Segre-Reinach 2018; Melchior 2011.

22. See, for instance, Tomc 2021; Ling and Segre-Reinach 2018.

23. Müller 2016.

24. Kalinina 2017.

25. Gurova 2019.

26. Suyarkulova 2016.

27. Novikov 2017.

28. Zelizer 2010.

29. Interviewees included twenty-two women and eight men.

30. Götz 2018.

31. Molnár 2016.

32. Götz 2018.

33. The Hungarian House has been a central institution of the Hungarian diaspora in New York City and in the United States since its founding in 1963.

34. Coffey and Atkinson 1996.

35. See, for instance, Bartlett 2019; F. Dózsa 1998; Ferencziné Sedlmayr 2006.

36. See https://www.nemzetisport.hu/sportszelep/2011/07/kalocsai-minta-hamilton-es-button-fl-es-ruhajan.

37. Western celebrities play a similar role in legitimizing traditional ethnic fashion in other parts of the world. Kidman wearing a qipao, a traditional Chinese dress, caused a similar reaction in China as her Kalocsa dress in Hungary, contributing to local repopularization (Chew 2007).

38. A dirndl is a traditional feminine dress based on peasant dress from the Alps worn in Austria, South Tyrol (Italy), and Bavaria (Germany).

39. Hampel refers to the fact that "true" Hungarian nationalists in the interwar period were anti-German and did not support Hungary's alliance with Nazi Germany precisely because they did not want to be dominated by other nations.

40. Bartlett 2019; Fülemile 2023.

41. F. Dózsa 1989.

42. Medvedev 2008: 253.

43. The "Bocskai" is named after István Bocskai, who was prince of Transylvania in 1605–1606 and led an important uprising against the Habsburgs. His was the first anti-Habsburg uprising led by Hungarian nobility against centralizing imperial rule. In the interwar period the Bocskai was particularly popular among university students, who basically wore it as a uniform.

44. Hampel 2013.

45. F. Dózsa 1998; Ferencziné Sedlmayr 2006.

46. March 15 is an important national holiday in Hungary commemorating the 1848 revolution. Before 1989 anticommunist activists and dissidents regularly held counter-celebrations in opposition to the official ceremonies organized by the government.

47. Molnár 2017.

48. Feischmidt and Pulay 2017; see https://www.youtube.com/watch?v=prNqrFIb8Hc.

49. Quote is from the brand's website as it appeared in 2014.

50. Muniz and O'Guinn 2001: 412.

51. Pasieka 2024; Wodak 2015.

52. Zelizer 2010.

53. Medvedev 2008.

54. Lázsiás is a type of folk jewelry made of coins that are no longer in circulation. The necklaces were particularly popular in the nineteenth century, and in some parts of Hungary they were produced until the end of World War I. The coins often contained the images of popular saints, guardian angels, and former emperors/empresses.

55. Various ethnic groups, though primarily Germans, were "invited" to settle in areas that became severely depopulated during the Ottoman period. Many of these ethnic enclaves were then subject to controversial bilateral population exchanges following the end of World War II, including the Slovak community of Tótkomlós.

56. See examples of women and men wearing traditional Matyó folk dresses in Mezőkövesd during Easter Monday celebrations at https://commons.wikimedia.org/wiki/File:Matyó_Húsvét.jpg.

57. See https://industry.notjustalabel.com/piroshka.

58. Quigley 2014; Taylor 2021.

59. Juhász 2017.
60. See https://www.instagram.com/p/DLen6U9oh0l/?hl.
61. Molnár 2023.
62. F. Dózsa 1989; Fülemile 2023; Medvedev 2008.
63. Anderson 2006.
64. Miller-Idriss 2018.
65. See, for instance, Mayer 2018; Filippello 2023.
66. Dietze and Roth 2020.

Chapter 4. "Making Hungary Great Again": Heritage Tourism and Symbolic Irredentism

1. The example is from a video recording of a literature class included in dossier hat-15-05-0180.
2. The ethnic/civic distinction in models of nationhood has been explored extensively in the literature on nationalism. For key definitions and debates, see Brubaker 1996, 2004; Brubaker et al. 2006; Zubrzykci 2001.
3. See, for instance, Marschall 2016; Peleikis 2010.
4. Bourdieu and Passeron 1990; Feldman 2008: 2.
5. Martin 2023.
6. Gellner 1983.
7. Brubaker et al. 2006.
8. Anderson 2006.
9. Lerch, Russell, and Ramirez 2017.
10. See, for instance, Dierkes 2010; Jaskulowski et al. 2018; Lerch, Russell, and Ramirez 2017; Tormey 2006; Schissler and Soysal 2005.
11. See, for instance, Lomsky-Feder 2004, 2011; Millei and Lappalainen 2020.
12. See, for instance, Bénéï 2005; Gholami 2017; Miller-Idriss 2009; Osler 2011; and Siebers 2019.
13. DeWitt and Storksdieck 2008; Michalkó, Rátz, and Keszeg 2016; Rátz, Michalkó, and Keszeg 2020.
14. El Haj 2001; Feldman 2002, 2008; Katriel 1995; Kelner 2010.
15. Katriel 1995; Feldman 2008.
16. Comaroff and Comaroff 2009; Surak 2010.
17. Lehrer 2013.
18. Brubaker 1996; see, for instance, Bhandari 2016; Carter 2004; Hughes and Allen 2010.
19. See, for instance, Aronczyk 2013, 2019; Bandelj and Wherry 2011; Kania-Lundholm 2014; Kowalski 2011; Rivera 2008.
20. Edensor 2001, 2007; Sumartojo 2016.
21. Attempts to bridge these approaches have been scarce. See Brubaker et al. 2006; Feldman 2008; and Surak 2012, 2017.
22. Brubaker and Kim 2011; Kim 2016; Lainer-Vos 2013.
23. Pogonyi 2015.
24. 101/2010 (X.21.) OGY.
25. The government established a range of institutions to translate this new vision into action. Between 2010 and 2013 and again since 2018, the *Határtalanul* program has been administered by one of these institutions, the Gábor Bethlen Alapítvány, a nonprofit organization. This fully government-financed NGO is entrusted with awarding state grants for the implementation of the government's long-term strategy for national minority politics. The grants, first and foremost, target transborder and diaspora ethnic Hungarians, providing support for the "cultural protection,

the material and spiritual growth, individual and collective prosperity" of these ethnic Hungarian communities that reside in the "external homeland" (*külhoni magyarok*).

26. For overviews, see Bárdi 2004; Csergő 2007; Hatvany 2006; Pogonyi 2013; Waterbury 2006.

27. See Pogonyi 2017. Although short of extending voting rights and formal citizenship, similar trends can be seen in other countries in the region. Poland introduced the Pole's card (*Karta Polaka*) in 2007, which grants the right of temporary or permanent residence in Poland as well as visa-free travel to applicants who are willing to demonstrate their Polishness.

28. Pap 2013: 25.

29. Csete 2011: 7.

30. Csete 2011. Csete is an expert in education development. He headed a state-owned nonprofit organization, the Apáczai Közalapítvány, providing Hungarian-language educational services and support for ethnic Hungarian diaspora communities in neighboring countries. This has remained his main area of expertise and inspired him to design the *Határtalanul* program. He is also the son of a prominent architect, György Csete, a central figure of the Hungarian organic architecture movement that openly rejected the state-backed modernist style already before 1989.

31. Csete 2011: 11.

32. Csete 2011: 12.

33. Csete 2011: 15.

34. This expectation might sound far-fetched at first, but students' class trip diaries frequently contain statements such as: "I am sure that everyone found a favorite place in Transylvania that they will return to in the future" (hat-14-01-0384).

35. See, for instance, Csurgó et al. 2018; Feischmidt 2005, 2008; Kürti 2001; Taylor 2021.

36. Discrimination against ethnic minorities was politically off-limits for debate in communist countries (Feischmidt 2005; Szabó 1989). Therefore, the dire situation of Hungarian (and other) ethnic minorities had to be kept under the rug in the name of socialist internationalism and brotherhood.

37. Zakariás 2018.

38. See Feischmidt 2008; Ilyés 2013. In 2019 Pope Francis attended the Pentecostal festival and officiated a mass as part of the festivities. Şumuleu Ciuc has been a Catholic pilgrimage site since the fifteenth century and particularly important for the Hungarian minority, given that most Romanians are Eastern Orthodox.

39. Csete 2011: 29.

40. The logo was changed to a schematic "Greater Hungary" image in 2019.

41. Csete 2011: 21.

42. Csete 2011: 25.

43. See Pap 2013.

44. In the 2013 sample, for instance, only three out of the thirty schools engaged with the language of the destination country: Preparatory activities at one school included a Romanian lesson to teach basic Romanian vocabulary to the participants (ha-13-01-167).

45. See, for instance, ha-13-01-207.

46. See, for instance, ha-13-01-142.

47. Edensor 2001, 2007; Sumartojo 2016.

48. Edensor 2007.

49. In 2019 the Slovak Parliament drafted a law to ban the public singing of the Hungarian anthem. The draft was passed by Parliament but vetoed by the president of the Republic, Andrei Kiska, who sent it back to the Parliament for revision. Szekler or székely denotes a subgroup of Hungarians who live in a loose diaspora enclave in the central mountainous region of Transylvania and not in transborder areas.

50. Nora 1996.

51. ha-13-01-133. Francis II. Rákóczi was a prince of Transylvania and the leader of the Hungarian uprising against the Habsburgs in 1703–1711. He died in exile in the Ottoman Empire in 1735 and was reburied in the St. Elisabeth Cathedral in Košice (Kassa) in 1906.

52. ha-13-01-175.

53. ha-13-01-162.

54. ha-13-01-175.

55. About 30 percent of the schools hire a travel agency to plan the trip for an extra charge not covered by state subsidies.

56. ha-13-01-228.

57. ha-13-01-228.

58. ha-13-01-175.

59. ha-13-01-175.

60. ha-13-01-265.

61. This is akin to how Jewish visitors on heritage tours to Poland avoid interactions with local Poles because they assume them to be antisemitic; the few interactions that do occur are often sought out to reinforce expectations of antisemitic behavior (Feldman 2008; Lehrer 2013).

62. hat-14-01-510.

63. ha-13-01-265.

64. There are only a few exceptions to this temporal frame, involving chiefly three prominent ethnic Hungarian writers, Sándor Márai, Albert Wass, and Áron Tamási, whose lives and careers were uprooted by the Treaty of Trianon. Wass is the most controversial among them, and the most frequently referenced on the class trips. His role will be explored in the next section on radical nationalist symbols.

65. Hobsbawm and Ranger 1983.

66. On such "poetic use of space," see also Smith 2004; Feischmidt 2008, 2020.

67. The majority Hungarian village of Ghimeş (Gyimes) in the Carpathian Mountains was one of the easternmost outposts of the Kingdom of Hungary and of the Austro-Hungarian Monarchy until 1920. Some of the actual boundary stones marking the border of the monarchy can still be seen near the village as well as its easternmost railway station (Ilyés 2013).

68. hat-14-01-0156.

69. Hovi 2014.

70. Only a couple of class trips mentioned or incorporated the Dracula story into their itinerary (e.g., ha-13-01-132, hat-15-05-0089).

71. See, for instance, ha-13-01-125.

72. Miller-Idriss 2018, 2019.

73. For more on these symbols, see Feischmidt et al. 2014; Molnár 2017, 2021.

74. The "other" category in table 4.1 includes well-known irredentist poems and pamphlets from the interwar period (e.g., Gyula Juhász: *Trianon*; Piroska Tábori: *Üzenet Erdélyből*; István Szathmáry: *Országzászló*) without providing any historical and political context for these works.

75. Given that the annual sample (N = 30) of dossiers is statistically representative of the overall class trips for each year, the percentage figures in the table can be generalized to the total population of class trips in respective years.

76. Feischmidt 2020.

77. See, for instance, ha-13-01-175, ha 13-01-213, hat-14-01-0510, hat-15-05-0452.

78. See, for instance, ha-13-01-213.

79. Molnár 2021.

80. See Molnár 2021 on the changing historical uses of the image.

81. ha-13-01-219.

82. In 2005 in the Hungarian equivalent of BBC's *Big Read*—a yearlong survey to find the nation's best-loved novel—three of Wass's novels made it into the top 100 list.

83. Feischmidt and Pulay 2017; Kürti 2012; Lange 2018.

84. ha-13-01-142.

85. ha-13-01-175.

86. See, for instance, ha-13-01-113, ha-13-01-162.

87. hat-15-05-0632.

88. Kelner 2010; Saxe and Chazan 2008.

89. Pap 2013.

90. Böröcz 1996.

91. Bhandari 2016: 925.

Chapter 5. Reinventing Nomadic Heritage: Anti-Westernism and Mythic Orientalism

1. As I explained in chapter 2, the right often uses the term "Carpathian Basin" to denote pre-Trianon, "Greater Hungary." In this chapter, it is used as a geographic designation.

2. The phrase was coined by the influential turn-of-the-twentieth-century poet, Endre Ady, who was incidentally the editor of the iconic literary magazine called *West*.

3. Hofer 1991: 158, 159.

4. Ablonczy 2021.

5. Matolcsy was also the president of Hungary's Central Bank between 2013 and 2025.

6. Laza 2012.

7. Laza 2012.

8. See, for instance, Bíró et al. 2009; Kremmler 2023; Maróti et al. 2022; Török 2022; Zsuppán 2024.

9. Zelizer 2010.

10. The introduction of *Hungarikum* classification was initiated in the early 2000s to collect and maintain an inventory of the most unique and distinguished national treasures and to safeguard these achievements. The *Hungarikum* list combines the logic of protected designation of origin labels that are common across the European Union and the UNESCO World Cultural Heritage classifications.

11. Sinkovics 2016.

12. Sinkovics 2016.

13. Ágoston 2017.

14. According to some reports, *The Horseback Archer*'s viewership exceeded the combined viewership total of all other Hungarian movies screened in 2016 (Ágoston 2017).

15. Ágoston 2017.

16. Pörzse 2016: 3.

17. Pörzse illustrates to what extent Kassai has mesmerized some right-wing intellectuals. Already in 2011, Pörzse described him as some kind of cultural savior. He suggested that Kassai "has given to Hungarians at least as much as Professor Szent-Györgyi [a Hungarian Nobel laureate in Physiology or Medicine for the discovery of Vitamin C], Ányos Jedlik [inventor of dynamo and electric motor], or Ernő Rubik [inventor of Rubic cube]," and he hopes that "his name will make it into school textbooks. Because Lajos Kassai is a DEMI-GOD! He created a world that works perfectly and everyone who lives in this world is happy. You cannot surpass this" (Pörzse 2011: 3).

18. Csákvári 2016.

19. Kassai 2019.

20. Kassai 2019: 18.

21. This is why figures 5.1 and 5.2 show typical details I saw in the Kassai Valley but use photographs I took at different events.

22. I use the term "Hungarian prehistory" to describe what in Hungarian is referred to as *magyar őstörténet*, denoting the study of the ethnogenesis of Hungarian people.

23. The pouches were originally made of leather, and their front was often covered by a richly decorated plate made of bronze or gilded silver. Such sabretache plates make up some of the most valuable archeological finds from the Conquest period. Some archeologists suggest that the plates were the insignia of high-ranking dignitaries (Virágos 2022). Re-creating the material culture of the Conquest period and Hungarian ancient history, a period from which very little actual artifacts remain, is a central preoccupation of this subculture.

24. An important milestone in this revival was the staging of a musical, "Stephen, the King," in 1983 and the subsequent film based on the recording of this premier, open-air performance that was watched by 120,000 people. The "rock opera," as it is called, follows the succession struggle for Hungary's throne between Stephen, who eventually becomes Hungary's first Christian king (and later its first saint), and his rival, Koppány, who vehemently opposes Hungary's Christianization and wants to preserve the settlers' paganism. Even though the story is set at the turn of the ninth and 10th centuries, the struggle between paganism and Christianity serves as a metaphor for Hungary's constant wavering between East and West and its independence struggles against foreign influence (Western European Christianity in this case). The film version of the rock opera was an enormous hit, and the opera has been widely performed in theaters and on open-air stages ever since its premier. To this day, it is the most successful Hungarian musical of all time. The visual world of the rock opera—its costumes in particular—made a huge impression on popular culture and gave a boost to popular interest in Conquest-era Hungarian history.

25. See also Molnár 2017.

26. The buildings were designed by Antal Grátz and Ákos Sziklai, both representatives of the organic architecture school and disciples of Imre Makovecz, its founder (Benkei 2012: 21). Organic architecture started as a countercultural movement in the 1970s that rejected the communist state-backed modernist doctrine and strove to develop a uniquely Hungarian architectural language (see Molnár 2019). Stemming from the anticommunist stance, organic architects and organic architecture as a style have been associated with the political right. In 2023 a new law on Hungarian architecture (*2023. évi C. törvény*) stipulated Makovecz's organic movement as the standard that national architecture should aspire to.

27. https://www.kertai.hu/.

28. See also Molnár 2017.

29. See also Benkei 2012.

30. See also Benkei 2012: 69–70.

31. Ágoston 2020: 26.

32. Benkei 2012: 33.

33. Kassai 2012: 2.

34. Zelizer 2010.

35. Most of the media coverage on horseback archery in general and Kassai in particular can be found in right-wing media sources, particularly in magazines such as *barikád*, *Demokrata* or *Heti Válasz*.

36. Partizán 2021.

37. Horseback archery enthusiasts also accuse the pre-1989 communist government of editing out some of the great victories of these Hungarian armies from the history curricula of public schools, most notably the Battle of Bratislava in 907 in which Hungarians won a decisive victory over the East Francian army, preventing a German invasion, to intentionally diminish Hungarian national self-esteem. They have blamed former communist and liberal governments for focusing

only on Hungary's lost battles, cultivating a kind of societal defeatism. Reenacting the Battle of Bratislava is therefore a popular, recurring event in horseback archery–themed festivals.

38. Kassai 2012:5.

39. Partizán 2021.

40. Ágoston 2020: 27.

41. This emphasis on competition performance goes somewhat against Kassai's mission statement that horseback archery follows the Eastern spirit and should be approached as a way of life and moral compass.

42. http://www.magtudin.org/Horkovics.htm.

43. https://magyarvar.hu/alapitvanyunk.

44. Szakács 2002.

45. It counts around 380 members. See https://www.nemethy.info/academy.html.

46. His father was a cavalry officer in the prewar Hungarian army and is closely related to Bertalan Nemethy, a central figure in prewar equestrian sports in Hungary and the show-jumping coach of the US Equestrian Team from 1955 to 1980.

47. Other military-themed heritage organizations (e.g., dedicated to Hungarian hussar traditions) have also gained in popularity and received increased public support since 2010.

48. See note 37.

49. Ethnosports are modern folk forms of sport intended for the preservation of traditional sports and games that are tied to specific ethnic groups as defined by UNESCO. Traditional physical activities are turned into modern sports through standardization of rules, equipment, scoring system, refereeing, and setting up formal institutions and international federations. Martial arts, belly dancing, and yoga are examples of ethnosports. Interest in ethnosports is particularly strong in places like Russia and Central Asia and was theorized extensively by a Russian anthropologist, Alexey Kylasov.

50. Mayhew 2024. Today they use a stuffed burlap sack as the goat's carcass.

51. In expressing this, he cited a famous nineteenth-century epic poem, *Toldi*, by one of the all-time great Hungarian poets, János Arany, about a real-life historical figure, Miklós Toldi, a legendary strong warrior hero from the fourteenth century. In describing how he felt, he referred to the scene when Toldi, the main protagonist, working in the fields, sees a group of warriors riding by and longs to join them, saying, "I wish I could be riding with you," but first he is snubbed by them as they think he is just a poor peasant.

52. The film was a flop even though it had an ample budget, featured the well-known Italian actor Franco Nero in the main role, and was directed by Gábor Koltay, who was also the director of the smash-hit rock opera about King St. Stephen and other important films that created the contemporary popular cultural iconography of the Conquest period that's so central to these right-wing subcultures in general and to horseback archery in particular.

53. László 2019 [1944].

54. Bar and Halewa 2025. For similar claims of autochthony and continuity on the Israeli side see, for instance, Shapira and Penslar 2013; Zerubavel 1995.

55. Bakay and Papp 2008.

56. Bakay and Papp 2008: 115.

57. Bakay and Papp 2008: 146. This comment is meant to counter negative perceptions disseminated by European chroniclers at the time who offered outlandish descriptions of the cruelties of Hungarian fighters, from killing babies to cannibalism.

58. Kummer 2021.

59. Kiszely 2012: 45; Hankó 2019: 40.

60. OGY határozat 32/2004 (IV.19).

61. Borbás 2024.

62. Kiss 2020.

63. V. Szabó, Kiss, and Tóth 2021.

64. Kiss 2022.

65. Borbás 2024.

66. According to the Hungarian-Turanic Foundation that organizes Kurultáj, the Hun-Turkic people comprise twenty-one different ethnic groups, including Turkish, Uzbek, Kyrgyz, Chechen, Azeri, Tatar, and Mongol.

67. Several clothing brands discussed in chapter 3 are sold at the fair.

68. See also Teisenhoffer 2024.

69. Povedák 2022; Teisenhoffer 2024.

70. Povedák 2022.

71. Povedák 2022: 82.

72. Some political analysts estimated the number of potential votes that could come from people involved in various prehistory-related subcultures to be around 100,000 (Ablonczy and Borbás 2024: 16). Fidesz wanted to snatch these sympathizers from Jobbik's political orbit.

73. Bódis 2024: 22.

74. By 2020 the contested ethnic origin stories embraced and spread by Kurultáj became part of school textbooks approved by the National Core Curriculum (Ablonczy and Borbás 2024: 19).

75. Nagy 2023.

76. Balogh 2022: 734; Dayioğlu 2022: 236.

77. Ablonczy 2022.

78. Akçali and Korkut 2012: 602.

79. Dayioğlu 2022.

80. Ablonczy 2021; Balogh 2022.

81. Balogh 2022: 735.

82. Balogh 2022: 736.

83. Ablonczy 2021.

84. Akçali and Korkut 2012.

85. Dayioğlu 2022.

86. As pointed out earlier, this also led to the general marginalization of academic research on Hungarian prehistory and the Conquest era.

87. Criticism of Finno-Ugric origin came up many times in my interviews from fashion producers to horseback archers and it was always presented as an anti-establishment, countercultural, anti-communist stance.

88. Ablonczy 2022.

89. Several of my interviewees, from fashion producers to horseback archers, noted that there was a palpable surge of interest in turning to Hungarian heritage-themed practices and artifacts around 2004, as cited earlier.

90. Ablonczy 2021.

91. Akcali and Korkut 2012: 600.

92. Balogh 2022: 739. The 2015 Syrian migrant crisis propelled Jobbik to give up its pro-Muslim stance.

93. Bíró et al 2009. There has been a resurgence of archeological research expeditions to Central Asia in the Turanian spirit since the 2010s, intertwined with the promotion of research on Hungarian prehistory (Ágoston 2013).

94. Kürti 2017. Just like in the case of Kassai, this allows and prompts Bíró to air his right-wing political convictions.

95. See also Kremmler 2022, 2023.

96. Ditzendy 2020.
97. Kürti 2017: 227.
98. Moreh 2016: 344.
99. Moreh 2016.
100. Laruelle 2012; Tüysüzoğlu 2014.
101. Zelizer 2010.

Chapter 6. Conclusion

1. Aspetsberger 2003.
2. The script was cowritten and the film was codirected by a key figure of Hungarian film history, Béla Balázs. Riefenstahl was credited as the writer because Balázs was Jewish. Upon the re-release of the film in 1938, the names of both Balázs and another Jewish Austrian writer, Carl Meyer, were removed altogether—most likely at Riefenstahl's request.
3. Hochschild 2016.
4. Spike and Riccardi 2025.
5. Creamer 2025.
6. PEN 2025.
7. DiMaggio and Powell 1983.
8. Geertz 1973.
9. Stanley 2024.
10. Hochschild 2016.
11. Zelizer 2010.
12. Lepore 2025.
13. See, for instance, Bar and Halewa 2025; Göçek 2014; Shapira and Penslar 2013; Zubrzycki 2020.
14. Stanley 2024.
15. Pinheiro-Machado and Vargas-Maia 2023.
16. See, for instance, Laruelle 2012; Levent 2016; Yavuz 2020.
17. Zhang 2023.
18. See, for instance, Nagle 2025; Mehmetcik and Çelik 2022.
19. Békés 2020, 2025; de Benoist 2017.
20. Hunter 1991; Gramsci 1971.
21. Bourdieu 1984; Banks 2024.

Methodological Appendix

1. Greskovits 2020; Molnár 2016.
2. See, for instance, Feischmidt and Pulay 2017; Miller-Idriss 2018; Teitelbaum 2017.
3. Zelizer 2010.
4. Blee 2007; Göppfarth 2020; Pasieka 2024; Teitelbaum 2017.
5. Blee 2007: 120.
6. Blee 2007.
7. See, for instance, Blee 1998.
8. Pasieka 2019.
9. See, for instance, Teitelbaum 2017.
10. See Teitelbaum 2017, 11–12, for examples.
11. Geertz 1973.

12. Charmaz 2006. Nine interviews were not recorded, either because the interviewee preferred not to be recorded or because circumstances made the recording unfeasible (e.g., at an outdoor horseback archery festival).

13. For a few notable exceptions, see Feischmidt et al. 2014; Feischmidt and Pulay 2017.

14. Small 2015.

15. See also Pasieka 2017, 2019, 2024.

16. See, for instance, Duneier 2000.

REFERENCES

Ablonczy, Balázs. 2021. "Hungarian Turanism: Eurasianism à La Hongroise?" In *The Return of Eurasia: Continuity and Change*, edited by G. Diesen and A. Lukin, 225–49. Singapore: Palgrave Macmillan.

Ablonczy, Balázs. 2022. *Go East! A History of Hungarian Turanism*. Bloomington: Indiana University Press.

Ablonczy, Bálint, and Barna Borbás. 2024. "Sámántánc az Országházban. Magyar eredetpolitika 2006–2024." *Válasz Offline* 2 (1): 11–21.

Adams, Laura L. 2010. *The Spectacular State: Culture and National Identity in Uzbekistan*. Durham: Duke University Press.

Ágoston, Balázs. 2013. "Sztyeppék titkai." *Demokrata*, July 3, https://demokrata.hu/magyarorszag/sztyeppek-titkai-82879/.

Ágoston, Balázs. 2017. "Százezren látták? Nem számít." *Demokrata*, March 22: 48–51.

Ágoston, Balázs. 2020. "A magyar nem szolgalélek." *Demokrata*, March 11: 26–27.

Akçalı, Emel, and Umut Korkut. 2012. "Geographical Metanarratives in East-Central Europe: Neo-Turanism in Hungary." *Eurasian Geography and Economics* 53 (5): 596–614.

Anderson, Benedict. 2006 [1983]. *Imagined Communities. Reflections on the Origin and Spread of Nationalism*. London: Verso.

Arato, Andrew, and Jean L. Cohen. 2022. *Populism and Civil Society: The Challenge to Constitutional Democracy*. Oxford: Oxford University Press.

Aronczyk, Melissa. 2013. *Branding the Nation: The Global Business of National Identity*. Oxford: Oxford University Press.

Aronczyk, Melissa. 2019. "Branding National Identity in an Unequal World." In *The Oxford Handbook of Consumption*, edited by F. Wherry and I. Woodward, 439–57. New York: Oxford University Press.

Aspetsberger, Friedbert, ed. 2003. *Der Bergfilm 1920–1940*. Wien: StudienVerlag.

Bakay, Kornél, and György Papp. 2008. *Lovasíjászat és őstörténet*. Budapest: Magyar Nyugat Könyvkiadó.

Bakos, István. 2011. "Bedő György és a Kairosz könyvkiadó méltatása." *Magyar Napló* 23 (3): 42–43.

Balogh, Péter. 2022. "Clashing Geopolitical Self-Images? The Strange Co-Existence of Christian Bulwark and Eurasianism (Turanism) in Hungary." *Eurasian Geography and Economics* 63 (6): 726–52.

Bandelj, Nina, and Frederick F. Wherry. 2011. *The Cultural Wealth of Nations*. Stanford: Stanford University Press.

Banks, Patricia A. 2024. "Race and Ethnicity in the Sociology of Cultural Production and Consumption." *Annual Review of Sociology* 50 (1): 229–49.

Bar, Neil, and Harel Chorev Halewa. 2025. "Constructed Autochthony: Palestinian Nationalist Historical Revisionism." *Journal of the Middle East and Africa* 16 (3): 181–201.

Bar-On, Tamir. 2021. "The Alt-Right's Continuation of the 'Cultural War' in Euro-American Societies." *Thesis Eleven* 163 (1): 43–70.

Bárdi, Nándor. 2004. "The History of Relations Between Hungarian Governments and Ethnic Hungarians Living Beyond the Borders of Hungary." In *The Hungarian Status Law: Nation Building and/or Minority Protection*, edited by B. M. Z. Kántor, O. Ieda, B. Vizi, and I. Halász, 58–84. Sapporo: Slavic Research Center, Hokkaido University.

Bartlett, Djurdja. 2019. *Fashion and Politics*. New Haven: Yale University Press.

Bayer, Zsolt. 2020. "Nem tanítok fasiszta írót!" *Magyar Nemzet*, February 7, https://magyarnemzet.hu/ahelyzet/2020/02/nem-tanitok-fasiszta-irot.

Beaman, Jean. 2015. "Boundaries of Frenchness: Cultural Citizenship and France's Middle Class North African Second Generation." *Identities* 22 (1): 36–52.

Beaman, Jean. 2016. "Citizenship as Cultural: Towards a Theory of Cultural Citizenship." *Sociology Compass* 10 (10): 849–57.

Békés, Márton. 2020. *Kulturális hadviselés: A kulturális hatalom elmélete és gyakorlata*. Budapest: Kkettk Alapítvány.

Békés, Márton. 2023. "Kultúrharcom legszebb nyara." *Látószög blog*. https://latoszogblog.hu/aktualis/kulturharcom-legszebb-nyara/.

Békés, Márton. 2025. *Nemzeti maximum*. Budapest: Kkettk Alapítvány.

Bénéï, Véronique. 2005. *Manufacturing Citizenship: Education and Nationalism in Europe, South Asia and China*. New York: Routledge.

Benkei, Ildikó. 2012. *A Völgy lovasa. Kassai Lajos lovasíjásszal beszélget Benkei Ildikó*. Budapest: Kairosz.

Bennett, Andy. 2011. "The Post-Subcultural Turn: Some Reflections 10 Years On." *Journal of Youth Studies* 14 (5): 493–506.

Berezin, Mabel. 2021. "Identity, Narratives, and Nationalism." In *Routledge Handbook of Illiberalism*, edited by A. Sajó and R. Uitz, 237–49. New York: Routledge.

Bevers, Ton. 2005. "Cultural Education and the Canon: A Comparative Analysis of the Content of Secondary School Exams for Music and Art in England, France, Germany, and the Netherlands, 1990–2004." *Poetics* 33 (5–6): 388–416.

Bhandari, Kalyan. 2016. "Imagining the Scottish Nation: Homeland Tourism and Homeland Nationalism in Scotland." *Current Issues in Tourism* 19 (9): 913–29.

Billig, Michael. 1995. *Banal Nationalism*. London: Sage.

Bíró, András Zsolt, A. Zalán, A. Völgyi, and H. Pamjav. 2009. "A Y-Chromosomal Comparison of the Madjars (Kazakhstan) and the Magyars (Hungary)." *American Journal of Physical Anthropology: The Official Publication of the American Association of Physical Anthropologists* 139 (3): 305–10.

Blee, Kathleen M. 1998. "White-Knuckle Research: Emotional Dynamics in Fieldwork with Racist Activists." *Qualitative Sociology* 21: 381–99.

Blee, Kathleen M. 2003. "Studying the Enemy." In *Our Studies, Ourselves: Sociologists' Lives and Work*, edited by B. Glassner and R. Hertz, 13–23. New York: Oxford University Press.

Blee, Kathleen M. 2007. "Ethnographies of the Far Right." *Journal of Contemporary Ethnography* 36 (2): 119–28.

Bódis, András. 2024. "Keleti nyitás Kurultájjal." *Válasz Offline* 2 (1): 22–23.

Bonikowski, Bart. 2016. "Nationalism in Settled Times." *Annual Review of Sociology* 42 (1): 427–49.

Bonikowski, Bart, and Paul DiMaggio. 2016. "Varieties of American Popular Nationalism." *American Sociological Review* 81 (5): 949–80.

Borbás, Barna. 2024. "A Magyar íjforradalom nyomában." *Válasz Offline* 2 (1): 169–73.

Böröcz, József. 1996. *Leisure Migration: A Sociological Study on Tourism*. Oxford: Pergamon Press.

Borvendég, Zsuzsanna. 2020. *A hálózat pénze. Magyarország kirablásának megszervezése*. Budapest: Kárpátia Stúdió.

Bourdieu, Pierre. 1984. *Distinction: A Social Critique of the Judgement of Taste*. Cambridge, MA: Harvard University Press.

Bourdieu, Pierre. 1985. "The Market of Symbolic Goods." *Poetics* 14 (1–2): 13–44.

Bourdieu, Pierre, and Jean-Claude Passeron. 1990. *Reproduction in Education, Society and Culture*. Vol. 4. Thousand Oaks: Sage.

Bowen, Sarah, and Marie Sarita Gaytán. 2012. "The Paradox of Protection: National Identity, Global Commodity Chains, and the Tequila Industry." *Social Problems* 59 (1): 70–93.

Brubaker, Rogers. 1996. *Nationalism Reframed: Nationhood and the National Question in the New Europe*. Cambridge: Cambridge University Press.

Brubaker, Rogers. 2004. "In the Name of the Nation: Reflections on Nationalism and Patriotism." *Citizenship Studies* 8 (2): 115–27.

Brubaker, Rogers, Liana Grancea, Jon Fox, and Margit Feischmidt. 2006. *Nationalist Politics and Everyday Ethnicity in a Transylvanian Town*. Princeton: Princeton University Press.

Brubaker, Rogers, and Jaeeun Kim. 2011. "Transborder Membership Politics in Germany and Korea." *European Journal of Sociology/Archives Européennes de Sociologie* 52 (1): 21–75.

Burawoy, Michael. 2019. *Symbolic Violence: Conversations with Bourdieu*. Durham: Duke University Press.

Bures, Eliah. 2020. "Beachhead or Refugium? The Rise and Dilemma of New Right Counterculture." *Journal for the Study of Radicalism* 14 (2): 29–64.

Bures, Eliah. 2023. "The Intellectual as Culture Warrior: Metapolitics and the European New Right." *Fascism* 12 (1): 1–26.

Camus, Jean-Yves. 2019. "Alain de Benoist and the New Right." In *Key Thinkers of the Radical Right*, edited by M. Sedgwick, 73–90. Oxford: Oxford University Press.

Carter, Sean. 2004. "Mobilizing Hrvatsko: Tourism and Politics in the Croatian Diaspora." In *Tourism, Diasporas and Space*, edited by T. Coles and D. J. Timothy, 188–202. London: Routledge

Castelló, Enric, and Sabina Mihelj. 2018. "Selling and Consuming the Nation: Understanding Consumer Nationalism." *Journal of Consumer Culture* 18 (4): 558–76.

Charmaz, Kathy. 2006. *Constructing Grounded Theory: A Practical Guide through Qualitative Analysis*. London: Sage.

Chew, Matthew. 2007. "Contemporary Re-emergence of the Qipao: Political Nationalism, Cultural Production and Popular Consumption of a Traditional Chinese Dress." *China Quarterly* 189: 144–61.

Childress, Clayton. 2017. *Under the Cover: The Creation, Production, and Reception of a Novel*. Princeton: Princeton University Press.

Clarke, John, Stuart Hall, Tony Jefferson, and Brian Roberts. 2011. "Subcultures, Cultures and Class." In *Cultural Criminology*, edited by K. Hayward, 47–116. London: Routledge.

Coffey, Amanda, and Paul Atkinson. 1996. "Concepts and Coding." In *Making Sense of Qualitative Data*, 26–52. London: Sage.

Comaroff, John L., and Jean Comaroff. 2009. *Ethnicity, Inc*. Vol. 236. Chicago: University of Chicago Press.

Corse, Sarah M. 1997. *Nationalism and Literature: The Politics of Culture in Canada and the United States*. Cambridge: Cambridge University Press.

Creamer, Ella. 2025. "A 'Great Shock': Julianne Moore's Children's Book Is Under Review by Trump Administration." *The Guardian*. February 17, https://www.theguardian.com/books

/2025/feb/17/a-great-shock-julianne-moores-childrens-book-under-review-by-trump-administration.

Csákvári, Géza. 2016. "Nagy nemzeti sikerfilm." *Népszabadság*. August 30.

Csergő, Zsuzsa. 2007. *Talk of the Nation: Language and Conflict in Romania and Slovakia*. Ithaca: Cornell University Press.

Csete, Örs, ed. 2011. *Határtalanul! Nemzeti Összetartozás az oktatásban*. Budapest: A határon túli magyar oktatásért Apáczai Közalapítvány.

Csurgó, Bernadett, Csongor Jánosi, Katalin Juhász, Vladas Sirutavičius, and Corneliu Pintilescu. 2018. "Folklore Revivalism and Ethnography: Alternatives to Everyday Culture." In *Handbook of COURAGE*, edited by B. Apor, P. Apor, S. Horváth, 573–601. Budapest: Institute of History, Research Center for the Humanities, Hungarian Academy of Sciences.

Dayioğlu, Attila Gökhun. 2022. "Hungarian Nationalism and Hungarian Pan-Turanism Until the Beginning of the Second World War." *Politics in Central Europe* 18 (2): 225–49.

de Benoist, Alan. 2017. *View from the Right: A Critical Anthology of Contemporary Ideas*. London: Arktos.

DeSoucey, Michaela. 2010. "Gastronationalism: Food Traditions and Authenticity Politics in the European Union." *American Sociological Review* 75 (3): 432–55.

DeWitt, Jennifer, and Martin Storksdieck. 2008. "A Short Review of School Field Trips: Key Findings from the Past and Implications for the Future." *Visitor Studies* 11 (2): 181–97.

Dierkes, Julian. 2010. *Postwar History Education in Japan and the Germanys: Guilty Lessons*. New York: Routledge.

Dietze, Gabriele, and Julia Roth, eds. 2020. *Right-Wing Populism and Gender: European Perspectives and Beyond*. Bielefeld: transcript.

DiMaggio, Paul J., and Walter W. Powell. 1983. "The Iron Cage Revisited: Institutional Isomorphism and Collective Rationality in Organizational Fields." *American Sociological Review* 48 (2): 147–60.

Ditzendy, Attila. 2020. "Az íjfeszítő népek családja." *Magyar Nemzet*, August 25: 18.

Dugin, Alexander. 2014. *Eurasian Mission: An Introduction to Neo-Eurasianism*. London: Arktos.

Duneier, Mitchell. 2000. *Sidewalk*. New York: Farrar, Straus & Giroux.

Edensor, Tim. 2001. "Performing Tourism, Staging Tourism. (Re)producing Tourist Space and Practice." *Tourist Studies* 1 (1): 59–81.

Edensor, Tim. 2002. *National Identity, Popular Culture and Everyday Life*. London: Routledge.

Edensor, Tim. 2007. "Mundane Mobilities, Performances and Spaces of Tourism." *Social and Cultural Geography* 8 (2): 199–215

El-Haj, Nadia Abu. 2001. *Facts on the Ground: Archaeological Practice and Territorial Self-Fashioning in Israeli Society*. Chicago: University of Chicago Press.

Elek, Nikoletta, and Orsolya Nagy. 2020. "Közel 70 ezren tiltakoznak az LMBTQ-mesekönyv terjesztése ellen." *Magyar Nemzet*, September 29, https://magyarnemzet.hu/belfold/2020/09/kozel-70-ezren-tiltakoznak-az-lmbtq-mesekonyv-terjesztese-ellen.

Erdei, Ferenc. 1987. *A magyar társadalomról*. Budapest: Magvető.

F. Dózsa, Katalin. 1989. *Letűnt idők, eltűnt divatok: 1867–1945*. Budapest: Gondolat.

F. Dózsa, Katalin. 1998. "A magyar ruha feltámadása. Népviselet és napi divat a harmincas években." *Rubicon* 7: 48–50.

Feischmidt, Margit. 2005. "A magyar nacionalizmus autenticitás-diskurzusainak szimbolikus térfoglalása Erdélyben." In *Erdély-(De)konstrukciók*, edited by M. Feischmidt, 7–32. Budapest-Pécs: Néprajzi Múzeum—PTE Kommunikáció- és Médiatudományi Tanszék.

Feischmidt, Margit. 2008. "The Hungarian Transylvania: Symbolic Reconstruction of Lost Territories." *Hungarian Studies* 22 (1–2): 119–33.

Feischmidt, Margit. 2020. "Memory-Politics and Neonationalism: Trianon as Mythomoteur." *Nationalities Papers* 48 (1): 130–43.

Feischmidt, Margit, Rita Glózer, and Zoltán Illyés. 2014. *Nemzet a mindennapokban: Az újnacionalizmus populáris kultúrája.* Budapest: L'Harmattan

Feischmidt, Margit, and Gergő Pulay. 2017. "'Rocking the Nation': The Popular Culture of Neo-Nationalism." *Nations and Nationalism* 23 (2): 309–26.

Feldman, Jackie. 2002. "Marking the Boundaries of the Enclave: Defining the Israeli Collective Through the Poland 'Experience.'" *Israel Studies* 7 (2): 84–114.

Feldman, Jackie. 2008. *Above the Death Pits, Beneath the Flag: Youth Voyages to Poland and the Performance of Israeli National Identity.* New York: Berghahn Books.

Ferencziné Sedlmayr, Krisztina. 2006. "Magyaros ruhamozgalom az 1930-as években." *Folia Historica* 24: 133–77.

Filippello, Roberto. 2023. "Fashion Statements in a Site of Conflict." *Fashion Theory* 27 (2): 205–35.

Finchelstein, Frederico. 2022. *Fascist Mythologies.* New York: Columbia University Press.

Finchelstein, Frederico. 2024. *The Wannabe Fascists: A Guide to Understanding the Greatest Threat to Democracy.* Berkeley: University of California Press.

Fox, Jon E. 2006. "Consuming the Nation: Holidays, Sports, and the Production of Collective Belonging." *Ethnic and Racial Studies* 29 (2): 17–36.

Fox, Jon E., and Cynthia Miller-Idriss. 2008. "Everyday Nationhood." *Ethnicities* 8 (4): 536–63.

Franka, Tibor. 2020. "A könyvesemberek fasizmusa." In *Magyar Nemzet*, September 30, https://magyarnemzet.hu/poszt-trauma/2020/09/a-konyvesemberek-fasizmusa.

Fukuyama, Francis. 1992. *The End of History and the Last Man.* New York: Free Press.

Fülemile, Ágnes. 2023. "Monarchs in National Dress—Sartorial Expressions of National Image in the Representational Practices of 19th-Century European Courts." *Acta Ethnographica Hungarica* 66 (2): 439–95.

Gajdics, Ottó. 2020. "A gyerekeket ne!" *Magyar Nemzet*, October 5, https://magyarnemzet.hu/ahelyzet/2020/10/a-gyerekeket-ne.

Gaugele, Elke. 2019. "The New Obscurity in Style. Alt-Right Faction, Populist Normalization, and the Cultural War on Fashion from the Far Right." *Fashion Theory* 23 (6): 711–31.

Geertz, Clifford. 1973. *The Interpretation of Cultures: Selected Essays.* New York: Basic Books.

Gellner, Ernest. 1983. *Nations and Nationalism.* Oxford: Blackwell

Gholami, Reza. 2017. "The Art of Self-Making: Identity and Citizenship Education in Late-Modernity." *British Journal of Sociology of Education* 38 (6): 798–811.

Göçek, Fatma Müge. 2014. *Denial of Violence: Ottoman Past, Turkish Present, and Collective Violence against the Armenians, 1789–2009.* Oxford: Oxford University Press.

Goff, Patricia M. 2005. "It's Got to Be Sheep's Milk or Nothing! Geography, Identity, and Economic Nationalism." In *Economic Nationalism in a Globalizing World*, edited by E. Helleiner and A. Pickel, 183–201. Ithaca: Cornell University Press.

Goncalves, Marcelo S. O., Isabelle Langrock, Jack LaViolette, and Katie Spoon. 2024. "Book Bans in Political Context: Evidence from US Schools." *PNAS nexus* 3 (6): 197.

Göpffarth, Julian Jasper. 2020. "Querdenker. Local Intellectuals, Far-Right Populism and the Politics of Aesthetics of *Kulturnation* in Germany." PhD dissertation, London School of Economics.

Gorski, Philip S., and Samuel L. Perry. 2022. *The Flag and the Cross: White Christian Nationalism and the Threat to American Democracy.* Oxford: Oxford University Press.

Götz, Eszter. 2018. *Kéz/Mű/Remek: Nemzeti Szalon 2018: Népművészet.* Budapest: Műcsarnok Nonprofit Kft.

Gramsci, Antonio. 1971. *Selections from the Prison Notebooks.* New York: International Publishers.

Greskovits, Béla. 2020. "Rebuilding the Hungarian Right through Conquering Civil Society: The Civic Circles Movement." *East European Politics* 36 (2): 247–66.

Gu, Xin, and Min Lu. 2021. "Re-Negotiating National Identity Through Chinese Fashion." *Fashion Theory* 25 (7): 901–15.

Gurova, Olga. 2019. "Patriotism as Creative (Counter-)Conduct of Russian Fashion Designers." *Research in Consumer Behavior* 20: 151–68.

György, Péter. 2012. "Neobarokk retró." *Népszabadság*. Budapest, May 28, http://nol.hu/velemeny/20120526-neobarokk_retro-1311241.

Hampel, Katalin. 2013. *Divatban az érték: Hampel Katalinnal beszélget Fazekas Valéria*. Budapest: Kairosz.

Hankó, Ildikó. 2019. "Magyar örökség: Lovasíjászat." *Demokrata*, August 7.

Hatvany, Csilla. 2006. "Legitimacy of Kin-State Politics: A Theoretical Approach." *Regio Yearbooks* 9: 47–64.

Hebdige, Dick. 1979. *Subculture. The Meaning of Style*. London: Routledge.

Helleiner, Eric. 2002. "Economic Nationalism as a Challenge to Economic Liberalism? Lessons from the 19th Century." *International Studies Quarterly* 46 (3): 307–29.

Helleiner, Eric, and Andreas Pickel. 2005. *Economic Nationalism in a Globalizing World*. Ithaca: Cornell University Press.

Henley, Jon. 2024. "Populist, Nativist, Neofascist? A Lexicon of Europe's Far Right." *The Guardian*, June 18, https://www.theguardian.com/world/article/2024/jun/18/populist-nativist-neofascist-a-lexicon-of-europes-far-right.

Hernádi, Zsuzsa. 2020. "A gyerek tabu!" *Demokrata*, November 2, https://demokrata.hu/magyarorszag/a-gyerek-tabu-306105/.

Hetzmann, Róbert. 2020. "Törvénymódosítás a normalitás megőrzéséért." *Magyar Nemzet*, October 12, https://magyarnemzet.hu/velemeny/2020/10/torvenymodositas-a-normalitas-megorzeseert.

Hír TV. 2020. "Credo: Brassótól Pozsonyig minden magyar iskolás ugyanabban a szellemiségben nevelkedhet." *Magyar Nemzet*, March 12.

Hobsbawm, Eric, and Terence Ranger. 1983. *The Invention of Tradition*. Cambridge: Cambridge University Press.

Hochschild, Arlie Russell. 2016. *Strangers in Their Own Land: Anger and Mourning on the American Right*. New York: New Press.

Hochschild, Arlie Russell. 2024. *Stolen Pride: Loss, Shame, and the Rise of the Right*. New York: New Press.

Hofer, Tamás. 1991. "Construction of the 'Folk Cultural Heritage' in Hungary and Rival Versions of National Identity." *Ethnologia Europaea* 21 (1): 145–70.

Hollander, Paul. 2019. "The One-Way Street: Misunderstanding Fascism." *Academic Questions* 32 (2): 271–75.

Horváth, József. 2020. "A tanterv támadása is a háború része." *Magyar Nemzet*, February 21, https://magyarnemzet.hu/velemeny/2020/02/a-tanterv-tamadasa-is-a-haboru-resze.

Hovi, Tuomas. 2014. "The Use of History in Dracula Tourism in Romania." *Electronic Journal of Folklore* 57: 55–79, https://www.folklore.ee/folklore/vol57/hovi.pdf.

Hubbes, László Attila. 2013. "New Hungarian Mythology Animated. Self-Portraits of the Nation." *Acta Universitatis Sapientiae, Philologica* 2: 223–40.

Hughes, Hugh, and Danielle Allen. 2010. "Holidays of the Irish Diaspora—the Pull of the 'Homeland.'" *Current Issues in Tourism* 13 (1): 1–19.

Hunter, James. 1991. *Culture Wars: The Struggle to Define America*. New York: Basic Books.

Ignatieff, Michael. 1993. *Blood and Belonging: Journeys Into the New Nationalism*. New York: Macmillan.

Ilyés, Zoltán. 2013. "A gyimesbükki „Ezeréves Határ" politikai instrumentalizálása." *ANTROPORT.HU* (Winter), http://www.antroport.hu/lapozo_archivum.php?akt_cim=340.

index.hu. 2020. "Závada Pál: Tömeges szülői tiltakozásra van szükség." *Index*, February 7, https://index.hu/kultur/2020/02/07/zavada_pal_nat_tanterv_irodalom_szulok_nemzeti_alaptanterv/.

Jaskułowski, Krzysztof, Piotr Majewski, and Adrianna Surmiak. 2018. "Teaching the Nation: History and Nationalism in Polish School History Education." *British Journal of Sociology of Education* 39 (1): 77–91.

Joób, Sándor. 2020a. "Kertész Imre és Ottlik Géza kihullott a Nemzeti Alaptantervből." *Index*, February 5, https://index.hu/belfold/2020/02/05/nemzeti_alaptanterv_iskola_magyar_irodalom_szerzok_kanon_wass_albert_nyiro_jozsef_tonke_dragt_herczeg_ferenc/.

Joób, Sándor. 2020b. "Nézzük meg mi szerepel a NAT-ban, és mi a baj vele." *Index*, February 13, https://index.hu/belfold/2020/02/13/nemzeti_alaptanterv_nat_magyar_irodalom_tortenelem_modszertan_tanari_szabadsag_oraszam/.

Juhász, Katalin. 2017. "От народного костюма до «этно-дизайна»—модные тенденции в фольклористическом движении «танцхаз» в позднесоциалистической Венгрии." (From national costume to ethno-design: fashion trends in the folk movement "táncház" in socialist Hungary.) *Teoriya Modi / Fashion Theory* 46: 12–45.

Kalinina, Ekaterina. 2017. "Becoming Patriots in Russia: Biopolitics, Fashion, and Nostalgia." *Nationalities Papers* 45 (1): 8–24.

Kaneva, Nadia, ed. 2011. *Branding Post-Communist Nations: Marketizing National Identities in the "New" Europe*. Vol. 33. New York: Routledge.

Kania-Lundholm, Magdalena. 2014. "Nation in Market Times: Connecting the National and the Commercial. A Research Overview." *Sociology Compass* 8 (6): 603–13.

Kárpáti, András. 2020. "A legszínvonalasabb szerzők szerepelnek az új NAT-ban." In *Magyar Nemzet*, February 13, https://magyarnemzet.hu/belfold/2020/02/a-legszinvonalasabb-szerzok-szerepelnek-az-uj-nat-ban.

Kassai, Lajos. 2012. "Kassai-féle lovasíjász módszer. Jelölés a kulturális örökség megőrzését szolgáló programok és tevékenységek nemzeti nyilvántartására." *Hungarikum application*. https://szellemikulturalisorokseg.hu/doks/nyomtatvanyok/kassai_fele_lovasijasz_modszer.pdf.

Kassai, Lajos. 2019. *Lovasíjászat*. Budapest: Püski.

Katriel, Tamar. 1995. "Touring the Land: Trips and Hiking as Secular Pilgrimages in Israeli Culture." *Jewish Folklore and Ethnology Review* 17 (1/2): 6–13.

Kékesi, Raymund. 2020. "Liberális mese és sötét valóság." *Pesti Srácok*, October 16, https://pestisracok.hu/liberalis-mese-es-sotet-valosag-a-felhaborodas-hatasara-gyorsan-kihuztak-az-ovodasokat-a-celcsoportbol/.

Kelner, Shaul. 2010. *Tours That Bind: Diaspora, Pilgrimage, and Israeli Birthright Tourism*. New York: NYU Press.

Kim, Jaeeun. 2016. *Contested Embrace: Transborder Membership Politics in Twentieth-Century Korea*. Stanford: Stanford University Press.

Kimura, Tets, William Peterson, and Shih-Ying Lin. 2022. "Fashion Nationalism in Asia: A Comparative Study of the Philippines' Terno and Taiwan's Qipao." *Asian Anthropology* 21 (2): 100–20.

Kiss, Attila. 2020. "'Íjuk mint Isten karja, és nyilaik elől nincs menekvés.' Sztyeppei típusú szaruin összetett íjak és nyílvesszők használati értékének vizsgálata." *Hadtörténeti közlemények* 133 (4): 953–97.

Kiss, Attila. 2022. *Altináj*. Budapest: Móra.

Kiszely, István. 2012. "A lovasíjászat egy gyémánt a koronából." *Demokrata*, January 11, 44–45.

Koch, Natalie. 2020. "The Corporate Production of Nationalism." *Antipode* 52 (1): 185–205.

Korompay, Csilla. 2020. "Tényleg Sorosék támogatják a nemzetellenes történészeket." *Magyar Hírlap*, February 6, https://www.magyarhirlap.hu/belfold/20200206-tenyleg-sorosek-tamogatjak-a-nemzetellenes-torteneszeket.

Kovács, János Mátyás, and Balázs Trencsényi, eds. 2020. *Brave New Hungary: Mapping the "System of National Cooperation."* Lanham: Lexington Books.

Kowalski, Alexandra. 2011. "When Cultural Capitalization Became Global Practice." In *The Cultural Wealth of Nations*, edited by N. Bandelj and F. F. Wherry, 73–89. Stanford: Stanford University Press.

Kőrösiné dr. Merkl, Hilda. 2016. "Széchenyi társaság díja 2016. Bedő György (posztumusz) és a Kairosz kiadó." Unpublished speech. http://www.szechenyiforum.hu/fileok/6/Kairosz-a.pdf.

Krekó, Péter, and Zsolt Enyedi. 2018. "Explaining Eastern Europe: Orbán's Laboratory of Illiberalism." *Journal of Democracy* 29 (3): 39–51.

Kremmler, Katrin. 2022. "'Eurasian Magyars': The Making of a New Hegemonic National Prehistory in Illiberal Hungary." In *Digging Politics: The Ancient Past and Contested Present in East-Central Europe*, edited by E. Hanscam and J. Koranyi, 181–216. Oldenbourg: Walter de Gruyter.

Kremmler, Katrin. 2023. "The Role of Culture in Illiberal Nation-Branding: The Making of Eurasian Civilizationism in Hungary." *Journal of Illiberalism Studies* 5 (May 5), https://www.illiberalism.org/the-role-of-culture-in-illiberal-nation-branding-the-making-of-eurasian-civilizationism-in-hungary/.

Kristóf, Luca, Dorottya Kisfalusi, and Eszter Vit. 2021. "Political Homophily in Cultural Reputational Networks." *Poetics* 89: 1–17.

Kubik, Jan. 1994. *Power of Symbols Against the Symbols of Power: The Rise of Solidarity and the Fall of State Socialism in Poland*. University Park: Penn State Press.

Kummer, Luca. 2021. "Kicsi a bors, de erős: a hucul ló." *A Magyar Állattenyésztők Lapja* 26 (9): 32–35.

Kürti, László. 2001. *The Remote Borderland: Transylvania in the Hungarian Imagination*. Albany: State University of New York Press.

Kürti, László. 2012. "Twenty Years After: Rock Music and National Rock in Hungary." *Region: Regional Studies of Russia, Eastern Europe, and Central Asia* 1 (1): 93–130.

Kürti, László. 2017. "Nomadism and Nostalgia in Hungary." In *Memories on the Move: Experiencing Mobility, Rethinking the Past*, edited by J. Tošić and M. Palmberger, 217–46. London: Palgrave Macmillan.

Lainer-Vos, Dan. 2013. *Sinews of the Nation: Constructing Irish and Zionist Bonds in the United States*. Cambridge: Polity.

Lamont, Michèle, and Virág Molnár. 2001. "How Blacks Use Consumption to Shape Their Collective Identity: Evidence from Marketing Specialists." *Journal of Consumer Culture* 1 (1): 31–45.

Lamont, Michèle, and Virág Molnár. 2002. "The Study of Boundaries in the Social Sciences." *Annual Review of Sociology* 28 (1): 167–95.

Lange, Barbara Rose. 2018. *Local Fusions: Folk Music Experiments in Central Europe at the Millennium*. Oxford: Oxford University Press.

Laruelle, Marlene. 2012. *Russian Eurasianism. An Ideology of Empire*. Baltimore: Johns Hopkins University Press.

Laruelle, Marlene. 2022. "Illiberalism: A Conceptual Introduction." *East European Politics* 38 (2): 303–27.

László, Gyula. 2019 [1944]. *50 Rajz a Honfoglalókról*. Budapest: Kairosz.

Laza, Bálint. 2012. "Megtaláltuk Matolcsy piros pöttyeit." *Index*. https://index.hu/tudomany/egeszseg/2012/11/19/megtalaltuk_matolcsy_piros_pottyeit/.

Lehrer, Erica T. 2013. *Jewish Poland Revisited: Heritage Tourism in Unquiet Places*. Bloomington: Indiana University Press.

Lepore, Jill. 2025. "The Trump Administration's Efforts to Reshape America's Past." *New Yorker*, August 25, 2025.

Lerch, Julia C., S. Garnett Russell, and Francisco O Ramirez. 2017. "Wither the Nation-State? A Comparative Analysis of Nationalism in Textbooks." *Social Forces* 96 (1): 153–80.

Levent, Sinan. 2016. "Common Asianist Intellectual History in Turkey and Japan: Turanism." *Central Asian Survey* 35 (1): 121–35.

Levitt, Peggy. 2015. *Artifacts and Allegiances: How Museums Put the Nation and the World on Display*. Berkeley: University of California Press.

Ling, Wessie, and Simona Segre-Reinach. 2018. *Fashion in Multiple Chinas: Chinese Styles in the Transglobal Landscape*. London: Bloomsbury Publishing.

List, Friedrich. 1885. *The National System of Political Economy (English Translation)*. London: Longmans, Green.

Löfgren, Orvar. 1989. "The Nationalization of Culture." *Ethnologia Europaea* 19: 5–23.

Lomsky-Feder, Edna. 2004. "The Memorial Ceremony in Israeli Schools: Between the State and Civil Society." *British Journal of Sociology of Education* 25 (3): 291–305.

Lomsky-Feder, Edna. 2011. "Competing Models of Nationalism: An Analysis of Memorial Ceremonies in Schools." *Nations and Nationalism* 17 (3): 581–603.

Lukácsy, György. 2016. "Kassai Lajos lovasíjász a siker titkáról." *Heti Válasz*, February 11, 38–40.

Magyar Nemzet. 2021. "Liberálisok, nácik és a szőnyegbombázás. Letters to the Editor." In *Magyar Nemzet*, March 16, https://magyarnemzet.hu/velemeny/2021/03/levelblokk.

mandiner.hu. 2021. "A Széchenyi Irodalmi és Művészeti Akadémia is nyilatkozott Tóth Krisztina ügyéről." *Mandiner online*, February 26, https://mandiner.hu/belfold/2021/02/a-szechenyi-irodalmi-es-muveszeti-akademia-is-nyilatkozott-toth-krisztina-ugyerol.

Marschall, Sabine. 2016. "The Role of Tourism in the Production of Cultural Memory: The Case of 'Homesick Tourism' in Poland." *Memory Studies* 9 (2): 187–202.

Maróti, Zoltán, et al. 2022. "The Genetic Origin of Huns, Avars, and Conquering Hungarians." *Current Biology* 32 (13): 2858–70. e7.

Martin, Cathie Jo. 2023. *Education for All? Literature, Culture and Education Development in Britain and Denmark*. Cambridge: Cambridge University Press.

Máté, Imre. 2004–2007. *Yotengrit 1–4*. Budapest: Püski.

Maxwell, Alexander. 2014. *Patriots Against Fashion: Clothing and Nationalism in Europe's Age of Revolutions*. Basingstoke: Palgrave Macmillan.

Maxwell, Alexander. 2021. "Analyzing Nationalized Clothing: Nationalism Theory Meets Fashion Studies." *National Identities* 23 (1): 1–14.

Mayer, Tara. 2018. "From Craft to Couture: Contemporary Indian Fashion in Historical Perspective." *South Asian Popular Culture* 16 (2–3): 183–98.

Mayhew, Bradley. 2024. "World Nomad Games: The Spectacular 'Olympics' of Central Asia." *BBC*. https://www.bbc.com/travel/article/20240912-world-nomad-games-the-spectacular-olympics-of-central-asia.

McKay, George A., and Michael N. Goddard. 2009. *Introduction: (Post-) Subculture Theory, and Practice in East-Central Europe*. Oxford: Peter Lang.

Medvedev, Katalin. 2008. "Ripping up the Uniform Approach: Hungarian Women Piece Together a New Communist Fashion." In *Producing Fashion: Commerce, Culture, and Consumers*, edited by R. L. Blaszczyk, 250–73. Philadelphia: University of Pennsylvania Press.

Meghji, Ali. 2021. *Decolonizing Sociology: An Introduction*. London: Wiley.

Mehmetcik, Hakan, and Arda Can Çelik. 2022. "The Militarization of Turkish Foreign Policy." *Journal of Balkan and Near Eastern Studies* 24 (1): 24–41.

Melchior, Marie Riegels. 2011. "From Design Nations to Fashion Nations? Unpacking Contemporary Scandinavian Fashion Dreams." *Fashion Theory: The Journal of Dress, Body & Culture* 15 (2): 177–200.

Mezey, Katalin. 2021. "Irodalmi minták gyermek olvasóknak." *Magyar Nemzet*, February 28, https://magyarnemzet.hu/velemeny/2021/02/irodalmi-mintak-gyermek-olvasok-szamara.

Michalkó, Gábor, Tamara Rátz, and Réka Keszeg. 2016. "A határokon átívelő tanulmányi kirándulások szerepe a nemzetépítésben: A 'Határtalanul!' program társadalomföldrajzi vizsgálata." *Kissebségkutatás* 25 (2): 36–58.

Millei, Zsuzsa, and Sirpa Lappalainen. 2020. "Learning Nation in Early Childhood Education: Multi-Sited Comparison Between Pedagogies of Nation in Australia and Hungary." *European Education* 52 (1): 33–47.

Miller-Idriss, Cynthia. 2009. *Blood and Culture: Youth, Right-Wing Extremism, and National Belonging in Contemporary Germany*. Durham: Duke University Press.

Miller-Idriss, Cynthia. 2014. "Marketing National Pride: Commercialization and the Extreme Right in Germany." In *Understanding Collective Pride and Group Identity. New Directions in Emotion Theory, Research and Practice*, edited by G. B. Sullivan, 149–60. New York: Routledge.

Miller-Idriss, Cynthia. 2018. *The Extreme Gone Mainstream: Commercialization and Far Right Youth Culture in Germany*. Princeton: Princeton University Press.

Miller-Idriss, Cynthia. 2019. "What Makes a Symbol Far Right?" In *Post-Digital Cultures of the Far Right: Online Actions and Offline Consequences in Europe and the United States*, edited by M. Fielitz and N. Thurston, 123–35. Bielefeld: transcript.

Molnár, Virág. 2005. "Cultural Politics and Modernist Architecture: The Tulip Debate in Postwar Hungary." *American Sociological Review* 70 (1): 111–35.

Molnár, Virág. 2013. *Building the State: Architecture, Politics, and State Formation in Postwar Central Europe*. New York: Routledge.

Molnár, Virág. 2016. "Civil Society, Radicalism and the Rediscovery of Mythic Nationalism." *Nations and Nationalism* 22 (1): 165–85.

Molnár, Virág. 2017. "The Mythical Power of Everyday Objects: The Material Culture of Radical Nationalism in Postsocialist Hungary." In *National Matters: Materiality, Culture, and Nationalism*, edited by G. Zubrzycki, 147–70. Stanford: Stanford University Press.

Molnár, Virág. 2019. "The Discontents of Socialist Modernity and the Return of the Ornament." In *Second World Postmodernisms: Architecture and Society Under Late Socialism*, edited by V. Kulić, 47–61. London: Bloomsbury.

Molnár, Virág. 2021. "The Toolkit of Nationalist Populism in Contemporary Hungary: Symbols, Objects, and Modalities of Circulation." *East European Politics and Societies* 35 (4): 948–74.

Molnár, Virág. 2023. "Class Trips Beyond Borders: Reimagining the Nation Through State-Sponsored Heritage Tourism." *Comparative Studies in Society and History* 65 (3): 557–86.

Moltke, Johannes von. 2022. "The Metapolitics of Identity: Identitarianism and Its Critics." *German Studies Review* 45 (1): 151–66.

Moltke, Johannes von, and Susanne Komfort-Hein. 2024. "'Where Woke Goes to Die': Transnationale Literaturpolitiken der Neuen Rechten." *Deutsche Vierteljahrsschrift für Literaturwissenschaft und Geistesgeschichte* 98: 619–38.

Moreh, Chris. 2016. "The Asianization of National Fantasies in Hungary: A Critical Analysis of Political Discourse." *International Journal of Cultural Studies* 19 (3): 341–53.

Morrison, Toni. 1988. "Unspeakable Things Unspoken: The Afro-American Presence in American Literature." *The Tanner Lectures on Human Values*, University of Michigan, October 7.

Mudde, Cas. 2004. "The Populist Zeitgeist." *Government and Opposition* 39 (4): 541–63.

Mudde, Cas. 2019. *The Far Right Today*. Cambridge: Polity Press.

Mudde, Cas. 2022. "The Far-Right Threat in the United States: A European Perspective." *The ANNALS of the American Academy of Political and Social Science* 699 (1): 101–15.

Mudde, Cas, and Cristóbal Rovira Kaltwasser. 2017. *Populism: A Very Short Introduction*. New York: Oxford University Press.

Müller, Jan-Werner. 2016. *What Is Populism?* London: Penguin UK.

Muniz, Albert M., and Thomas C. O'Guinn. 2001. "Brand Community." *Journal of Consumer Research* 27 (4): 412–32.

Nagle, John. 2025. "Framing Irredentism: Ancient Statehood, Sacred Lands and Causes and the National Family." *Nations and Nationalism* (online first): 1–11. https://doi.org/10.1111/nana.13101.

Nagy, Zsolt. 2023. "Balázs Ablonczy. Go East! A History of Hungarian Turanism Translated by Sean Lambert. Bloomington: Indiana University Press, 2022." In *Austrian History Yearbook* 54: 206–7.

narancs.hu. 2020a. "Szakács Árpád, a kultúrharc sámánja alufóliás teóriával állt elő a NAT-tal kapcsolatban." *Magyar Narancs*, February 10, https://magyarnarancs.hu/feketelyuk/szakacs-arpad-a-kulturharc-samanja-alufolias-teoriaval-allt-elo-a-nat-tal-kapcsolatban-126738.

narancs.hu. 2020b. "A könyvdaráló Dúró Dóra és Szakács Árpád megvédik a megtámadott anyákat." *Magyar Narancs*, October 1, https://magyarnarancs.hu/feketelyuk/a-konyvdaralo-duro-dora-es-szakacs-arpad-megvedik-a-megtamadott-anyakat-133654.

narancs.hu. 2020c. "Plakátokkal bélyegzik meg a Meseország mindenkié című könyvet áruló boltokat." *Magyar Narancs*, October 6, https://magyarnarancs.hu/belpol/plakatokkal-belyegzik-meg-a-meseorszag-mindenkiet-arulo-boltokat-133775.

NAT. 2020. Nemzeti Alaptanterv, Article 5/2020 (I.31.) Kormány rendelet. *Magyar Közlöny* 17: 1–31.

Németh, György. 2021. "A család az család—de mi a kérdés?" *Magyar Nemzet*, March 6, https://magyarnemzet.hu/velemeny/2021/03/a-csalad-az-csalad-de-mi-a-kerdes.

Nora, Pierre. 1996. *Realms of Memory: Rethinking the French Past*. New York: Columbia University Press.

Norris, Pippa, and Ronald Ingelhart. 2019. *Cultural Backlash: Trump, Brexit and Authoritarian Populism*. Cambridge: Cambridge University Press.

Novikov, Anna. 2017. "The Visual Language of Neo-Nationalism: Patriotic Fashion in East Central Europe and Central Asia." *TRAFO—Blog for Transregional Research*. https://trafo.hypotheses.org/7082.

Olay, Ferenc. 2023. *Magyarország a külföldi tankönyvekben*. Budapest: Kárpátia Studió.

Osler, Audrey. 2011. "Teacher Interpretations of Citizenship Education: National Identity, Cosmopolitan Ideals, and Political Realities." *Journal of Curriculum Studies* 43 (1): 1–24.

Ott, Anna. 2021. "Tizenegyes—Mit olvas az író Tóth Krisztina?" *Könyves Magazin*, February 11, https://konyvesmagazin.hu/friss/tizenegyes_ott_anna_toth_krisztina_olvasas.html.

Paál, Zoltán. 2005. *Arvisura - Igazszólás: mondák, regék, népi hagyományok a palóc kézművesek világából I-II. 3. Kiadás*. Budapest: Püski.

Paksa, Rudolf. 2012. *A magyar szélsőjobboldal története*. Budapest: Jaffa Kiadó.

Pap, Szilárd István. 2013. "Encountering the Nation Beyond National Borders: Hungarian High School Students, Tourism and the Micromanagement of Nation Building." MA thesis, Central European University, Budapest.

Partizán. 2021. "Interview with Lajos Kassai." https://www.youtube.com/watch?v=ILc_OY_VVIo.

Pasieka, Agnieszka. 2017. "Taking Far-Right Claims Seriously and Literally: Anthropology and the Study of Right-Wing Radicalism." *Slavic Review* 76 (S1): 19–29.

Pasieka, Agnieszka. 2019. "Anthropology of the Far Right: What If We Like the 'Unlikeable' Others?" *Anthropology Today* 35 (1): 3–6.

Pasieka, Agnieszka. 2024. *Living Right: Far-Right Youth Activists in Contemporary Europe*. Princeton: Princeton University Press.

Pataki, Tamás. 2021. "Bán Mór: Jókait nem lehet kirekeszteni a magyar irodalomból." *Magyar Nemzet*, February 22, https://magyarnemzet.hu/kultura/2021/02/ban-mor-jokait-nem-lehet-kirekeszteni-a-magyar-irodalombol.

Peleikis, Anja. 2010. "Heritage and the Making of (Trans-)Local Identities: A Case Study from the Curonian Spit (Lithuania)." In *Translocality*, edited by U. Freitag and A.v. Oppen, 229–47. Leiden: Brill.

PEN. 2025. *Cover to Cover: An Analysis of Titles Banned in the 23–24 School Year*. February 27, https://pen.org/report/cover-to-cover/.

Pesl, Martin. 2021. "Ungarn Ist Ein Toxisches Land." *Falter* 11: 28–30.

Peterson, Richard A., and Narasimhan Anand. 2004. "The Production of Culture Perspective." *Annual Review of Sociology* 30 (1): 311–34.

Petrovics, Gabriella. 2021. "Amit most látunk az egyfajta irodalmi 'szobordöntögetés.'" *Magyar Nemzet*, February 27, https://magyarnemzet.hu/kultura/2021/02/amit-most-lattunk-az-egyfajta-irodalmi-szobordontogetes.

Piela, Anna. 2021. *Wearing the Niqab: Muslim Women in the UK and the US*. London: Bloomsbury Publishing.

Pilkington, Hilary, Elena Omel'chenko, and Al'bina Garifzianova. 2010. *Russia's Skinheads: Exploring and Rethinking Subcultural Lives*. New York: Routledge.

Pinheiro-Machado, Rosana, and Tatiana Vargas-Maia. 2023. *The Rise of the Radical Right in the Global South*. Abingdon: Routledge.

Pogonyi, Szabolcs. 2013. "National Reunification Beyond Borders: Diaspora and Minority Politics in Hungary Since 2010." *European Yearbook of Minority Issues* 10: 535–62.

Pogonyi, Szabolcs. 2015. "Transborder Kin-Minority as Symbolic Resource in Hungary." *Journal on Ethnopolitics and Minority Issues in Europe: JEMIE* 14 (3): 73–98.

Pogonyi, Szabolcs. 2017. *Extra-Territorial Ethnic Politics, Discourses and Identities in Hungary*. London: Palgrave Macmillan.

Poole, Steven. 2025. "Banned! The Twenty Books They Didn't Want You to Read." *The Guardian*, August 23, https://www.theguardian.com/books/2025/aug/23/banned-the-20-books-they-didnt-want-you-to-read.

Portes, Alejandro, and Robert D. Manning. 2005. "The Immigrant Enclave: Theory and Empirical Examples." *The Urban Sociology Reader* 38: 583–94.

Pörzse, Sándor. 2011. "A Kassai." *barikád*, August 11, 3.

Pörzse, Sándor. 2016. "Két filmről szubjektíven." *barikád*, February 18, 3.

Povedák, István. 2022. "'Come, Look and Hear How the Past Has Been and the Future Will Be!' Festival Culture and Neo-Nationalism in Hungary." In *Festival Cultures: Mapping New Fields in the Arts and Social Sciences*, edited by M. Nita and J. H. Kidwell, 65–86. London: Palgrave Macmillan.

Quigley, Colin. 2014. "The Hungarian Dance House Movement and Revival of Transylvanian String Band Music." In *The Oxford Handbook of Music Revival*, edited by C. Bither and J. Hill, 182–204. Oxford: Oxford University Press.

Rátz, Tamara, Gábor Michalkó, and Réka Keszeg. 2020. "Educational Tourism and Nation Building: Cross-Border School Trips in the Carpathian Basin." *Hungarian Geographical Bulletin* 69 (1): 57–71.

Rivera, Lauren A. 2008. "Managing 'Spoiled' National Identity: War, Tourism, and Memory in Croatia." *American Sociological Review* 73 (4): 613–34.

Rosenthal, Lawrence. 2020. *Empire of Resentment: Populism's Toxic Embrace of Nationalism*. New York: New Press.

Rubinstein, Julian. 2004. *Ballad of the Whiskey Robber: A True Story of Bank Heists, Ice Hockey, Transylvanian Pelt Smuggling, Moonlighting Detectives, and Broken Hearts*. New York: Back Bay Books.

Rydgren, Jens. 2006. *From Tax Populism to Ethnic Nationalism: Radical Right-Wing Populism in Sweden*. New York: Berghahn Books.

Sajó, András, Renáta Uitz, and Stephen Holmes. 2021. *Routledge Handbook of Illiberalism*. London: Routledge.

Saxe, Leonard, and Barry Chazan. 2008. *Ten Days of Birthright Israel. A Journey in Young Adult Identity*. Waltham: Brandeis University Press.

Scheppele, Kim Lane. 2013. "The Rule of Law and the Frankenstate: Why Governance Checklists Do Not Work." *Governance* 26 (4): 559–62.

Schissler, Hanna, and Yasemin Nuhoglu Soysal. 2005. *The Nation, Europe, and the World: Textbooks and Curricula in Transition*. New York: Berghahn Books.

Schwenck, Anna. 2023. *Flexible Authoritarianism: Cultivating Ambition and Loyalty in Russia*. Oxford: Oxford University Press.

Sedgwick, Mark. 2019. *Key Thinkers of the Radical Right: Behind the New Threat to Liberal Democracy*. Oxford: Oxford University Press.

Sewell Jr., William H. 1992. "A Theory of Structure: Duality, Agency, and Transformation." *American Journal of Sociology* 98 (1): 1–29.

Shapira, Anita, and Derek J Penslar, eds. 2013. *Israeli Historical Revisionism: From Left to Right*. London: Routledge.

Siebers, Hans. 2019. "Are Education and Nationalism a Happy Marriage? Ethno-Nationalist Disruptions of Education in Dutch Classrooms." *British Journal of Sociology of Education* 40 (1): 33–49.

Sinkovics, Szilvia. 2016. "Pozitív életszemlélet, lendület, tiszta energia." *barikád*, January 21, 32–35.

Small, Mario L. 2015. "De-Exoticizing Ghetto Poverty: On the Ethics of Representation in Urban Ethnography." *City & Community* 14 (4): 352–58.

Smith, Anthony D. 2004. *The Antiquity of Nations*. Cambridge: Polity.

Snyder, Timothy. 2017. *On Tyranny: Twenty Lessons from the Twentieth Century*. New York: Crown.

Spektorowski, Alberto. 2003. "The New Right: Ethno-Regionalism, Ethno-Pluralism and the Emergence of a Neo-Fascist 'Third Way.'" *Journal of Political Ideologies* 8 (1): 111–30.

Spike, Justin, and Nicholas Riccardi. 2025. "How Hungary's 'Electoral Autocracy' Parallels Trump's Return." *AP News*, February 15, https://apnews.com/article/trump-orban-hungary-autocracy-authoritarian-republicans-dfdf6299a614ec4e364be37c1132e446.

Stanley, Jason. 2018. *How Fascism Works: The Politics of Us and Them*. New York: Random House.

Stanley, Jason. 2024. *Erasing History*. New York: Simon & Schuster.

Stanton, Zack. 2021. "How the Culture War Could Break Democracy." *Politico*, May 20, https://www.politico.com/news/magazine/2021/05/20/culture-war-politics-2021-democracy-analysis-489900.

Sumartojo, Santi. 2016. "Commemorative Atmospheres: Memorial Sites, Collective Events and the Experience of National Identity." *Transactions of the Institute of British Geographers* 41: 541–53.

Surak, Kristin. 2010. "The Business of Belonging." *New Left Review* 63: 151–59.

Surak, Kristin. 2012. *Making Tea, Making Japan. Cultural Nationalism in Practice*. Stanford: Stanford University Press.

Surak, Kristin. 2017. "Engaging Objects: The Phenomenology of the Tea Ceremony and Japaneseness." In *National Matters: Materiality, Culture, and Nationalism*, edited by G. Zubrzycki, 173–93. Stanford: Stanford University Press.

Suyarkulova, Mohira. 2016. "Fashioning the Nation: Gender and the Politics of Dress in Contemporary Kyrgyzstan." *Nationalities Papers* 44 (2): 247–65.

Szabó, Miklós. 1989. "Magyar nemzettudat problémák a huszadik század második felében." In *Politikai kultúra Magyarországon 1896–1986*, edited by M. Szabó, 225–52. Budapest: Medvetánc Könyvek.

Szakács, Gábor. 2002. "A Magyar Vár Alapítvány." *Demokrata* 45: 54–55.

Szakács, Árpád, and Zsolt Bayer. 2019. *A kultúra diktatúrája*. Budapest: Kárpátia Stúdió.

Szilvay, Gergely. 2021. "A Háttér Társaság és a tudományos kirekesztés módszertana." *Mandiner*, February 1, https://mandiner.hu/velemeny/2021/02/hatter-tarsasag-kirekesztes.

Szily, László. 2020. "Toldozott-foltozott, nevetséges rendőrnyelven megírt szöveget akarnak eladni Nemzeti Alaptantervként." *444.hu*, February 7, https://444.hu/2020/02/07/toldozott-foldozott-nevetseges-rendornyelven-megirt-szoveget-akarnak-eladni-nemzeti-alaptantervkent.

Szőke, Tibor. 2020. "Mitől válik egy mesekönyv szellemi hormonkezeléssé?—Interjú Pécsi Rita neveléskutatóval." *SZEMlélek*, October 8, https://szemlelek.blog.hu/2020/10/08/mitol_valik_egy_mesekonyv_szellemi_hormonkezelesse_interju_pecsi_rita_neveleskutatoval.

Szombati, Kristóf. 2018. *The Revolt of the Provinces: Anti-Gypsyism and Right-Wing Politics in Hungary*. Vol. 23. New York: Berghahn Books.

Taylor, Mary N. 2021. *Movement of the People: Hungarian Folk Dance, Populism, and Citizenship*. Bloomington: Indiana University Press.

Teisenhoffer, Viola. 2024. "Pagan Revival, Re-Enchantment, and New Forms of Rituality in Hungary: The Case of the Kurultaj Festival." *Religion* 54 (1): 62–87.

Teitelbaum, Benjamin R. 2017. *Lions of the North: Sounds of the New Nordic Radical Nationalism*. Oxford: Oxford University Press.

Tomc, Sandra. 2021. *Fashion Nation: Picturing the United States in the Long Nineteenth Century*. Ann Arbor: University of Michigan Press.

Tormey, Roland. 2006. "The Construction of National Identity through Primary School History: The Irish Case." *British Journal of Sociology of Education* 27 (3): 311–24.

Török, Tibor. 2022. "Relations Among the Historical Populations of the Carpathian Basin in Light of Recent Archaeogenetic Findings." December 16, https://doi.org/10.53644/MKI.Kas.2022.351.

Tóth, Krisztina. 2021. "A műveimben jórészt olyan elesett emberek szerepelnek, amilyenek most a véremet akarják venni." *Mandiner online*, April 3, https://mandiner.hu/kultura/2021/04/a-muveimben-joreszt-olyan-elesett-emberek-szerepelnek-amilyenek-most-a-veremet-akarjak-venni.

Trump, Donald. 2024. "Donald Trump's Victory Speech in Full: Transcript." *Newsweek*, November 6, https://www.newsweek.com/donald-trump-victory-speech-full-transcript-1981234.

Turner, Terence S. 2012. "The Social Skin." *HAU: Journal of Ethnographic Theory* 2 (2): 486–504.

Tüysüzoğlu, Göktürk. 2014. "Strategic Depth: A Neo-Ottomanist Interpretation of Turkish Eurasianism." *Mediterranean Quarterly* 25 (2): 85–104.

Urbinati, Nadia. 2019. *Me the People: How Populism Transforms Democracy*. Cambridge, MA: Harvard University Press.

V. Szabó, Gábor, Attila Kiss, and Zoltán Henrik Tóth. 2021. "Rekonstruált szkíta kori íjakkal és nyilakkal végzett lőkísérlet a Dédestapolcsány-Verebce-Bérci koravaskori ostrom kapcsán." *Magyar Régészet* 10 (3): 43–52.

Ventsel, Aimar. 2014. "'That Old School Lonsdale': Authenticity and Clothes in German Skinhead Culture." In *The Paradox of Authenticity in a Globalized World*, edited by Russell Cobb, 261–275. Basingstoke: Palgrave Macmillan.

Ventsel, Aimar. 2022. *Punks and Skins United: Identity, Class and the Economics of an Eastern German Subculture*. Oxford: Berghahn Books.

Virágos, Gábor, ed. 2022. *Tarsolylemezek. A honfoglaló elit kincsei*. Budapest: Magyar Nemzeti Múzeum.

Waldinger, Roger. 1993. "The Ethnic Enclave Debate Revisited." *International Journal of Urban and Regional Research* 17: 444–52.

Waterbury, Myra A. 2006. "Ideology, Organization, Opposition: How Domestic Political Strategy Shapes Hungary's Ethnic Activism." *Regio Yearbook* 9: 68–86.

Williams, Jeffrey J. 2022. "The Culture Wars." In *The Encyclopedia of Contemporary American Fiction 1980–2020*, Vol. 1, edited by P. O'Donnell, S. J. Burn, and L. Larkin, 1–9. Hoboken: Wiley.

Wodak, Ruth. 2015. *The Politics of Fear: What Right-Wing Populist Discourses Mean*. London: Sage.

Yavuz, M. Hakan. 2020. *Nostalgia for the Empire: The Politics of Neo-Ottomanism*. Oxford: Oxford University Press.

Young, Jessica K. 2023. "Memory Studies on the Frontlines of the Culture Wars." *Memory Studies* 16 (6): 1702–8.

Zakaria, Fareed. 1997. "Illiberal Democracy." *Foreign Affairs* 76 (6): 22–43.

Zakariás, Ildikó. 2018. *Jótékony nemzet. Szolidaritás és hatalom a kisebbségi magyarok segítésében*. Budapest: MTA TK Kissebségkutató Intézet—Kalligram.

Zelizer, Viviana A. 2010. *Economic Lives: How Culture Shapes the Economy*. Princeton: Princeton University Press.

Zerubavel, Yael. 1995. *Recovered Roots: Collective Memory and the Making of Israeli National Tradition*. Chicago: University of Chicago Press.

Zhang, Chenchen. 2023. "Postcolonial Nationalism and the Global Right." *Geoforum* 144:103824, doi: https://doi.org/10.1016/j.geoforum.2023.103824.

Ziblatt, Daniel, and Steven Levitsky. 2018. *How Democracies Die*. New York: Penguin Books

Zimmerman, Jonathan. 2022 [2002]. *Whose America? Culture Wars in the Public Schools*. Chicago: University of Chicago Press.

Zubrzycki, Geneviève. 2001. "'We, the Polish Nation': Ethnic and Civic Visions of Nationhood in Post-Communist Constitutional Debates." *Theory and Society* 30 (5): 629–68.

Zubrzycki, Geneviève. 2020. "A New Polish Nationalist Law Strives to Create a Revisionist Narrative." In *Historical Revisionism*, edited by B. Krasner, 141–45. New York: Greenhaven Publishing.

Zsuppán, András. 2024. "Csontokból nyert tudás. Mende Balázs a genetikai múltról." *Válasz Offline* 2 (1): 129–32.

Primary sources

Chapter 4 uses unpublished primary data from the class trip dossiers (e.g., student diaries, class materials, images). Dossiers are cited by the archival reference number assigned to the dossier by the state monitoring agency (e.g., ha-13-01-265, hat-15-05-0180).

INDEX

A NOTE ON THE TYPE

This book has been composed in Adobe Text and Gotham. Adobe Text, designed by Robert Slimbach for Adobe, bridges the gap between fifteenth- and sixteenth-century calligraphic and eighteenth-century Modern styles. Gotham, inspired by New York street signs, was designed by Tobias Frere-Jones for Hoefler & Co.

GPSR Authorized Representative: Easy Access System Europe - Mustamäe tee 50, 10621 Tallinn, Estonia, gpsr.requests@easproject.com

www.ingramcontent.com/pod-product-compliance
Lightning Source LLC
LaVergne TN
LVHW100306050926
847404LV00026B/216

* 9 7 8 0 6 9 1 2 9 0 3 8 6 *